Kabbalah in Print

Kabbalah in Print

The Study and Popularization of Jewish Mysticism in Early Modernity

Andrea Gondos

Cover: Thomas Wyck (ca. 1616–ca. 1677), *A Scholar in His Study*
Hallwyl Museum, Stockholm, Sweden.

Published by State University of New York Press, Albany

For information, contact State University of New York Press, Albany, NY
www.sunypress.edu

Library of Congress Cataloging-in-Publication Data

Name: Gondos, Andrea, author.
Title: Kabbalah in print : the study and popularization of Jewish mysticism in early
    modernity / Andrea Gondos, author.
Description: Albany : State University of New York Press, [2020] | Includes
    bibliographical references and index.
Identifiers: ISBN 9781438479712 (hardcover : alk. paper) | ISBN 9781438479736
    (ebook)
Further information is available at the Library of Congress.

10 9 8 7 6 5 4 3 2 1

Library of Congress

2021   443776

I dedicate this book to the memory of my
Grandmother, Dr. Julianna Gál (z"l)
whose love of books and thirst for knowledge
inspired my own intellectual quest

A book is like a magic garden carried in your pocket.

—Chinese Proverb

I MUST Create a System, or be enslav'd by another Man's;
I will not Reason and Compare: my business is to Create.

—William Blake, *Jerusalem*

What a glorious gift is imagination, and what satisfaction it affords!

—Thomas Mann, *Confessions of Felix Krull, Confidence Man*

Contents

Contents

Illustrations

Acknowledgments

The preparation of this book benefited from the indispensible support of several organizations and individuals. The Canadian Graduate Scholarship awarded by the Social Sciences and Humanities Research Council of Canada (SSHRC) allowed me to develop much of my research between 2006 and 2009. A postdoctoral fellowship (2014–2016) granted by the Azrieli Foundation made it possible for me to conduct extensive research in Israel at the National Library in Givat Ram, especially in its important repository of mystical texts, the Scholem library. I thank the librarians who have aided my research on a daily basis, Dr. Zvi Leshem and Yuval de Malaḥ, as well as the always gracious staff. My research questions and methodological paradigm were informed by two academic workshops I participated in 2009: the annual workshop on The History of the Jewish Book at the Herbert D. Katz Center of Advanced Judaic Studies at University of Pennsylvania and the workshop on Reading across Cultures: The Jewish Book and Its Readers in the Early Modern Period, organized at the Radcliffe Institute for Advanced Studies at Harvard University. I am grateful to the workshop directors for the financial assistance and the scholarly opportunities these workshops afforded in my professional development.

Over the years I have benefited from conversations with a number of scholars, whose insights and guidance were invaluable to the development of my own work: Daniel Abrams, Adam Afterman, Yossi Chajes, Avriel Bar-Levav, Bernard Dov Cooperman, Rachel Elior, Iris Felix, Jonathan Garb, Yehudah Galinsky, Pinchas Giller, Matt Goldish, Zeev Gries, Gershon Hundert, Boaz Huss, Moshe Idel, Yoed Kadary, Maoz Kahanah, Ruth Kara-Ivanov Kaniel, Yehudah Liebes, Haviva Pedaya, Elchanan Reiner, Biti Roi, Moshe Rosman, David Ruderman, Bracha Sack, Adam Shear, Norman Stillman, Steven Weitzman, and Elliot R. Wolfson.

I would like to express my gratitude to the anonymous readers of the manuscript for their suggestions and careful reading of the manuscript, which significantly improved the final work. Thank you also to Diane Ganeles and the editorial team at SUNY for their assistance in preparing the work for publication.

The supervisor of my doctoral work, Ira Robinson, was so much more than a mentor; I owe him my deepest gratitude for the countless hours that we spent on working through difficult passages and texts and for providing an intellectual space for developing my own voice. Similarly, my research as an Azrieli postdoctoral fellow in Israel under the supervision of Ronit Meroz at Tel Aviv University was invaluable in both shaping the arguments of this book as well as charting new paths for my future research. I am grateful for everything I learned from her during our weekly discussions as she drove us from Mevaseret Zion to Tel Aviv University. The hours and minutes during our conversations, like the discourses of the *zoharic* rabbis during their many peregrinations, just collapsed into the space of inventing and discovering *ḥidushim*.

I would like to express gratitude to two special friends and mentors, Professor Norma Joseph and Rabbi Howard Joseph, for all the wonderful study sessions we engaged in over the course of many years, raising questions and debating theological issues, which were always complemented by outstanding food, thus feeding both body and soul.

I thank my parents, Dr. George and Dr. Csilla Gondos, who supported my intellectual pursuits throughout my life. They taught me the value of hard work and kindness in all things I undertake.

My deepest gratitude is saved for my husband, Dr. Csaba Nikolenyi, who gave me strength when I was weak and who aroused me when I slumbered. Many of the ideas in this book were formed in the crucible of our walks and night vigils when mind embraced mind and the boundary between I and Thou silently dissipated.

Introduction

This book sets a new direction for the study and development of Kabbalah in the early modern period by understanding the printing, reorganization, and transmission of kabbalistic knowledge and textual practice. First, I seek to refocus attention on the profile and unique characteristics of Kabbalah in East-Central Europe—Poland, Moravia, and Bohemia—in early modernity, geographical areas largely understudied in contemporary academic scholarship.[1] Second, I move the methodological emphasis from the theosophical and symbolic understanding of kabbalistic works to the cultural, intellectual, and pedagogic concerns that informed their composition and textual organization. I argue that the democratization of knowledge spurred by printing impelled new authors—the secondary elites—in Ashkenazi lands to reframe the Zohar, and other foundational works of Kabbalah, in new and creative ways making them more accessible for a lay reading audience or those less versed in this lore.

Shifting the methodological focus from the semantic to the structural and didactic characteristics of kabbalistic texts can help us understand better the proliferation of kabbalistic study guides in the sixteenth and seventeenth centuries in East-Central Europe, Italy, and Safed, as well as the role secondary elites played as cultural intermediaries in this process. The kabbalistic study guide, a new genre in the Jewish literary canon, appeared for the first time shortly after the printing of the classical works of Jewish mysticism in the late sixteenth century and sought to popularize and render previously esoteric knowledge exoteric. Thus, these reference tools, which were meant to create greater access to the foundational texts of Kabbalah, such as the medieval classic, the Zohar, constitute a unique window into cultural production at the nonelite, more popular, but still educated levels of Jewish society. A detailed investigation of how Jewish

1

esoteric knowledge was organized and presented in these learning aids
also provides important insights into early modern reading practices,
attitudes toward epistemic organization and transmission, the circulation
of earlier kabalistic textual material, and authority and authentication of
legitimate sources of Jewish mystical speculation.

In this book, I will examine the literary strategies and creative
technical adjustments the authors of these guides adopted for mediating
a restricted body of knowledge from the exclusive domain of elites to a
broader readership. A detailed investigation of the four works written by
R. Yissakhar Baer (ca. 1580–ca. 1629), an author active in early-seventeenth-
century Prague, and other compilers who shared his educational and
intellectual goals, sheds light on the literary strategies, pedagogic concerns,
and religious motivations of secondary elites, a new cadre of authors
empowered by the opportunities that the technological innovation of
printing opened up for them. The book highlights the emergence of three
interconnected factors that became intertwined with the transmission of
Kabbalah in early modernity: (1) the rise of secondary elites as cultural
and literary mediators of kabbalistic knowledge; (2) the appearance of
new genres, specifically the kabbalistic study guide, that reframed esoteric
knowledge in more accessible ways; and (3) shifting intellectual and cultural boundaries, as the transmission of Kabbalah became a meeting point
connecting various strata of Jewish society and forming an intellectual
bridge between Jewish and Christian readers.

At the same time, the present study points beyond the narrow field of
Kabbalah and intellectual history in the early modern period contributing
to a broader discussion regarding communication, knowledge organization,
and transmission, expanding our understanding of how various forms
of media shape religious institutions, communities, and authority in the
postmodern world.[2] Carpenter and McLuhan have already underscored
that the "packaging and distribution of ideas and information" transformed
human consciousness, modes of interaction, and identity.[3] They further
advocated for a methodological shift examining one particular medium
of communication by using another: analyzing print from the perspective
of electronic media and television seen through the lens of print.[4] They
argued that the computer and modern mass media in comparison to
printed matter allow for "light-through rather than light-on" approach,
contrasting the content driven analytical mode of literacy with the state
of perpetual connectedness, an "all-at-onceness," that electronic media
affords human societies in the postmodern world. The global village

phenomenon we live today is akin to preliterate human consciousness when the mythological narrative created a network of connections that illuminated all aspects of human experience.

Drawing on the observations of Carpenter and McLuhan, this book posits that printing itself fostered a sense of connectedness and contributed to the formation of "imagined communities," members of which participated in a broader cultural dialogue that surpassed geographical or religious borders and boundaries.[5] Using the term, *textual communities* deployed by Brian Stock, Boaz Huss describes the kabbalistic circles of Safed in the sixteenth century as "zoharic communities" connected to each other through intense engagement with the Zohar as a book and a repository of ancient secrets.[6] The movement of individual agents of culture and the portability of the book as a physical object in the age of print transformed the paradigm of learning from a communal approach centered on a master-teacher, who decoded and transmitted knowledge to a select group of disciples, to the emergence of individualized study environments with an emphasis on private deinstitutionalized intellectual space.[7] In this personalized reading environment, kabbalistic study guides connected Christian Hebraists with Jewish readers, while at the same time offered intellectual tools and a system of simplifying and decoding ancient Jewish mystical lore. United by their common interest in and pursuit of kabbalistic knowledge, members of this imagined community were plugged into a greater cultural network of printers, agents, book dealers, scholars, ecclesiastical censors, and expurgators, whose encounters, albeit mostly indirect, formed a critical juncture in the intellectual development of early modernity.

A striking feature of these study guides was the attention their authors, printers, and editors paid to managing and organizing information on the page. As in the electronic age when the technical feature of hypertext allows us to shift between multiple screens and sources of information, speed constituted an important consideration in the organization and visual presentation of content in kabbalistic learning aids. In the case of the Sulzbach edition of the Zohar (1684), for instance, the printing of Yissakhar Baer's *zoharic* lexicon, *Imrei Binah*, at the bottom of each page as a running text was a harbinger of the technical innovation of the hypertext that allowed readers to access parallel sources simultaneously.[8] The technological adjustment of presenting the secondary text of the study guide in close spatial proximity and in the framework of the same page of the primary narrative of the Zohar visually linked these two texts and

offered an effective pedagogical tool to decode and explicate the original.[9]
The linking of various genres through the application of innovative technology creates multivocality[10] and intertextuality[11] among distinct textual
sources effacing conventional forms of linear thought and "reconceiving
assumptions about authors and readers and the texts they write and read."[12]
The editorial decision to print two different textual sources on the same
page highlights the imbricated nature of technology and writing expanding the cognitive focus beyond content and rhetoric to considerations of
"physical and cognitive execution of text production."[13] The technological
innovation of the Sulzbach Zohar, therefore, reinforces the notion that
technology, whether applied to print matter or the computer, functions
not as an object but as a "vital system" embedded in a specific phase of
human history conditioned by the complex interaction between cultural
agents, creative motives, and cognitive demands.[14]

The organization, management, and rapid retrieval of information
that we expect of computerized technology today were already of central
concern for the authors of kabbalistic study guides in the premodern era
as well. The sixteenth-century mystic, R. Moses Cordovero, perceiving the
chaos and confusion generated by the circulation of Jewish esoteric texts
both in manuscript and print, devised systematic methods for coping with
the multiplicity of resources. In his defining work, the *Pardes Rimonim*,
he devotes an entire chapter (Gate 23) to the encyclopedic treatment of
kabbalistic terms and symbols arranged in alphabetical order to promote
easy consultation. As Walter Ong notes, alphabetic indexes represent a point
of transition between oral and visual cultures. While in the manuscript
age, rhetoric provided the loci or places for cross-referencing, in the era
of printed books, these indicators become visually and spatially localized.[15]

In compiling the *Pardes*, Cordovero embodied not only the prevailing
attitude of the typographic age but also our own predilections at the time
of computers and digital technologies to regard knowledge as infinite and
learning not as memorization but broad, expansive reading, and a systematic
management of resources.[16] Although he enjoined the reader not to simply
skip from topic to topic, nevertheless the arrangement of his chapters by
clear topical headers facilitated consultation and easy referencing of various
subjects in the Jewish mystical arcana, making a large library of kabbalistic resources available in one volume. Cognizant of the ever-expanding
repository of kabbalistic texts, Cordovero as an editor and author sought
not so much to reduce and digest available information so as to create
order in it and access to it. Interspersing the literary genre of anthology,

known in Christian textual circles as the *florilegia*, with other genres such as an alphabetized index of key kabbalistic terms, Cordovero presents the reader interested in Jewish mysticism with a single book aimed to present an inclusive and authoritative resource for the study of Kabbalah.

The activities of secondary elites as cultural agents need to be framed in the broader context of matters concerning authority, textual control, and canonization.[17] Michel Foucault's important study, "What Is an Author" (1977) provides a historical analysis of the invention of the "author" as a construct. Foucault shows that the preoccupation with authorship, that is so endemic to our understanding of any literary composition, is a relatively recent development stemming from the Enlightenment, with its focus on the individual. Yet, while authors may not always be clearly identified in sixteenth- and early-seventeenth-century works, the examination of abridgements to Moses Cordovero's *Pardes Rimonim*, extant in several print and manuscript versions, reveals how authorial voice changed from one digest to another reflecting unique hermeneutic, pedagogic, and cultural concerns and paradigms. The forty-eight manuscript variants of the *Pardes Rimonim* at the National Library of Israel's collection, half of which come from the sixteenth century along several abridgments of the work in print and manuscript, demonstrate that the *Pardes* generated intense literary activity by secondary elites. We may further posit, based on David Stern's conceptualization of anthologies, that the primary function of abridgments to the *Pardes* served the function of canonization and demarcation of what constituted legitimate forms of Kabbalistic knowledge, while delegitimating competing variants.[18]

The tendency to devise effective methods of knowledge organization found parallel expression in the intellectual pursuits of early modern Christian writers as well. In the field of education for instance, the early-seventeenth-century German Calvinist, Johannes Henricus Alsted, composed several works that proposed new systems and methodologies to information organization and resource management. His two works, *Consiliarius Academicus et Scholasticus* and *Systema Mnemonicum Dupex*, attempt to digest and create topical categories, alphabetical indexes, and commonplace books in order to navigate the confusing networks of information produced by print matter.[19] Central to the systematic methods of both the Christian theologian, Alsted, as well as the adept of Jewish mystical lore, Moses Cordovero, is an eye for pedagogical considerations and the gradual transmission of knowledge that is always commensurate with the development and expected competence of the reader.

Computer technology has unlocked vast resources to represent knowledge visually and enhance the assimilation of information. The visual representation of kabbalistic ideas, symbols, and processes begins already in the manuscript age in the thirteenth century but receives creative impetus following the death of the Safed kabbalist, R. Isaac Luria Ashkenazi (Ari), in 1572. As Chajes notes, tree diagrams or *Ilanot* that mapped the entire divine being and interdivine dynamics in precise and comprehensive ways become increasingly more ramified and complex in their presentation as we move from thirteenth-century manuscripts to Lurianic models from the sixteenth century onward.[20] Relating to the natural world these diagrammatic depictions deploy geometrical forms and embedded textual excerpts to create pictorial images of the structures and processes in godhead while retaining fluid communication between image and verbal communicative elements. The synchronic presentation of verbal and visual ciphers enhanced the performative intent of these diagrams whether as mnemonic devices, meditational mandalas or amulets.[21]

The presence of visual diagrams in printed study guides to Kabbalah is relatively scant due to several reasons. First, these books were written either for beginners or for preachers and teachers who needed tools for easier referencing of the Zohar and other works of Kabbalah and thus lacked complex theoretical depictions of the divine or a performative dimension that would have necessitated the use of pictorial images. Second, kabbalists who penned some of these guides, such as Menaḥem Azariah da Fano, in the late sixteenth to early seventeenth century, exercised theological conservatism in using pictorial images to depict the divine and therefore were reluctant to include such visual representations in printed works accessible to a broad readership. It is indicative of this tendency that when Fano edits and reprints Samuel Gallico's précis of Cordovero's *Pardes Rimonim* (1623), he omits all pictorial images included in the first edition of the book (1601). Third, the use of images in printed books increased expenses for the printer, and since the publishing of study guides was aimed at wide circulation and a less specialist audience, these works tended to be smaller, often pocket-size, with visual material kept to the minimum.

The appearance of kabbalistic study guides in the early modern period introduces new questions and methodological perspectives that move the academic discussion from the history of ideas and psychohistory,[22] exemplified by the scholarship of Gershom Scholem, to asking questions about how changes in material culture impacted the diffusion of Kabbalah at this time.[23] A marked increase in the genre of kabbalistic learning aids, following the publication of some of the most important classics of kabbalistic literature, shows that changes and shifts in material culture and the attendant knowledge explosion were defining factors the efflorescence of kabbalistic literary activity in the sixteenth and seventeenth centuries. Scholem regarded kabbalistic literary activity as informed and shaped primarily by historical antecedents. Kabbalistic doctrines, such as the transmigration of souls (metempsychosis), *tikkun* (cosmic restoration), and Messianic speculations, that became recurrent topoi in the compositions of the Safed kabbalists, represented spiritual panacea to the sufferings of so many Jewish exiles. Scholem's overemphasis of the psychological consequences of the Expulsion, fails to sufficiently account for the ways in which broader institutional, ideational, and technological forces shaped the development of post-Expulsion Kabbalah.[24]

This book aims to broaden our understanding of the cultural processes that influenced literary production and knowledge transmission in the early modern period. It will do so by engaging the works of Yissakhar Baer as a point of reference for examining parallel attempts by writers of kabbalistic manuals in order to highlight the diversity of intellectual models and responses that authors deployed to enhance the transmission of this knowledge and its general study. Yissakhar Baer's literary creativity as a compiler was singular in that he maintained a consistent effort to integrate traditional rabbinic genres with new types of compilatory formats reflecting a holistic approach to knowledge precisely at a time when other early-modern thinkers also endeavored to accentuate the interplay between the natural world, science, religion, and the esoteric.[25] His four compositions display an attitude consonant with the ethos of the seventeenth century that technology offered a remarkable opportunity for the correlation and democratization of the intellectual and theological disciplines. In the chapters that follow, I provide a focused examination of Yissakhar Baer's compositions, always contextualizing them within broader intellectual developments among Jews and Christians so as to underscore the various intersecting influences that impacted the variety of organizational models for reframing extant Jewish mystical texts and ideas.

The Intellectual Climate in Prague at the Dawn of the Seventeenth Century

While Poland constituted an important center of Jewish life in early modern Eastern Europe, Prague—the seat of the imperial capital of the Habsburg Empire between 1583 and 1611—boasted of having the second-largest

urban Jewish community in all of Europe.[26] Political sovereignty over
Prague was in hands of the Kings of Poland and Hungary until 1526, when
the city, as well as the rest of Bohemia, became eventually absorbed by
the Habsburg Empire. The fortunes of the Jewish community in Prague
depended on the positions and the attitude of the emperor: whereas the
reign of Ferdinand I (1526–1564), who had assumed control over Bohemia
following the demise of King Louis the Jagellonian at the battlefield of
Mohács against the armies of the Ottoman Empire in 1526, was marked
by a series of harsh measures against the Jews of Prague. These included
the edicts of expulsion in 1541 and 1557, as well as the ordinance of
1561, which required Jewish families in the city to attend a weekly Jesuit
sermon. In a sharp reversal of imperial policy, Ferdinand's successors,
Maximilian II (1564–1576) and Rudolph II (1576–1611) adopted a much
more friendly attitude toward the Jews of Bohemia in general and those
of Prague, in particular. In 1566 Maximilian decreed that the Jews of
Prague would never again be expelled from the city and four years later,
in 1571, he paid a historic visit to the ghetto.

The golden age of Prague Jewry, however, was associated with the
reign of Maximilian's son, Rudolph II, who consolidated the political and
legal framework that allowed the flourishing of the Jewish communities
of Bohemia.[27] In 1577 the emperor confirmed and reinforced his father's
pledge never to allow the expulsion of the Jews from Prague or from
the entirety of the Bohemian kingdom. Furthermore, he lifted existing
restrictions on Jewish trades, allowing in particular Jewish participation
in the jewelry, gold, and silver businesses. Rudolph's policies resulted in a
phenomenal growth in the size of Prague's Jewish population from a few
hundred in the middle of the 1500s to approximately 3,000 by the turn
of the century. Most of the migrants came from Eastern Europe, princi-
pally Poland and Lithuania, or the German principalities. The growing
wealth of the Prague community was marked by the rise to prominence
of Mordechai Meisel, a Court Jew, who received special protection and
trading privileges from the Emperor in 1592, and played a central role
in the organization of the Empire's financial system.[28] As the wealthiest
resident of the entire city, Meisel was also major benefactor of Prague
community and in this capacity sponsored the construction of the synagogue that bears his name.[29]

The increased westward mobility of Polish Jewry led to the development of an important transregional nexus connecting Prague with the
centers of Jewish learning in Poland. Important examples of this network

include the movement of David Gans, the author of *Ẓemaḥ David*, a prominent chronicler of Jewish and universal history, who arrived and settled in the imperial capital after years of study at the Krakow *yeshivah* of Moses Isserles. Similarly, after having served as chief rabbi of Moravia, then all of Bohemia, the Maharal moved to his native Poznań in 1592. His successor was Mordechai Yaffe (*Levush*), a native of Prague, who had given up his post in Poznań and whose earlier appointments included the Rabbinate of Grodno (1572), Lublin (1588), and Kremenets. The *Levush* received his training in Jewish law and rabbinics from the leading Polish rabbis of the time, Moses Isserles and Solomo Luria.[30] Yaffe's majestic work, the *Levushim*, a halakhic work that responded both to Joseph Qaro's *Shulhan Arukh* and the Moses Isserles's *Mappah* by providing interpretations and explanations that expanded what he considered unnecessarily concise codes, was printed in the Polish presses of Krakow and Lublin over a period of fourteen years between 1590 and 1604. In an interesting turn of events, the Maharal and the *Levush* changed positions one more and final time in 1597; the Maharal returned to and remained in Prague until his death in 1609 while the *Levush* returned and served in Poznań until his death in 1613.[31]

Perhaps the most important symbolic manifestation of the Emperor Rudolph's friendly attitude toward the Jews of his capital city was his legendary meeting with the chief rabbi of the community, the Maharal, in 1592. In spite of the significance of the encounter, its details are not known. The celebrated chronicler of the time, David Gans, writes the following about the event in his *Ẓemaḥ David*:

> Out of his beneficence and out of his desire to learn the truth, our sovereign, the Emperor Rudolph, a just ruler, the source of great and brilliant light, may his glory be exalted, called to him the *Gaon*, our teacher Rabbi Loew ben Bezalel, and received him most graciously, speaking to him face to face as a man speaks to his equal. As for the substance and purpose of this dialogue, it remains a secret, which the two men decided not to disclose. This event took place in Prague on Sunday, the third of Adar 5352.[32]

As mentioned above, soon after this meeting, on the 4th day of Iyar, the Maharal, left his rabbinic post in the city.

Apart from indicating the Emperor's friendly predisposition toward the Jewish community, the meeting between Rudolph and the Maharal

also speaks of another extremely important cultural characteristic of the
Imperial Court of the day: its openness to and active support of scientific, magical and occult studies and practices. Almost all of the leading
scientists of contemporary Europe, including the astronomers and mathe-
maticians Johannes Kepler, Tycho Brache, and John Dee, visited or stayed
at the Imperial Court.[33] Since the lines between scientific knowledge and
inquiry on the one hand and magic and occult arts on the other were
not so clearly drawn in the early modern period, it was not surprising
to find that Rudolph was interested in both. He encouraged visits by and
conversations with Christian Kabbalists and even appointed as his personal
confessor Johannes Pistorius, who compiled the largest compendium of
Christian Kabbalistic works of the time, *Artis Cabalisticae*, printed in Basle
in 1587.[34] Rudolph was particularly interested in collecting books and
manuscripts about occult secrets as well as works that discussed Jewish
mystical matters.[35]

It is precisely in the context of this interest in esotericism that the
Maharal's visit with the emperor needs to be particularly appreciated as it
coincided with a revival of the study of Kabbalah not only in the Jewish
community of Prague but also among the Jews of Poland. However, in
contrast to Poland, the Jews of Prague existed in an environment where
the same intellectual current, the interest in mysticism and esotericism,
defined both the Jewish and the majority Christian societies. The Hebrew
printing presses of Prague, similarly to those in Poland, produced a
growing number of kabbalistic works including the writings of the leading rabbinic authorities of the time and alongside those written by the
gradually growing class of secondary elites. In short, as Davies notes, the
"rise of kabbalah was the most significant change in the intellectual life
of Ashkenazi Jews of the seventeenth century . . . it displaced philosophy
and, through a process of reinterpretation swallowed midrash as well. It
became the dominant theology of Jewish pietism; it became, indeed, a
force and a system of thought that could challenge the Talmud for the
pre-eminent place in Ashkenazi Judaism."[36]

The scholars of Prague played a pivotal role in the process of kabbalistic revival in the late sixteenth and early seventeenth centuries. However,
it is important to emphasize that this development unfolded neither in
isolation from the rest of Ashkenazi Jewry nor was it a process without
internal opposition. The leading lights of Prague's rabbinic aristocracy,
including leaders such as the Maharal (1525–1609),[37] Isaiah Horowitz
(1550–1630), and Yom Tov Lippmann Heller (1578–1654) were all masters

of Kabbalah who moved between Prague and Poland at various times during their rabbinic careers. While realigning the status of Kabbalah, their fundamental position toward the revelation and popularization of mystical ideas was characterized by conservatism in contrast to the much more open position of the secondary elites, preachers, beadles, and scribes, who relied on the medium of the printing press to spread Kabbalah to a steadily growing broader readership. The conflict between the rabbinic and the secondary religious elites was not limited solely to their views on Kabbalah; the former also strongly objected to the new genre of abridgments that became especially popular in the aftermath of the publication and circulation of the *Shulḥan Arukh*.[38] Kabbalistic abridgments were regarded with particular suspicion by the primary elite because they revealed esoteric material to the masses without the mediation of the trained teacher through oral discourse. The complaint of Rabbi Berekhia Berakh, in 1662, about the printing of Kabbalistic literature on a wide scale in seventeenth-century Eastern Europe illustrates very clearly the concerns of those who shared the position of the conservative Kabbalists.

I have seen a scandalous thing in the matter of kabbalistic studies . . . for the very name *kabbalah* (received tradition) indicates that it was transmitted individually and that it must not be revealed [publicly]. . . . But now there have appeared presumptuous men who abuse the crown [of heavenly wisdom], turning it into a spade with which to feed themselves. They wrote books on kabbalistic subjects, obtain permission to print them, and then hawk them around to "divide [that is, distribute] them in Jacob." . . . They reveal hidden and secret things to great and small, and even mingle the invention of their hearts with [authentic] kabbalistic teachings, until it becomes impossible to distinguish between the words of the kabbalist masters and their own additions. . . . Thus they speak grievous things against God [by revealing] that which He has hidden. But even if they contended themselves with merely copying faithfully the words of kabbalist masters, their sin would be too great to bear, for they make public this wisdom and turn it into common talk, all the more so as they stretch out their hands against the Sanctuary. I know that the rabbis of old kept aloof from this science because they feared it might have been adulterated by unqualified persons, as indeed we now see it has been. . . . May the sages of our generation forgive me if I say that they are responsible for this abuse, because they grant approbations and licenses for printing [these books], commending, justifying, and extolling them to heaven, whereby they make themselves like false witnesses on behalf of liars.[39]

It is important to emphasize that the conservative Kabbalists of Prague and Poland in the early modern period took a strong stance against the unmediated study of Kabbalah by individuals and emphasized the tradition that, as Berakh's comment shows, maintained and reinforced the central role of the master who controlled the form and content of its transmission. In his introduction to the *Levush*, Mordechai Yaffe clearly explains that one cannot properly grasp the teachings of Kabbalah without having first studied the natural sciences and astronomy.

Every student . . . who wishes to ascend 'the ladder which stands on the earth, but whose head reaches to the heaven' (Gen. 28:12) must ascend to the . . . uppermost heights on which God, may He be blessed, stands. . . . First [the student] must learn the sciences of philosophy and nature . . . all of which are included in . . . the *Guide of the Perplexed* [by Maimonides]. And afterwards he must ascend and study . . . astronomy . . . and afterwards he must ascend even higher and enter into the wisdom of the kabbalah; then he will merit the apprehension of the First Cause, Who stands above [the spheres].[40]

In addition to the need for a gradual preparation prior to one's immersion into mystical studies, the above quote shows the ongoing influence of the Maimonidean rationalistic tradition of Jewish philosophy at the time when prominent members of the rabbinic aristocracy also shared such sentiment. The Maharal's educational reforms, for instance, endorsed the concomitant study of both philosophy and science in the *yeshivot* of Prague.[41] At the same time, Moses Isserles was fervently admonished by Solomon Luria (the Maharshal) for supporting the study of Aristotelian philosophy.[42] These three members of Prague's rabbinic court joined hands in approving and supporting the publication of *Givat Hamoreh* by Joseph ben Isaac Halevi, a unique philosophical work in the Ashkenazi world that explicitly built on the rationalistic tradition.[43] Moses Isserles declared in two well-known statements in his *Torat ha-Olah* (1562) that "the methods

of the Kabbalah are essentially the same as the methods of philosophy"
and that "Kabbalah and philosophy are one and the same. The difference
is that the two are expressed in different languages."[44]

By the second decade of the 1600s the influence of philosophy had
started to decline. With the Maharal's death in 1609 the school of rabbinic
thinkers who tried to reconcile philosophy, rabbinic literature and Kabbalah
lost its most powerful and authoritative champion. The election of Isaiah
Horowitz, as the chief rabbi of Prague in 1614 ushered in a new period
where the rationalistic tradition would be clearly superseded by mysticism. In a strange turn of political events, the Emperor Rudolph was also
deposed at this time with his eventual demise in 1612, marking the end
of an era of prosperity in the intellectual and cultural history of Prague.

The Cultural Context:
Secondary Elites and the Popularization of Kabbalah

In the first decade of the seventeenth century two prominent printers,
Gershom ben Beẓalel Katz and his kin, Moshe ben Beẓalel Katz, published
four works by the kabbalist, Rabbi Yissakhar Baer ben Petaḥya Moshe, in
the city of Prague. The aim of these works, as the author argued in his
introductions, was to offer educational tools to readers who were interested
in entering the world of Kabbalah but lacked the specialized knowledge
required of them for this endeavor. Yissakhar Baer's literary activity
denotes a moment in intellectual history that had already witnessed the
publication of major works of Kabbalah in the middle of the sixteenth
century, such as the Zohar, Sefer Yeẓirah, Ma'arekhet ha-Elohut, and the
works of Joseph Gikatilla, Menaḥem Recanati, Moses Cordovero, and Meir
ibn Gabbai. While printing made these works available to larger segments
of Jewish and Christian readers, these texts remained largely closed and
incomprehensible due to their enigmatic language, idiosyncratic ideas,
and unusual symbolism, all of which seemed, to some extent, strange
and unfamiliar to those not accustomed to studying the Jewish mystical
corpora. Yissakhar Baer's works, therefore, signify a critical juncture in the
cultural production of kabbalistic texts as these ideas transitioned from
constituting closely guarded esoteric secrets in the Middle Ages, transmitted
largely orally or transcribed in manuscript form, to sustained efforts of
opening this lore through the medium of print in the sixteenth century.[45]
Yet, while printing signified an important stage in opening Kabbalah to

a wider readership, it was the emergence of a new literary genre—the kabbalistic study guide—that was tasked to mediate Jewish mystical texts and knowledge to a broader audience of nonspecialists.

Following the printing of a large number of kabbalistic works in the sixteenth century, study and absorption of this material unfolded along two trajectories: a direct and an indirect, or mediated, paths. Jewish social elites, who had both the intellectual and the economic acumen to pursue full-time and in-depth study of Kabbalah turned to direct study of the classical sources and when they could, augmented their learning with the oral explication of a kabbalistic master.[46] By contrast, other segments of Jewish learned society, the secondary elites, who displayed competence in all aspects of the traditional rabbinic curriculum, Tanakh, Mishnah, and Talmud, but were forced to eke out a living by serving as beadles, teachers, itinerant preachers, and healers,[47] lacked both the time and the financial resources to engage Kabbalah full time and with the assistance of a qualified teacher. This social class acquired kabbalistic teachings primarily in an indirect manner mediated through printed works and occasionally, when the opportunity arose, with a qualified master. With the diffusion and broader circulation of printed works of Kabbalah and the increased cultural prestige associated with this body of knowledge, secondary elites recognized a unique opportunity for creating a new cultural product that mediated between the kabbalistic corpora and a new community of readers. Members of this secondary elite simplified complex ideas and produced digests and study guides in order to enhance the practical dimensions of daily ritual life. Unlike the traditional rabbinic elite, who took a conservative position to what they defined as authoritative and legitimate sources of Jewish knowledge, the secondary elites proposed a new cultural agenda that emphasized people's right "to choose whether to learn, what they wanted to learn and how they wanted to learn it."[48] The literary innovation of this new group of authors stemmed not from the production of scholastic or theologically complicated treatises, but rather from the textual strategies they adopted to mediate between high and low culture.[49]

The study of Yissakhar Baer and his works makes an important contribution to our understanding of the social and intellectual developments in early modern Ashkenazi culture in its transition from a manuscript to a largely print-based society.[50] Decidedly understudied within the academic scholarship, both in the field of Kabbalah and in cultural history, secondary elites emerge as important intermediaries and negotiators between elite and popular culture.[51] They were poised to gain considerable social prestige and economic benefit from the diffusion of printed books and the greater accessibility to certain bodies of knowledge. For them, books constituted a cultural product that made independent learning possible and thus effectively broadened the intellectual horizons of the laity. Because this segment of Jewish society worked primarily as educators, their strategies of disseminating newly available texts, ideas, and learning came to be reflected in the innovative pedagogical tools they adopted to facilitate the communication of this new information.

The re-presentation of esoteric knowledge and classical works of Kabbalah in the form of intellectual study guides served to commercialize knowledge through mass printing and distribution and address a new nonelite consumer, for whom book learning offered the possibility for social mobility and cultural empowerment. Undaunted by pressures to produce works with original insights and innovative conceptual systems, these authors gained cultural prestige in Jewish society by assuming the role of a pedagogue whose cultural product, the kabbalistic study guide, became the intellectual compass with which readers could gain a foothold in an otherwise complex and often unfamiliar terrain. They saw themselves as mediators of Kabbalah, whose intellectual agency and innovative methodology in providing cognitive shortcuts reached a popular level of consumers and thus enabled them to introduce an alternative voice to elite cultural hegemony, which came under attack in the dissemination of printed matter.[52]

Each of Yissakhar Baer's four printed works constitutes a deliberate strategy to promote a new cultural program for the transmission of kabbalistic knowledge. First, in *Pithei Yah* (1609), the abridgment form enabled him to condense Moses Cordovero's kabbalistic encyclopedia, the *Pardes Rimonim*, into a concise guide to the most fundamental principles of Kabbalah. Second, in *Yesh Sakhar* (1609), the fusion of the halakhic statements of the Zohar with the literary framework of the *Shulḥan Arukh* served to harmonize the legal and mystical dimensions of Judaism and to empower ordinary Jews to enhance their daily performance of the commandments by comprehending the attendant kabbalistic overtones. Third, in composing a lexicon to the Zohar, in *Imrei Binah* (1610), he aimed to ease the user's access to the Aramaic original, which presented a considerable cognitive barrier to the nonelite reader. Finally, elucidation of the *peshat* or literal meaning of *zoharic* words and expressions in his *Meqor Ḥokhmah* (1610), provided a tool for the novice in kabbalistic studies to augment the weekly reading of the Torah with insights into its deeper, mystical, registers.

The literary-pedagogic resources generated by Yissakhar Baer present an intellectual program informed by three interrelated objectives. First, he aimed to connect and join different genres in the classic rabbinic literary canon, and thereby unify disparate elements of study, into one Torah. Thus, rather than presenting Kabbalah as a compartmentalized and extraneous system outside the scope of rabbinic Judaism, he regarded it as a quintessential element underlying all fields of Jewish knowledge that needs to be integrated into its regular study. Second, perceiving the gap between the transmission of Kabbalah through print and the difficulty of its cognitive assimilation, he proposed an innovative pedagogical solution through the reorganization, explication, and simplification of the original works. He was an exponent of the idea that Jewish esoteric knowledge was not to be transmitted in an unmediated fashion to the nonelite reader. As editor, abridger, and anthologizer, he saw his task in composing reference tools designed to enhance a neophyte's absorption and comprehension of Jewish mystical texts and concepts. Third, he articulated a perception of messianic expectations based not on historico-political events or intense psycho-spiritual experiences, but rather on cultural and technological developments, such as the widespread use of printing, that engendered greater access to previously closed bodies of knowledge. The unexpected access his generation enjoyed to kabbalistic corpora that had been closely guarded by the sages of the past, was interpreted by him as a sign that ushered in the end of times and the immanent coming of the Messiah. In turn, access demanded participation of Jews at all levels of society not merely by the elites.[53] In this sense, he saw his own creative efforts as instruments that abet the perfection of the generation in anticipation of a Messianic renewal.

A detailed discussion of Yissakhar Baer's works and intellectual milieu will contribute to our understanding of a body of literature—the kabbalistic study guide—the goal of which, as authors frequently reveal in their introductions, was not so much to offer an original work, but rather to create better organizational structures for the processing of information in Kabbalistic works that had already appeared in print. It is not accidental that several study guides are printed within a century following the first major publishing wave of kabbalistic texts as each author vied and competed for presenting a superior product to the interested reader.[54] What distinguished one kabbalistic guide from another and hence bolstered both its popularity and commercial success was the methodology authors adopted for the management and presentation of esoteric content. This sentiment is captured in authors' introductions as they justified the superiority of their product based on educational and technical improvements they offered compared to competing works in the field.

Apart from a few attempts to offer brief summaries of kabbalistic study guides, a detailed examination of the literary strategies authors adopted has not yet been undertaken by scholars. This is a particularly important desideratum as such information would reveal not only the religious and cultural models these authors worked with but also how they conceptualized the pedagogical dimensions of Kabbalah study. Engaging questions endemic to the field of cultural studies Boaz Huss has published a number of works that investigate the reception history of the Zohar. In his book, *Like the Radiance of the Sky*,[55] Huss traces the confluence of discrete cultural and social processes that facilitated the reception of the Zohar providing an extensive overview of secondary literature of commentaries and learning tools that expedited this process. However, while he offers a comprehensive and detailed enumeration of these sources among them the works of Yissakhar Baer, he stops short of providing an in-depth evaluation of how information was organized in these texts and the various strategies that authors adopted for teaching and transmitting kabbalistic knowledge.[56] Similarly, Zeev Gries and Yaakov Elbaum devote short discussions to Yissakhar Baer in their respective works, both of which are only available in Hebrew, yet while the former places him in the context of popularization of kabbalistic customs through the writing of conduct literature (*sifrei ha-hanhagot*), the latter discusses him in relation to the circulation and printing of kabbalistic literature in Eastern Europe in the early modern period.[57] The methodological approach of all three authors is informed by a preference for surveying evidence at the macrolevel—discussing general trends and providing a cross section of compositions—and not at the microlevel, where the close examination of authorial strategies reveals the pedagogic considerations that animated the approach of secondary elites to how Kabbalah should be disseminated and taught.

Shifting Intellectual Boundaries: Transnational Kabbalistic Networks in Early Modernity

In framing Yissakhar Baer's literary activity at the turn of the seventeenth century it is useful to consider larger cultural developments and patterns that influenced and, to a large extent, defined early modern Jewry. Three elements identified by David Ruderman—the technological invention of the printing press, the rise of a secondary elite, and enhanced mobility—will serve as important pivots for my investigation of Yissakhar Baer's imprint on Jewish and Christian literature and culture.[58] In addition, several scholars have noted that the rise of Kabbalah constituted a significant change in intellectual life in this period providing a cultural bridge not only between the elite and the less-educated strata of Jewish society but also between Jews and Christians, who also hoped to learn this particular lore and synthesize it with Christian beliefs.[59] The incorporation of Yissakhar Baer's works into compositions compiled and edited by Christian, as in the Sulzbach edition of the Zohar (1684), and the appearance of his books on the bookshelves of renowned Christian Hebraists of the time, like Johannes Buxtorf and Stephanus Rittangelius, underlines the unique role Kabbalah played as a mediating force in the cultural exchange between Jews and Christians in this period. The notion of "connected histories" that Ruderman adopts as a critical question in his discussion is particularly valuable for contextualizing Yissakhar Baer's attempt to reach out, communicate, and connect diverse reading communities with a new body of knowledge. Employing the concept of connectedness allows us to argue that the study of Kabbalistic texts and ideas created a unique intellectual space within early modern European society that offered a place of meeting and mixing between Jews and Christians, whether this encounter transpired in the ateliers of printing houses, study halls, or book fairs. The learning aids offered by Yissakhar Baer and made available through the medium of print to consumers of different religious and educational backgrounds help us understand that in the early modern era cultural and intellectual boundaries shifted and at times became more porous and ambiguous than the more clear demarcation envisioned by elites.

Mobility of people, books, and ideas connecting communities and individuals reached a peak in the Galilean hilltown of Safed, which by the second half of the sixteenth century emerged as the prominent center for the transmitting and innovating kabbalistic ideas and practice. The intellectual and pietistic legacies of Safed's leading kabbalists, Moses Cordovero and Isaac Luria, attracted students eager to immerse themselves in its spiritual ambiance and esoteric resources from all corners of the Jewish world. Many espoused to learn from the masters or their disciples and undertook what can be called a *peregrinatio kabbalistica* to come into direct contact with the authentic teachings of Safed Kabbalah. R. Solomon Shlomiel of Dresnitz from Moravia, Menachem Azariah da Fano from Italy, and Abraham Azulai from Fez, all made the journey to Safed in the hope of acquiring teachings and books. In turn, Menachem Azariah attracted followers from distant lands, such as Poland, who undertook the peregrination in order to study with him in Italy. Those historians, who argue for a transnational paradigm of Jewish history and view political and geographical borders dividing Jewish communities in early modernity as porous and flexible, claim that the popularization of Kabbalah and the wide-scale diffusion of kabbalistic ideas highlight the existence of powerful intellectual networks that connected authors and readers of diverse locales and traditions.[60]

Kabbalah in Print thus adds a largely unexplored dimension to the scholarly understanding of intellectual networks by examining the movement of kabbalistic traditions from Safed and Italy to Ashkenazi lands.[61] The works of Yissakhar Baer also expose that the theosophic layers of Lurianic Kabbalah proved too complex and difficult for the popularization of Jewish mysticism within a broader readership at this time. The study guides surveyed here refrain from any meaningful engagement with conceptual aspects of Lurianic Kabbalah and therefore there is a conspicuous absence beyond the occasional reference to Ḥayyim Vital in these study guides. R. Solomon Shlomiel's extant letters, one of which was addressed to Yissakhar Baer, provide a valuable account of the development of Safed Kabbalah, its defining personalities, and the intellectual tension that arose among the kabbalists in advocating and authorizing the Lurianic over the Cordoverean system as the Kabbalah of choice.[62]

Yet, R. Solomon Shlomiel constitutes more than just a biographer of Safed and its kabbalistic community, he also assumes prominence as a point person for aspiring authors of Kabbalah back in the communities of Ashkenazi lands, like Yissakhar Baer, who sends him a manuscript of *Yod'ei Binah* his large commentary on the Zohar for approval (*haskamah*) of the Safed kabbalists. R. Solomon Shlomiel's reply to Yissakhar Baer reveals that at the beginning of the seventeenth century the Safedean kabbalistic elite was reluctant to approve the works of authors who espoused the Cordoverean and not the Lurianic theological system.[63] The importance of Cordoveran Kabbalah at this point time in Ashkenaz has been noted by Moshe Idel, who showed that "the greatest part of kabbalistic literature that was disseminated and influential at the end of the sixteenth and the beginning of the seventeenth century was derived from Cordoverean sources."[64] Yissakhar Baer's literary output demonstrates that this was especially true for secondary elites who lacked direct access to Lurianic manuscripts that were circulated in extremely limited circles, whereas several works of Moses Cordovero had already appeared in print and therefore constituted a more accessible source material for these authors.

Overview

Chapter 1 examines the impact of the printed book on shaping Christian and Jewish culture and religious consciousness. The diffusion of the new technology of print reconfigured not merely the technological, intellectual, and educational, but also the religious landscape of Europe. While not everyone had equal access to books, the production of cheaper pamphlets and new ways of knowledge sharing through lending and borrowing, ensured the entry of heterodox ideas into the religious fabric of European society that challenged the Catholic doctrinal hegemony on religious beliefs. New movements, such as the Reformation, used the mass production of print matter in vernacular languages to transition religion from the exclusivity of the Church into the private and direct domain of believers. Carlo Ginzburg's study of a sixteenth-century Italian miller, a representative of popular culture highlights the power of print in abetting intellectual creativity even in those segments of Christian society, that were traditionally not associated with book learning. At the same time, this chapter highlights that at the level of high culture among the learned humanists of Italian society, Hebrew books and more specifically the field of Jewish mysticism came to represent vestiges of an ancient civilization, which they longed to rediscover and appropriate. The printing of the Zohar and other kabbalistic texts in the middle of the sixteenth century reflects a growing demand not only by larger segments of Jewish society but also by an emerging Christian readership. Yet, printing could only partially open this corpus of esoteric knowledge. To facilitate greater access to Kabbalah, learning tools and educational guides had to be developed to navigate the literary and conceptual challenges of these texts; it is in the transition from high to low, and from Jewish to Christian culture that the role of secondary elites, like Yissakhar Baer, becomes accentuated.

Chapter 2 describes the cultural and social milieu in which to frame Yissakhar Baer and other secondary elites' literary activity focusing on

Prague and Poland. Following a detailed overview of the characteristics of early modern Ashkenaz, I will turn to a brief description of the scant information that is available about Yissakhar Baer's life. The chapter will end with a discussion about the agents who played an instrumental part in making Yissakhar Baer's work reach their intended readers: the printers themselves. In particular, I will examine the place of Yissakhar Baer's efforts to popularize mystical works in the broader context of his printers' publication programs.

Chapter 3 examines Yissakhar Baer's first published work, *Pithei Yah*, which recasts Moses Cordovero's encyclopedic compilation, the *Pardes Rimonim*, into a digest of ten short chapters. In analyzing *Pithei Yah*, this chapter focuses on how the genre of abridgment functioned in reorganizing information. This chapter also provides a brief overview on the role and development of digests in Christian religious texts to show that this genre served an important pedagogic role among the learned segments of both Jewish and Christian society. In my investigation, I am specifically interested in how the abridgment, as a literary genre, functioned for an author who represented the secondary elite and wished to address a readership similar to him. Raising questions regarding the concepts that his abridgment chose to elucidate and the techniques he engaged for this purpose reveals what was lost in content and what was gained by the adoption of a new form in mediating elite culture to nonelite readers. Finally, I offer some comparative insights between *Pithei Yah* and the abridgment strategies adopted by two Italian kabbalists, Menahem Azariah da Fano in *Pelah ha-Rimon* and Samuel Gallico in *Assis Rimonim*, works that were printed less than a decade before Yissakhar Baer's own compendium.

Chapter 4 considers the form and the content of Yissakhar Baer's, *Yesh Sakhar*. In its content, *Yesh Sakhar* draws on the *ta'amei ha-mitzvot* literature, a distinct kabbalistic genre prevalent in the Middle Ages that seeks to uncover the mystical reasons for the commandments in Jewish law. In composing *Yesh Sakhar*, the author orders the laws of the Zohar following the thematic layout of Joseph Qaro's *Shulhan Arukh*, a codification of Jewish law printed in the sixteenth century. Arguably, Qaro's work also addressed a new audience that was no longer inclined toward an in-depth study of the masters of Jewish jurisprudence but wished merely to receive a practical guide for the observance of Jewish law. I argue that Yissakhar Baer's adoption of the codifying format of the *Shulhan Arukh* implies that he shares Qaro's goal to address a wider audience by simplifying halakhic discourse. At the same time he goes beyond

Qaro's work by infusing discussion of Halakhah with its corresponding kabbalistic explanation. By so doing he, as an author, shapes a new idea and ideal: Jewish mysticism cannot remain on the margins restricted to elite circles but, instead, needs to be made accessible to a wider audience. He achieves this goal by synthesizing the most fundamental realm of Judaism, Halakhah, with its most esoteric one, Kabbalah.

Chapters 5 and 6 explore Yissakhar Baer's works that engage specifically the linguistic and semantic aspects of the Zohar. His *Imrei Binah* seeks to clarify the difficult words (*milim zarot*) that appear throughout the Zohar. His aim is to both clarify these neologisms that have as well as to provide other kabbalistic sources that are helpful in clarifying these expressions. In contrast to other similar lexicons that take an alphabetical approach to arranging these words, Yissakhar Baer's literary strategy is to offer a concise definition and explanation of these terms following the layout of the Zohar itself, in the order of Biblical chapters (*parashiyot*). In *Meqor Hokhmah*, he turns to translating, summarizing, and explicating the literary layer of the Zohar, which he embellishes with brief kabbalistic commentaries. In *Meqor Hokhmah*, he turns to explicating the literal meaning (*peshat*) of *zoharic* pericopes. The main methodological focus for chapter 6 is to provide a renewed appreciation for the genre of anthology, which has historically suffered from neglect and depreciation in academic discourse not merely in Jewish but also in general literary studies. The chapter will provide comparative insights into the strategies that other authors adopted for presenting the exegetical content of the Zohar. This comparative analysis will demonstrate that as a literary form anthologies exhibit elasticity and originality in shaping and reframing the boundaries of existing texts and areas of knowledge. Editors of kabbalistic anthologies employed various techniques to create their own product by adopting strategies that they deemed apposite to address a specific readership through the deliberate reconfiguration of original texts. Thus no two anthologies appear identical. By uncovering Yissakhar Baer's strategies of recombining the Zohar's semantic and linguistic dimensions, chapters 5 and 6 will provide insights into the way that the author introduced, presented, and re-presented the Zohar to new readers.

Chapter 7 discusses the reception history of Yissakhar Baer's works, especially among Christian readers, demonstrating that "reading takes no measures against the erosion of time,"[65] and that new readers rediscover and reappropriate in creative ways the written compositions of earlier generations.[66] This section will conclude by contextualizing the scholarship of Isaiah Tishby and Daniel Matt's recent translation of the Zohar into English, as creative steps in the popularization of Kabbalah continuing the efforts of such early modern figures as Yissakhar Baer in the creative re-presentation of the Zohar.

Chapter 1

Print Technology and Its Impact
on Religious Consciousness

A man's knowledge can reach only so far as his books extend. Sell,
therefore, everything you have in order to buy books . . . "The more
books, the more knowledge."

—Isaac Companton

Printing and Its Impact on Christianity

Book printing, which began in the middle of the fifteenth century with
Gutenberg's invention of the movable type, transformed the access to
knowledge and information management on an unprecedented scale.[1]
Whereas the assessment of scholars varies considerably regarding just
how revolutionary printing was compared to manuscript culture,[2] there is
strong consensus regarding the transformative affects of the printed book
on the production, circulation, and accessibility of written matter.[3] Those
who prefer to highlight the evolutionary rather than the revolutionary
character of printing underline that the basic structure and appearance of
the printed book was modeled largely on the layout, writing hands, and
organization of content, already in place for the production of manuscripts.[4]
Like manuscripts, books were also comprised of sheets assembled into
quires and carefully bound by a cover. In addition, the continuity from
scribal to print culture is evinced by the use of referencing techniques
and indexing developed already in the scriptoria but extended and further enhanced in the print shop.[5] Nevertheless, others maintain that in

spite of structural and formal similarities between manuscript and print
matter, the technical innovation of the movable type precipitated certain
cultural transformations that arose directly from the invention of a new
commercial medium.

One area unequivocally impacted by the diffusion of the printing
press, was the unprecedented increase in the circulation of books. The
low cost of paper in contrast to the vellum,[6] used for the production of
manuscripts, made it possible for books to reach new audiences and for
new readers to access a far greater amount of books.[7] Printing, in contrast
to scribal copying, dramatically decreased the amount of time required
for reproducing a text thus making a large number of copies available
in a significantly shorter time.[8] The consumer was exposed to a "more
varied literary diet than had been provided by the scribe," more books
became available for purchase which a person could own and incorporate
into one's private collection, read from time to time, and consult in the
comfort of one's home and personal library.[9] In fact, the possession and
gradual expansion of a personal library became an important intellectual
endeavor not merely for the clerical, scholarly and aristocratic strata in
European society but also for lay individuals.[10] Once acquired, the book
was seen as something more than a material object lining the shelves of
libraries, it assumed intimate and personal dimensions and "served as the
record of one's life, a chart of one's network of literary connections, and a
confidant of one's feelings."[11] Humanist readers of the fifteenth and early
sixteenth century regarded the volumes they purchased as extensions of
their lives, as a kind of diary that ran alongside the formal printed text, in
which the empty spaces beckoned the owners to contemplate and record
important events in their lives or their intellectual ruminations.[12] The
publicly traded book thus became refashioned into a treasured possession
that reflected not merely the features assigned to it in printers workshops,
but also the owner's personal associations, concerns, and *modus vivendi*.

Printing also played a crucial role in aiding cultural preservation.
Ludovico Domenichi, the renowned Renaissance translator, called attention
to the preservative power of printing in the sixteenth century when he
lamented that if printing had been available for the ancients their works
would not have disappeared.[13] Another important case in point was the
conservation of large books, which took a long time and considerable
expense to produce in the scriptoria. On occasion, scribes were called
upon to copy but a fragment of a manuscript original in accord with the
demand and interest of the commissioner.[14] Therefore, large books had a

very limited circulation and were particularly vulnerable to decline in the manuscript age. Printing, however, made the reproduction of oversized books possible and thus contributed to their conservation and circulation among a broader group of readers. Larger print runs and additional marketing strategies were developed to make oversized books more appealing to potential consumers and therefore increase profitability for the printers who invested substantial sums in producing them. *Cosmographia*, a large book with extensive illustrations, was printed in 1550 and at 3,600 copies represented a considerable increase from the print run of 500–1,000 for average oversized books.[15] Technical improvements, such as title pages and indexes, became novel features in the book production process implemented by eager printers who hoped to turn a profit on their investment. The title page, appearing first with the printed book, served as an important advertising tool, introducing briefly the author and announcing the title and publisher of the text. Indexes were key selling features for potential buyers in the sixteenth century, and printers invested considerable money to include them even in popular works composed in the vernacular.[16] Printing, therefore, generated not merely a quantitative explosion but an equally important qualitative transformation in the management and organization of information: "printing shaped both the nature of the information explosion, by making more books on more topics available to more readers, and the methods for copying with it, including a wide range of printed reference tools."[17]

Textual production in the early decades of printing gradually transitioned from the scriptoria, located in university towns and patrician villas controlled largely by the ecclesia, to the workshops of profit-driven book sellers, operating in major urban centers of Europe.[18] At the same time, a high percentage of *incunabula* reflected the preponderance of religious works printed, not in vernacular languages, but in Latin.[19] In the early years, printers were quick to realize that the majority of their customers came from among the Catholic clergy, and therefore religious literature would turn a dependable profit. The Bible was in great demand by all strata of society—from churchmen, university professors, students, and the laity—and it should not be surprising that in the fifteenth century alone, more than one hundred different editions of the Bible were issued by various European printshops.[20] In the sixteenth century this figure jumped to 437, four times the output of the fifteenth century.[21] Clearly, the main priority for printers in the first centuries of production was to firmly lodge the Bible not only in educational and clerical institutions but also on the bookshelves of the pious laity, who for the first time were able to access this text in vernacular languages.[22]

Alongside the Bible, other genres of devotional literature also began to circulate, some of which targeted the religious specialist, while others appealed to a general readership. Collections of sermons, handbooks on the remedies of the human soul, and guides on confessionals intended for priests were as much in demand as books on the lives of saints, and the cult of the Virgin, which were popular for urging piety among lay believers. Printing intensified the preoccupation with religious questions and opened up "a distinct arena of possibility . . . for religious agents to debate opponents, win converts, or consecrate their own legitimacy and authority by claiming to speak in the name of the masses."[23] Printing brought religion with all of its unresolved theological contradictions and dilemmas into the daily lives of ordinary people and at the same time books devoted to religious topics appeared in libraries of lay individuals.

Inquisitional records about the life and religious concerns of a six-teenth-century Italian miller, Domenico Scandella, expose the depth to which religious texts and questions pervaded the lives and preoccupied the thoughts of common individuals who were far removed from circles of clerical, scholarly, or aristocratic elites. Menocchio, as Scandella was commonly called, was convinced that the Catholic Church was doctrinally obsolete, with the priests and the Inquisition acting like parasites, con-trolling the minds and lives of the masses: "Priests want us under their thumb, just to keep us quiet while they have a good time."[24] The only way to neutralize the influence of the Church, maintained Menocchio, was to acquire knowledge from books and one's own intellect and marshal a counternarrative to the hegemonic dogma of the ecclesia. Empowered by access to printed books, which he either purchased or borrowed, and popular oral traditions, presumably influenced by contemporary Anababtist or Lutheran religious ideologies, Menocchio audaciously revealed his own idiosyncratic cosmogony and set out to proselytize others to his version of theological *veritas*. According to Menocchio's reformulation of the Biblical genesis narrative, in the beginning only chaos existed with the four elements—earth, fire, water, and air—comingled in it; and from it "a mass formed—just as cheese is made out of milk—and worms appeared in it and these were the angels . . . and among the number of angels there was also God."[25]

At the fulcrum of the confrontation between Menocchio and the Church, was the question of legitimacy and authority in accessing, expounding, and disseminating correct religious knowledge. Following the Counter-Reformation, the Church was particularly sensitive to doctrinal heterodoxy and the Inquisition was swift to thwart any attempt that sought to undermine the supremacy of Catholic theology. The Church correctly identified that the malaise, which informed the heretical views of Menocchio, was largely attributable to the diffusion of printed matter, which, if left uncensored, had the potential to cultivate subversive ideas and heretical tenets. Thus, from the sixteenth century on, especially in Italy, the enthusiasm for printing was concomitantly tempered with ecclesiastical attempts to control the circulation of uncensored texts, leading to public and private book burnings and the compilation of an incessantly revised and constantly expanding *Index Librorum Prohibitorum* (Index of Prohibited Books).[26]

For Menocchio, however, the availability of printed matter signified freedom from the chains of clerical oppression and an invitation to engage creatively with diverse ideas. Having acquired a modest library, half of which consisted of bought books while the other half was borrowed, Menocchio set out to read and synthesize these heterogeneous strands of knowledge into what seemed to him a coherent and innovative conceptualization of the world and his place in it. Textual sources, such as the Bible in vernacular, the Qur'an in Italian translation,[27] Boccaccio's *Decameron*, a travel book by Sir John Mandeville transcribed into Italian, and other accounts of lives of saints and popular legends,[28] served as raw material, which combined with oral traditions circulating at the time, provided the framework for Menocchio's theological iconoclasm. The books he read pushed Menocchio toward new cultural vistas, and challenged him to reevaluate his beliefs in light of a variegated reality that stared back at him from the printed page. For an uneducated miller, whose daily routine transpired squarely within the confines of the small village of Montereale, Mandeville's *Travels* embodied an invitation to see the world, virtually of course, but nonetheless, to visit remote islands and encounter unusual people, such as the Pygmies, and the revolting flesh-eating ceremonies of the cannibals. Menocchio's exclamation, "So many kinds of races . . . and different laws," "many islands where some lived in one way, some in another," "out of many different kinds of nations, some believe in one way, some in another,"[29] voices the profound astonishment of the self-taught plebian, for whom the printed book became the gateway to profound cultural transformation. By the time Menocchio was burned at the stake by the Inquisition in 1599, he had endured seven interrogations and a two-year prison sentence, yet defiantly held true to his treasured beliefs, which embodied for him nothing less than his cultural acumen. Printing, as Menocchio's story emphatically highlights, comprised a powerful cultural tool that influenced not merely an elite readership but reshaped and profoundly imprinted the religious and intellectual panorama of the lower classes.

In the early modern period, printing intensified the role of religion in society and posed a particularly acute challenge to the religious hegemony of the Catholic Church. Menocchio's appropriation of the printed medium for a fundamental overhaul of his own religious system may have been conditioned by another transformation more systematic in its scope and much grander in its scale, the onset of the Protestant Reformation, which, beginning with the first decades of the sixteenth century, radically recon- figured the religious landscape of early modern Europe. That the success of the Reformation owed as much to Luther's zealous disparagement of the indulgences and the general corruption rampant within the Catholic Church, set down and immortalized in his *Ninety-five Theses*, as it did to the technological opportunities provided by the printing press, has been extensively underscored by scholars.[30] Access to God unmediated by the Catholic ecclesia was at the forefront of Luther's religious revision, which he hoped to attain by placing the Gospels directly into the hands of the laity in vernacular languages that could be accessed by all. Divesting the Catholic Church of its power to act as interlocutor between Heaven and Earth, Luther harnessed "spiritual aspirations to an expanding capitalistic enterprise" and enlisted printers to flood Europe with cheap pamphlets that spread the Protestant propaganda to all parts of the continent.[31] The Reformation placed religious knowledge and expertise in the hands of every householder and spiritualized the Protestant household.[32] In Catholicism, the devout could not access God directly without the mediating efforts of ordained priests who ministered in Latin on one's behalf, dispensing both the catechism and the sacraments necessary for proper religious conduct. By contrast, printing in Protestant circles transferred religion from the control of institutions and specialists to the family household. Fathers, as heads of their domicile, were entrusted with the responsibility of ensuring that members of their family received proper religious educa- tion and that they conducted regular worship services at home. Printed Bibles, prayer books, and "numerous pocket-size manuals that came off the printing presses"[33] were important educational tools, made available by the new technology, to aid the transition of religion from the public space of churches to the privacy of the home. Through the wide diffusion of printed matter in vernacular languages, Protestant reformers strove to spread religious ideas beyond a scholastic elite to a broader populace of uneducated laypeople.

> Through prayer and meditation, models for which they could find in scores of books, the draper, the butcher . . . soon learned to approach God without ecclesiastical assistance . . . The London citizen learned to hold worship in his own household . . . the private citizen had become articulate in the presence of the Deity.[34]

Luther recognized that the use of vernacular languages in place of Latin together with the technological innovation of printing, which enabled the quick and cheap production of religious texts, would transport religious ideas and ideals to new reading communities.[35] However, the use of vernacular languages for the presentation of the Bible and religious concepts was not without controversy and reluctance. Luther expressed a sense of profound trepidation and agony over forcing what in his eyes seemed vulgar and unsanctified on the sacred as he undertook the monumental task of translating the Bible into German: "I bleed blood and water to give the Prophets in the vulgar tongue. Good God, what work! How difficult it is to force the Hebrew writers to speak German! Not wishing to abandon their Hebrew nature, they refuse to flow into Germanic barbarity."[36] Nonetheless, Luther's priority was to communicate the new religious ethos of the Reformation to all strata of society, and therefore when it came to rendering the Bible into German, he displayed a keen eye to people's use of the German vernacular.[37]

In the first half of the sixteenth century, Christian responses to print technology were ambiguous at best. On the one hand, printing made it possible for Protestant reformers to disseminate new religious ideas to distant lands and to a broader circle of readers. Luther took full advantage of the availability of new technological and cognitive tools and extolled the communicative values of cheap pamphlets and the use of vernacular languages in advocating a theologically reformulated Christianity on the European continent. Religion became democratized when lay individuals could own a piece of it in the form of vernacular Bibles, prayer books, and collected sermons. At the same time, while the Protestant reformers strove to replace the rosary with the book, the Catholic Church adopted several measures in the first decades of the sixteenth century to quell the uncontrolled circulation of heterodox religious ideas and regulate the dissemination of knowledge. Papal Bulls, Inquisitional inquiries, and indexes of forbidden books, colluded to enforce the perpetuation of Catholic dogma and erect a powerful barrier against the free diffusion of new intellectual and religious systems. An educational consequence of the differing attitude toward the printed book between Protestants and Catholics resulted in encouraging reading among the former, while restricting it among the latter.[38] The concomitant responses of enthusiasm and anxiety exhibited by the two rival Christian factions concerning the educational opportunities inherent in print technology found expression among contemporary Jews as well. In the next section, I will trace the diverse attitudes espoused by Jews toward the printed word.

Trajectories of Hebrew Printing

The gradual transition of the written word from manuscript to the printed page, that unfolded gradually and became indelibly entrenched in Christian Europe amid the religious crisis of the Protestant Reformation and the subsequent political upheavals that engulfed the European continent, set the stage—the limitations and opportunities—for the emergence of Hebrew printing in the early modern period. As I trace the development of Hebrew printing and more specifically the appearance of kabbalistic literature in the sixteenth and seventeenth centuries, it is important to remain mindful of cultural reciprocity that persistently informed and molded Christian and Jewish attitudes toward this new technological medium. The tension between Christian elite demands for the use of Latin in print versus growing interest in books in vernacular languages resonated in debates over Hebrew versus Yiddish printing, as new readers in Jewish communities, such as women, children, and uneducated men, turned to texts expressed in languages they could comprehend. The powerful restraining force of the Catholic Church in the wake of the Counter Reformation that led, on the one hand, to the public burning of the Talmud along with other Jewish books, while at the same time, it commissioned indexes that itemized forbidden Hebrew material, stymied the efflorescence of Hebrew printing in the sixteenth century, and altered its future direction. At the same time, printing brought Hebrew books into the libraries of Christian readers, especially at the elite and scholarly levels, and facilitated cultural exchanges and intellectual cooperation. The study of Hebrew printing, therefore, needs to carefully isolate internal Jewish developments, while simultaneously recognizing the influence of broader social, cultural, and political factors.

Within three centuries, from the incunabula period to the end of the seventeenth century, Hebrew book production went from 139 titles in the fifteenth century, 2,700 titles in the sixteenth century, to as high as 3,526 titles in the seventeenth century.[39] The first Hebrew books printed were Rashi's *Commentary on the Pentateuch* and Jacob ben Asher's *Arba'ah Turim*.[40] Increased output was also accompanied by important organizational transformations in Hebrew printing. What used to be a largely peripatetic profession of pioneering entrepreneurs in the early decades of printing solidified into established large printing houses by the first half of the sixteenth century. Gershom Soncino, an important Jewish printer, traveled extensively in search of both new textual sources as well as more favorable economic conditions to sell his print matter: "I toiled and found books that were previously closed and sealed . . . I traveled to France, Chambery, and Geneva, to the places of their origin."[41] Soncino printed books in Hebrew, Latin, Greek, and Italian, and was able to keep his expenses low by employing mostly his family and casual cheap labor. By contrast, as large Hebrew presses proliferated in the sixteenth century, they were increasingly owned and operated by Christian printing magnates whose financial investment and operational output were many times higher than that of Gershom Soncino.[42]

Daniel Bomberg, one of the most profitable and prestigious Christian printers of Hebrew books in the early modern period, availed himself of various technical, commercial, and marketing advantages to make his enterprise competitive and qualitatively superior to other presses. Originally from Antwerp, he established his printing house in Venice and after a brief partnership with an apostate Jew, Felice da Prato, he applied to, and received exclusive monopoly from, the Venetian Senate for the printing of Hebrew books for two decades.[43] He employed a large staff of scholars, proofreaders, correctors, typesetters, and editors. In addition, he invested substantial sums of money in compiling advertising catalogues that reached distant Jewish communities in as diverse geographical locations as Syria, the Crimea, Egypt, Africa, and India, informing commercial agents and potential customers about new titles and their respective prices.[44] He printed approximately 228 books during his printing career, which constituted one of the most impressive production outputs of his time, including rabbinical classics such as the *Mikra'ot Gedolot* and the *editio princeps* of both the Babylonian (1519/1520–1523) and the Jerusalem (1522–1524) Talmuds. The press also maintained very strict standards both in regard to paper quality as well the aesthetic appearance of its books, so that when the Venetian Senate decreed a fine of 100 ducats, the revocation of privileges, and public burning of books for presses that did not abide by certain quality-control measures, the Bomberg press was always beyond reproach.[45]

While the Bomberg press was an industry leader both in magnitude of book production and visual presentation, it nonetheless was compelled to share the Venetian print market with three other competitors—the Giustiniani, the Bragadin, and the di Gara printing houses. In fact, this quartet enjoyed such unparalleled market advantage that their combined publishing output accounted for the majority of all the Hebrew books printed in the course of the sixteenth century.[46] The Venetian printers were famed in Jewish communities all over the world for their expert imprints and meticulous proofreading, which made their products and services highly sought after.[47]

> It is well publicized and known to all exiles that the imprints
> from Venice are the most correct and exact of all the imprints
> made today under the heavens. For if you take a Humash
> printed in Salonica, you will find every sort of sin (i.e. numer-
> ous mistakes), which is not the case of the Venice imprints.[48]

When mystical works by Safed kabbalists began to appear in print toward the end of the sixteenth century, they did not issue from presses operating in the Ottoman Empire, which were known to have printed kabbalistic material at this time, but instead were prepared for print by Italian presses. Thus, when Gedalyah Cordovero decided to print his father's works, he sent them to the Venetian presses, whose reputation for quality far surpassed their Ottoman rivals in Salonica and Constantinople. Similarly, Cordovero's student, Elijah de Vidas, entrusted the manuscript of his seminal work, *Reshit Ḥokhmah*, with the di Gara press in Venice, which printed it in 1579, five years after its completion by the author.[49]

In addition to being a prominent printing center at the time, Venice also functioned as a cultural hub for the production of important manuscripts. Venetian ateliers employed copious scribes to copy Greek manuscripts and to generate handwritten newsletters with military and political updates that could bypass censorial control. Alongside printed books, certain literary genres continued to be disseminated in manuscript form, including magical texts, political satires, anticlerical works, and tractates about sexuality. Thus, authors who were likely to expose ideas that would elicit the condemnation of Inquisitional censors were confined to manuscripts with limited and carefully circumscribed circulation.[50]

The price of books, in relation to other commodities in Italy, offers an important indicator concerning the affordability and ownership of printed matter among Jews in Cinquecento Italy. We saw in the case of Menocchio, that a Christian miller in the sixteenth century owned privately between five to eight books and had access to another six to eight borrowed volumes. Hebrew book costs were subject to periodical fluctuations throughout the century, conditioned at times by production shortages, competition among rival presses, and ecclesiastical decrees that delimited the circulation of certain texts. The burning of the Talmud in 1553 lead to a sudden drop in the price of Talmudic tractates as owners rushed to sell their own copies of the forbidden text. However, as the printing and circulation of the Talmud ceased in the second half of the sixteenth century, demand for forbidden, and therefore rare, books drove the prices up again.[51]

The Bomberg catalog for the years 1542–1543, mentioned earlier, represents a rare and invaluable source of information for disclosing the price of Hebrew books at the time, and provides a point of departure for determining their relative value compared to average salaries and the price of other goods and services. The catalog was acquired by the famous humanist scholar, Conrad Gesner, in 1543, during his stay in Italy, and subsequently published in one of his books. According to the catalog, the cost of the Babylonian Talmud was 22 ducats, which represented the equivalent of more than three months of work for an average manual laborer. To purchase Bomberg's *Multi-Commentary Bible* at 10 ducats, the laborer had to work for a month and a half. Large books, therefore, were expensive, and their circulation was limited to the libraries of well-to-do patrons, for whom the Babylonian Talmud cost 15 percent and Alfasi's legal code 12 percent of their annual income. Thus, members of the Jewish community, even in the highest income category of over 150–200 ducats a year,[52] had to set aside a substantial portion of their annual income to afford large-sized books. By comparison, a horse or a slave cost only marginally more than the Talmud at 22–24 percent of one's annual income.[53] The occupational sectors most frequently associated with the acquisition and regular consultation of books were physicians, scholars, rabbis, and students, professions that historically displayed highly variegated wage scales. Rabbi Yizhak de Lattes, a celebrated rabbi of his day, was offered extraordinary compensation by the community in Pesaro, which included 100 gold scudi, the equivalent of 126 ducats, and accommodation "suited to his rank." By comparison, the community rabbi in Verona earned a meager 6 ducats, which allowed him just enough money to cover basic necessities.[54] Physicians fared just marginally better, and were often required to supplement their regular income with other revenue-generating activities, such as making house calls. A community physician, who attended to the poor, earned an annual income of only 15 scudi, while others were able to attain salaries more commensurate with their Christian counterparts at 100–300 annually. Paradoxically, many readers who arguably stood to benefit most from purchasing and reading large-sized Hebrew books were economically prevented from doing so. The fact that they did own large books in their libraries suggests that they may have either received them as gifts from the community or wealthy patrons, or assumed a considerable financial burden by purchasing these books on their own.[55]

A 1595 edict by Pope Clement VIII, which forced the relatively large Jewish community of Mantua to deliver its library holdings to the Inquisition's headquarters for examination and, when necessary, expurgation, provides a rare glimpse into the number and types of books Jews owned and read in the Duchy. The inventory drawn up by the community contained a total of 21,142 copies of works comprised mainly of printed books, with a small number of manuscripts (14%),[56] and 1,234 titles in three languages, Hebrew, Yiddish, and Italian.[57] The analysis of book ownership in the sixteenth century demonstrates that an average Jewish household had 50 volumes, wealthier libraries 100–300, and lay or economically disadvantaged families 1–10 books.[58] Among Christians, urban households owned more sizable library collections than the rural ones, and while the nobility, clergy, and judges acquired hundreds of tomes, the merchants and laity availed themselves of more modest library collections, with 1–10 books, which represented a considerably smaller number than their Jewish counterparts.[59]

The reading interest of the Jews of Mantua displays a penchant for books that regulated and impacted the course of daily ritual life, such as liturgical (34.6%) and halakhic texts (10.7%), along with the most fundamental and sacred book in Judaism, the Pentateuch and its commentaries (22.2%). In fact, the Torah and the prayer book were ubiquitous in every household. The most popular titles in the inventory included the *Pirkei Avot* (43.9%), legal codes such as Maimonides' *Mishneh Torah* (43%), the Mishnah (39.8%), R. Jacob ben Asher's *Arba'ah Turim* (35.1%), R. Joseph

Qaro's *Shulhan Arukh* (33.7%), an ethical tractate titled *Menorat ha-Maor* (26.5%), R. Moses Qimḥi's grammar book, *Mehaleq Shvili ha-Da'at*, and the homiletical compilation of Midrash Tanhuma (20.1%). Works of philosophy and Kabbalah circulated at approximately 10 percent and appeared mainly in the libraries of scholars (70%). At the same time, it is revealing that the Zohar (10.5%) enjoyed wider diffusion and popularity than Maimonides' philosophical work, *The Guide of the Perplexed* (9.5%).[60] The fact that copies of the Zohar could be found in one out of every ten households just four decades after its printing, attests to the great cultural currency it commanded among the Jews of Mantua at the end of the sixteenth century, a phenomenon that I will discuss more fully below. The library holdings of the Mantua Jews reflect as much the reading interests as the cultural priorities of the community and therefore the predominance of Hebrew books, with only a marginal representation of non-Jewish, Italian literature (2.4%),[61] accentuate the preservative value the printed medium afforded to the Mantuan Jewish community. Books for women and children were few, but included *Misvot Nashim*, a women's guide on Jewish religious and ritual life written in Yiddish, and *Or Lustro* and *Davar Tov*, small format polyglot lexicons for children, written usually in Hebrew, Italian and Yiddish.[62]

A brief examination of the library inventory of the Mantua Jewish community at the end of the sixteenth century demonstrates that the increased circulation of books transformed people's access to knowledge in profound ways. Whereas in the preprint era, knowledge was controlled by and confined largely to rabbinic elites, the diffusion of printed texts made it possible to standardize both ritual and liturgy and made these available and accessible to the laity. As with the Protestant Reformation in the Christian world, the demand for vernacular texts, in Italian and Yiddish, with an appeal to new readers, such as uneducated men, women, and children, opened up cultural opportunities of self-study. Furthermore, the democratization of knowledge through print unlocked access to thereto restricted and previously supervised areas of wisdom and made the mystical tradition of Judaism, the Kabbalah, directly available to an interested and eager-to-learn nonelite readership.

Christian Consumers of Kabbalistic Books

The intellectual synthesis of diverse religious systems and ancient philosophical schools, which was advocated by humanist thinkers from the fifteenth century on, became intensified by the technological opportunities that printing proffered in the last decades of that century. Humanism, which originated from Italy and gradually conquered the intellectual centers of Europe, was a movement that called for a profound overhaul of the regnant educational curriculum.[63] In the process, the humanists discovered that educational reform and cognitive renewal were ultimately predicated on revisiting the cultural legacy of the past—the literary remnants of vanquished, but once glorious, civilizations. The quest of Christian humanists to rediscover the gnosis the ancients possessed and to reexamine the arcane sources of knowledge, led to fervent scholarly activities and compelled the monumental translation efforts of Marsilio Ficino (1433–1499), who transposed entire bodies of wisdom from Greek and Hebrew into Latin. Ficino was in the employ of Medicis—the powerful Florentine banking dynasty—who commissioned him to translate the complete works of Plato, printed in 1484, and a much treasured, newly acquired manuscript by the Medicis, the *Corpus Hermeticum*. The latter was a set of tractates attributed to Hermes Trismegistus, the mythical Egyptian magus and prophet, who for the Renaissance humanist represented the revival of an all but forgotten lore that originated from the dawn of humanity.[64] Trismegistus, or "thrice great," Hermes mastered all three realms of natural and divine knowledge, kingship, priesthood, and philosophy,[65] and thus personified for the humanists the highest ideal of unifying separate domains of wisdom into one universal truth.

According to an emerging new philosophical formulation, articulated for the first time by Ficino and later embraced by other Renaissance thinkers, all human wisdom originated from a primal revelation of truth, which he called *prisca theologia* (ancient theology). This archaic stratum of human consciousness, conditioned by a basic notion of the Divine, informed the religious and intellectual systems of all pagan authors, including Plato, Zoroaster, Hermes, Orpheus, and Pythagoras. Ficino's conceptualization of ancient theology erased the boundary separating religion and philosophy and presented these disciplines as sharing a spiritual core, whether it was centered on belief in the Trinity, an Aristotelian maxim, an Orphic hymn, or a kabbalistic text. To locate the original wellspring of truth, the humanist sifted through the layers of historical epochs and their idiosyncratic religious and cultural manifestations, and arrived at the Mosaic tradition, equating the ultimate source of ancient wisdom with the revelation of the Hebrew Bible.[66]

The Christian humanists' attraction to the Bible was not motivated by a desire to discover rabbinical scriptural exegesis or jurisprudence, but

rather to remove the veil that covered the Bible's cryptic language and
to uncover the primordial mysteries concealed therein.[67] They regarded
the Kabbalah, as the repository of the most authentic layer of Judaism,
revealed by God to Moses and the Jewish people, and passed down orally
from one generation to another. Kabbalah thus emerged as a great equal-
izer, a universal code that formed the nucleus from which all subsequent
religions and philosophies derived. Whereas, rabbinic texts such as the
Talmud accentuated Jewish particularity and enforced the primacy of laws
and rituals in shaping Jewish religious identity, the Kabbalah muted the
theological schism between Judaism and Christianity and created a common
universal language. Pico della Mirandola (1463–1494),[68] Marsilio Ficino's
student and a prominent Christian kabbalist of the Renaissance period,
voiced the theological utility of kabbalistic literature for Jewish-Christian
debate and discourse: "Taken together, there is absolutely no controversy
between ourselves and the Hebrews on any matter, with regard to which
they cannot be refuted and gainsaid out of the cabalistic books, so there
will not even be a corner left in which they may hide themselves."[69]
Christian appropriation of the Kabbalah was tantamount to removing the
divine essence from Judaism, which bereft of its life line would with time
cease to exist and eventually merge with the true and universal doctrines
of the Catholic Church.[70]

The concept of ancient theology became a ubiquitous cultural force
in the fifteenth and sixteenth centuries and constituted a catalyst for intellectual syncretism that brought Jews and Christians into dialogue with
the pagan seers and religious systems of the primordial past. The image
of Hermes Trismegistus carved into the marble floor near the entrance
at the Cathedral of Siena, typifies the incorporation of a sacred figure of
pagan history as a prefiguration to the advent of Jesus and Christianity.[71]
The inscription below his feet says, "Hermes Mercurius Trismegistus, the
contemporary of Moses." To the left of him, a bearded man garbed in
oriental robes and a turban, visibly shorter and smaller than Trismegistus,
stands in a reverent posture and hands him an open book. This figure
likely represents Moses, as Jews in the fifteenth century were frequently
portrayed in Christian iconography as assuming an Ottoman style.[72] The
book held simultaneously by Moses and Hermes reads: "Take up your
letters and laws, Egyptians!" On his right, Trismegistus leans on a tablet
held by two sphinxes, which carries an inscription: "God the Creator
of all / Made the second God, visible and sensible / He made him first
and singular / Delighted and exceedingly loved his own son / Who is

called the Sacred Word."[73] The placement of this mosaic at the entrance
of the cathedral, served as a visual affirmation of the universal truth of
the Christian religion, the origins of which are rooted in ancient divine
mysteries, represented by Hermes Trismegistus, who mediates between
the laws and letters of the Hebrews on his left and the Christian Trinity
of God, Son, and the Holy Spirit (the Word), on his right.[74]

The cultivation of an integrated systems of thought informed not
only the decorations of sacred Christian space, but infiltrated also printing
workshops, university lecture halls, and the private studies of Jewish and
Christian intellectuals. Translation and the printing press made vast volumes of human knowledge available and expanded the cultural horizons
of individuals. In the urban centers of Europe, like Venice, Amsterdam,
Prague, and Florence, Christian and Jewish thinkers strove to cultivate
comprehensive learning of theology, philosophy, science, and medicine.
The idea of the "Renaissance man" or universal sage was espoused not
only by Christian humanists such as Pico and Ficino in Italy, and Johannes
Reuchlin in German lands, but also by their Jewish contemporaries like
Judah Messer Leon, his student Yohanan Alemanno, and Abraham Yagel.[75]
The admission of Jewish students to the medical faculty at the university
of Padua in the early sixteenth century exposed Jews not only to a new
academic curriculum but also to new expressions of culture and art while
still remaining observant of the religious demands of traditional Jewish
life: "Theoretically, at least, after class a Jewish medical student could
enjoy both a hearty kosher lunch in the adjacent ghetto and an edifying
excursion to view Giotto's paintings in a nearby church."[76]

It is not surprising therefore, that in the first half of the seventeenth
century, a prominent graduate of the Padua Medical School, Joseph
Delmedigo, was so inspired by his studies in Italy that he undertook the
composition of a major encyclopedic work, *Ya'ar Levanon* (*The Forest of
Lebanon*), in which the natural sciences were explicated alongside the
tenets of philosophy.[77] The Italian Jewish polymaths of the early modern
period frequently engaged the encyclopedic genre for the organization and
presentation of multiple systems of thought.[78] The integration of Kabbalah
into the academic curriculum of the Christian humanist, was predicated
first and foremost, on the availability of books and second, on the guidance of teachers who were expert both in the Hebrew language and in
the principles of Kabbalah. The pursuit of Hebrew texts led Christian
scholars to the printing houses, while the need for tutorials in Semitic

languages and Jewish mystical theosophy brought them into dialogue with the leading Jewish intellectuals of their time.

Grammar books devoted to the detailed exposition of the Hebrew language began to appear in print in the fifteenth century and became important reference tools for Christian Hebraists in the following centuries. It was the printing of the medieval Provencal grammarian and Bible commentator, David Qimhi's magnum opus titled *Sefer Mikhlol* (*Comprehensive Book*), comprised of two sections—a complete dictionary of Biblical Hebrew, *Sefer Shorashim* (*Book of Roots*) and a systematic handbook on Hebrew grammar titled, *Mikhlol*—that established these texts as standard reference tools for the study of the Hebrew language.[79] The demand for the *Shorashim* in Italy was so urgent in the incunabula period that it was reprinted four times in quick succession, from 1469 to 1471 in Rome, and in 1479, 1490, and 1491, in Naples. In the sixteenth century, it enjoyed unprecedented popularity[80] and was frequently consulted, translated, and appropriated by Christian Hebraists as the authoritative guide to learning and teaching Hebrew grammar. The influence of Qimhi's works was so pervasive among Christian scholars and theologians that until the nineteenth century they constituted the decisive texts on the Hebrew language studied in European universities.[81] David Qimhi's brother, Moses, was also credited with writing a book on Hebrew grammar, *Sefer Diqduq*, which enjoyed wide circulation and popularity in the Renaissance period. The *editio princeps* was printed by Joshua Soncino in 1488, and was subsequently reprinted eleven times in the fifteenth century.[82]

The acquisition and study of Hebrew grammar books complemented the pursuit of Jewish mystical theology in the curriculum of Christian Kabbalists. The prominent German Hebraist and avid student of Kabbalah,[83] Johannes Reuchlin, took advantage of his posting at the embassy in Rome in 1498, representing the Elector Philipp of the Palatinate, to acquire Hebrew books as well as to immerse himself in intensive Hebrew studies with one the most renowned Biblical commentators of the period, Obadiah Sforno. It is of note that the "book hound" who was hired to track down and obtain relevant books on Reuchlin's behalf, returned with none other than David Qimhi's classic exposition of Hebrew grammar, the *Sefer Mikhlol*.[84] It is also interesting that the first section of the *Mikhlol* was obtained as a manuscript, while the second part, the Hebrew lexicon, was an imprint, highlighting the continuity of manuscripts alongside printed editions of a given work at end of the incunabular age. The acquisition

of Hebrew books constituted a considerable challenge for Reuchlin, and
he frequently complained that Jews were averse to selling their books
to Christians. The success of his book hunt was in no small part facilitated by Lawrence Behem, the majordomo of the Vatican under Pope
Alexander VI, whose considerable influence opened important doors in
Reuchlin search. The acquisition of Qimḥi's *Mikhlol* proved essential for
Reuchlin's subsequent scholarly endeavors and formed the foundation for
his own exposition of the Hebrew language, the *Rudiments of Hebrew
Grammar*.[85]

To supplement his book learning, Reuchlin's affiliation with the
papal court enabled him to engage the young but already highly esteemed
Obadiah Sforno in individual tutorials. He took daily classes with Sforno
for little more than a year and paid top price for the private instruction
at one gold piece per lesson. Sforno was not merely a prodigious scholar
of the Bible but had also mastered the humanist curriculum, including
proficiency in the Latin language, which made him particularly well posi-
tioned to teach Hebrew studies to interested Christian disciples. Sforno
maintained close association with the papal court and actively promoted
scholarly and theological exchange between Jews and Christians. In his
interpretation of Exodus 24:12, he revealed that God desired the study of
both the oral and written Torah by non-Jews, and therefore Christians are
called on to cultivate their knowledge of the Hebrew language.[86]

While Reuchlin's studies of the Hebrew language appealed to his
interest in philology, his turn to the study of Kabbalah engaged Reuchlin,
the theologian. He wrote two tractates on Kabbalah, the *Miracle-Making
Word*, printed in 1494 and composed before his extended sabbatical
in Rome, and *Art of the Kabbalah*, appearing in 1517, which displays
Reuchlin's mastery of both the Hebrew language and diverse sources of
medieval Kabbalistic theosophy. For the systematic presentation of disparate
kabbalistic theories in *Art of the Kabbalah*, Reuchlin relied primarily on
manuscripts in their Hebrew or Aramaic original and to a lesser extent
on printed works available in Latin translation, such as Joseph Gikatilla's
Sha'arei Orah, translated by the celebrated convert to Christianity, Paulus
Ricius.[87] In his survey of the major tenets of Kabbalah, Reuchlin synthesized an impressive array of medieval kabbalistic classics, including the
Sefer Yeẓirah, the *Bahir*, the Zohar, with the works of prominent medieval
philosophers and kabbalists, such as Maimonides, Nachmanides, Abraham
ibn Ezra, Azriel of Gerona, and Todros Abulafia. He may have also relied
on anthological compilation of kabbalistic texts, a manuscript example of

which can be found at the Jewish Theological Seminary (MS Halberstam 444).[88] It is noteworthy that Reuchlin's highest praise is reserved not for the mythical or theosophic-theurgical kabbalistic system espoused by the Zohar and other works but rather for Joseph Gikatilla's *Ginat Egoz*, a work devoted to the exposition of linguistic mysticism and the magical operations that arise from the proper understanding of the Hebrew alphabet and the activation of its metaphysical potential.[89] Reuchlin's attraction to the magical possibilities inherent in a divine language reflected a more universal principle shared by prominent Christian Kabbalists of the Renaissance period.[90] Reuchlin argued, based on a theory originally developed by Marsilio Ficino and further refined by Pico della Mirandola, that words correspond to natural powers and the artful combination and manipulation of the elements of a divine language such as Hebrew can produce powerful magical outcomes.

> What a certain noble philosopher recently proposed in Rome has not seemed unlearned to me: No names in a magical and licit operation have the same power as those in Hebrew or those closely derived from Hebrew, because of all things, these are firstly formed by God. That in which nature chiefly practices magic is the voice of God.[91]

Thus, an intellectual and religious reorientation among an increasing number of Christian humanists and Kabbalists led them to foment close contacts with their Jewish counterparts.[92] A discovery of the magical properties intrinsic to the Hebrew language, impelled the Christian Hebraists to integrate intensive study of Hebrew with the contemplative inquiry into Kabbalistic theology and practical magic.[93] The demand for textual sources compelled Christian intellectuals in Italy to seek out and acquire whatever Hebrew resources they could find in both manuscript and printed forms. The printing of grammar books and kabbalistic texts therefore became critical not only for a Jewish but also for a growing Christian reading community.

Wealthy Christian humanists such as Reuchlin and his revered Italian colleague, Count Pico della Mirandola, had access not only to the best Jewish scholars of their generation but in addition possessed the means to acquire a substantial portion of the extant kabbalistic literature in Latin translation, which further aided their study and knowledge of these texts.[94] Kabbalah and the Hebrew language formed a cultural bridge

between intellectuals from the two religious communities and spurred an
efflorescence of intellectual creativity, which culminated in the emergence
of new ideational currents, such as the phenomenon of Christian Kabbalah. The intimacy and mutual respect between the Christian scholar,
Pico della Mirandola, who sought to establish the true meaning of one
of the most recondite books of the Hebrew Bible, the Song of Songs,
and his willing teacher Yohanan Alemanno, is faithfully documented in
Alemanno's account.

> When I came to take shelter in the shadow of this cherub,
> crowned with divine lights, a prince perfect in knowledge
> of the Lord, who shields him and his intelligence day and
> night and is never separated from him, stirred his mouth and
> tongue to ask me if, in my vain life, I had seen any brilliant
> light among the commentators on the Song that is Solomon's
> that would distinguish between the various things that are so
> confusingly mixed in it . . .
>
> He said, "Please let me also hear, for I have labored over
> all the commentators who have written in Greek and Latin,
> but I am not satisfied about the order of progression rightly
> to be found in it."
>
> So I, as a servant before his master, read out its arrange-
> ment, which I had established among its symbols and, praise
> to the living God! He thought of me as of someone who has
> found a great treasure [. . .]
>
> This is my lord, called Count Giovanni della Mirandola
> and I am Yohanan, son of Isaac of Paris, called Ashkenazi, in
> Hebrew, and Aleman in the language of the people among
> whom I live.[95]

The elegiac undertone in Alemanno's depiction of his relationship with Pico,
calls to mind the concept of *amicitia* or friendship, which the Renaissance
humanists enthusiastically embraced as an essential component in the
pursuit of knowledge. Ancient Greek literary models based on Aristotle,
Seneca, and Cicero advocated the cultivation of friendship among scholars,
which would in turn lead to the formation of intellectual communities
that would function independent of other social institutions. The pursuit
of universal truth, the *prisca theologia*, brought Christian humanists closer
to their Jewish counterparts, whom they regarded less as rivals and more

as intellectual collaborators and colleagues sharing the path in the quest for knowledge.[96]

Close cultural encounters and collaborations between Jews and non-Jews, however, were not unequivocally endorsed in Jewish circles. The Rabbis were painfully aware that familiarity with the intellectual and theological legacy of medieval and ancient rabbinic speculations would open the door for Christians to engage Jews in dialogue and discussion with the ulterior motive of converting them to the Christian faith.[97] The discovery of kabbalistic texts and ideas by the Renaissance humanists, as is evident in the theological efforts of Pico della Mirandola, invited them not only to present Kabbalah as the most ancient and authentic layer of the Mosaic revelation, but also to argue that properly elucidated kabbalistic doctrines reinforce the truth of both the Christian religion and the matter of the Trinity.[98]

> No Hebrew Kabbalist can deny that the name Jesus, if we interpret it according to Kabbalist principles and methods, signifies God, the Son of God, and the wisdom of the Father through the divinity of the third person . . .[99]

Rabbinic caution and reticence against the uncontrolled exposition of certain doctrines of Judaism informed the composition of a responsum by Rabbi Elia Menaḥem Ḥalfan in Venice, in 1544. Based on precedent and evidence drawn from both Talmuds, Rabbi Ḥalfan argued that while Jews were certainly permitted to teach Hebrew to non-Jews in order to enable them to comply with the seven Noahide laws, any instruction regarding the oral and esoteric traditions of Judaism was expressly forbidden.[100] That neither ecclesiastical proscription nor rabbinic indictment could halt the printing of kabbalistic literature and their assiduous study by Jews and non-Jews alike is evinced by the fervent activity to print both first, as well as rival, editions of kabbalistic texts in the second half of the sixteenth century.

The high cultural acumen associated with the ancient Jewish lore that represented the theological repository of both Judaism and Christianity, impelled the followers of these religions to invest considerable time and effort to acquire and study these texts.[101] By the time the French priest, Jacques Gaffarel purchased several kabbalistic books from Mirandola's library for Cardinal Richelieu, in the first half of the seventeenth century,[102] Kabbalah ceased to be confined to the libraries of Jewish and Christian elites and gradually conquered the public dimensions of religious life. With the Zohar's appearance in print, in the middle of the sixteenth century, Kabbalah began to penetrate all aspects of Jewish life, from sermons, liturgy, and rituals to even the halakhic (legal) stratum.[103] For Christians, Kabbalah, came to embody the most valuable part of Judaism that had to be saved from the Inquisitorial bonfire and held up as the most potent weapon Christians can engage in their theological crusade for the conversion of Jews, as reflected in the callous statement of Sixtus of Siena: "By means of the Kabbalah 'Christians can stab Jews with their own weapon.' "[104]

Printing Jewish Mysticism:
The Zohar and Other Works

A major milestone in the dissemination of kabbalistic texts was the printing of the Zohar between 1558 and 1560. Before its appearance in print, the Zohar enjoyed only limited and restricted circulation in the form of fragmentary manuscripts without a clearly defined literary framework that would delineate the content of the zoharic corpus.[105] Thus, prior to the middle of the sixteenth century, those who collected zoharic fragments never possessed a unified canon, each person owned a different manuscript variant, hundreds of which circulated at the end of the Middle Ages and into the early modern period. R. Yehudah Ḥayyat describes his own persistence to gradually acquire as many units of the text as he could: "I resolved to seek wisdom . . . gathering whatever [parts] of the aforementioned book [the Zohar] could be found. I collected a bit here and a bit there, until most of what is extant of it was in my possession."[106]

The first literary evidence that incorporates the largest amount of extant *zoharic* material is Moses Cordovero's *Or Yakar*, an encyclopedic commentary on the Zohar that remained in manuscript until its publication in the twentieth century.[107] It was in Cordovero's meticulous editorial hands that for the first time distinct units and passages of the *Zohar* were collated and reworked into an actual book and literary corpus.[108] The transformation of the Zohar into a sacred and authoritative text alongside literary representatives of the Oral Torah such as the Mishnah, the various Midrashic compilations, and the Talmuds unfolded as a gradual but sustained process in which the actual printing of the text denoted not the beginning of canonization but rather its culmination.[109] The printing of the Zohar, in fact, could be conceptualized as an indispensable and final step in establishing it as the authoritative source of kabbalistic speculation, for in the absence of a closed corpus both authority and canonicity could be more easily disputed.[110] In addition, emerging from the Iberian Jewish intellectual tradition, the Zohar was destined to cement the cultural hegemony of Spanish Jewry and present Kabbalah in its unadulterated authenticity without the admixture of philosophy and magic, which were so closely intertwined in the speculative system of the Italian Kabbalists.[111]

In the fifteenth and sixteenth centuries, the authority of the Zohar was mediated through the introduction of zoharic ideas and passages into commentaries, sermons, liturgy, customs, and halakhah. One of the first kabbalists to incorporate substantial portions of the Zohar into his works was Menaḥem Recanati, who wrote his *Commentary on the Torah* in Italy at the end of the thirteenth century. The early printing of his work in Venice in 1523, even prior to the printing of other kabbalistic classics, such as *Ma'arekhet ha-Elohut* (1557, Ferrara; 1558, Mantua), *Sefer Yeẓirah* (1562, Mantua), Gikatilla's *Sha'arei Orah* (1559, Mantua), and *Sha'arei Zedek* (1561, Riva di Trento), underlines the emergence of a growing demand to access the Zohar, albeit in an indirect and excerpted fashion. At the end of the fifteenth century, with the influx of a large contingent of refugees from the Iberian Peninsula, the Zohar became so pervasive that nearly every kabbalistic work included some exegesis on it.[112]

At the same time, a growing number of sermons in the sixteenth century began to reference the Zohar and other kabbalistic sources targeting both elite and nonelite audiences. Isaac de Lattes, the Italian rabbi closely involved with the printing of the Zohar, delivered an impassioned sermon to the Jewish community of Bologna in 1559, asking them for donation of funds at a time when the community experienced economic and political turmoil. In the course of his sermon, De Lattes' frequent allusion to lengthy and theologically complex passages from the Zohar, which he had to have delivered in translation, underscores the depth to which the Kabbalah in general and the Zohar in particular penetrated the Jewish community of Bologna and the intensity with which it resonated for its members.[113] A survey of homiletical works printed between 1540 and 1640 indicates that out of 193 sermons, 25 or close to 13 percent, displayed some kabbalistic content.[114]

In the area of halakhah, the Zohar became an important source of authority and *zoharic* customs and decisions governing Jewish life and conduct eventually became incorporated into normative legal codes.[115]

Rabbi Joseph Qaro in his comprehensive compendium on Jewish law, the *Beit Yosef*, takes decisive steps to align the halakhic portions of the Zohar with Jewish practice:

> And thus I have observed the Ashkenazim who were in the habit of washing their hands for the priestly blessing, even though they had already washed their hands in the morning. However, I did not know the origin of this matter that the Levites wash the hands [of the Kohen], until by God's grace I found it explained in the Zohar in *Parashat Naso*.[116]

On another occasion, Qaro legislated in both the *Beit Yosef* and the *Shulḥan Arukh* that a synagogue should have twelve windows based on the Zohar's mystical interpretation of this precept, a question that received no legal treatment by either the medieval legal decisors or the Talmud.[117] Beginning with the early sixteenth, and becoming more amplified in later centuries, the Zohar's idiosyncratic interpretation of halakhah provided a counterpoint to major Ashkenazi law codes, such as the *Arba'ah Turim*,[118] and impelled legists and kabbalists to evaluate and to take a position concerning the relationship between these two discrete but equally fundamental fields within Judaism. Meir ibn Gabbai, for instance, sharply repudiated the opinion of the *Tur*, and enthusiastically embraced the halakhic position expressed by R. Shim'on bar Yohai in the Zohar concerning the question whether one is allowed to pray in an audible voice.

> Thus I have seen in the homily of Rashbi, peace be upon him, and it is proven from his words that it is forbidden, whether in public or not in public, to let others hear one's prayer. And this is not as the opinion of R. Jacob the son of the Rosh . . . and in such matters that are not found in our Talmud, we should rely on the tradition of [Kabbalah] the holy light, Rashbi, peace be on him.[119]

Kabbalists in the sixteenth century, especially the Safed mystics, proposed a number of liturgical innovations based on the Zohar's unique theological formulation that highlighted the theurgical efficacy of prayer, which had to be recited with proper intention and concentration. Thus, Elijah de Vidas in his *Reshit Ḥokhmah* highlights the reciprocal relationship between human action and its metaphysical consequence. The unification of thought, speech, and action during a person's recitation of prayer, functions as a shield against the demonic side, which is diminished by it, while holiness and the Divine are strengthened and restored to ontological unity and perfection.

> A person, whose actions are for the sake of Heaven and for the mystery of unification of the Name, that is the [*Sefirah* of] *Malkuth*, [with] Heaven, [the *Sefirah* of] *Tiferet*. When a person begins by saying, 'for the sake of heaven,' in everything he does, the demonic immediately departs. However, if his actions are not for the sake of heaven, evil resurges and accompanies that action. Therefore, a person should direct his deeds for the sake of heaven: in thought—so that mind and action would be united for the sake of the unification of his Master [God] as is known; in speech—he should recite [the formula] 'for the sake of the unification of the Blessed Holy One and his *Shekhinah*'; and in doing—so that his deeds would not be futile, for speech and thought will not suffice when the vessel [itself] is repulsive.[120]

Another liturgical insertion widely observed in contemporary Jewish communities was the recitation of a passage derived from the Zohar delivered just before the Torah scroll was removed from the Ark beginning with "Blessed Be His Name" (*Berikh Shmei*).[121]

Jewish circles, enthusiastic about the printing of the Zohar along with other kabbalistic texts, were motivated by three interrelated principles. First, that printing would democratize access to thereto restricted texts and knowledge. Second, printing would contribute to the preservation of a Jewish legacy that was perceived to be under constant threat of extinction and oblivion due to political persecutions and dislocation of the Jewish people at the time, including the painful memory of the large-scale expulsion of Jews from the Iberian Peninsula. Thus, while manuscripts were often unreliable, filled with errors and easily lost in the wandering, printing produced fixed texts, in larger quantity, that enjoyed broader circulation.[122] Third, the appearance of Kabbalah in general, and the Zohar in particular, in print signaled for many the spiritual apogee of Jewish history, the last generation and the imminent arrival of Messianic redemption. In his introduction to *Minḥat Yehudah*, R. Yehudah Ḥayyat expressed two interrelated principles: he maintained, on the one hand, that access to the Zohar and, in fact the very existence of the text in his generation, bears eschatological significance; on the other hand, the popularization, dispersion and intensive study of this lore would hasten the coming of the Messiah.

> [F]or until the last generation, in which we live today . . . this book was intended to be hidden, and until that time, only the supernal beings, the angels, were to benefit from it, until the last generation, when it would be revealed to the lower beings. And through the merit of those who delve into it and immerse themselves in it, the Messiah will come, for because of it, the land shall be filled with the knowledge of God,[123] and this will be the reason for His coming, as it is written, through it "you shall return, every person, to his possession."[124]

Hayyat further argues that not only does the Zohar affect the general course of Jewish history, it also offers apotropaic dimensions in the individual Jew's life.[125] He attributes surviving the expulsion from Spain and the subsequent vicissitudes he suffered at sea and in North Africa to his relentless study of Kabbalah, in general, and the Zohar, in particular:

> I believe in perfect faith that this [the Zohar] is the merit that helped me in all the predicaments that befell me during the expulsion from Spain. If my power was the power of rocks, if my flesh was capable of suffering all these tribulations, it is surely because of the effort I exerted in following this wisdom. This is what strengthened and kept me as I have kept it, when nobody else did.[126]

Isaac de Lattes in his imprimatur to the Mantua edition of the Zohar, draws on the messianic sentiment he knows would resonate with the readers in order to theologically justify and arouse urgency for the printing of the Zohar.

> Behold, the seventh year, the year of *shemitah*[127] is approaching. When will we prepare for our future? And when will the verse be fulfilled concerning is: "And the land shall be filled with knowledge of the Lord?' 'If not now, when?"[128] In the seventh millennium when the world will be destroyed? Almost a third

of the sixth millennium has passed by, and our souls disdain honey, mistaking the sweet for the bitter. We treat as moldy bread the noble bread on which the highest angels are fed. We do the commandments as an act of habit, arbitrary laws with no explanations . . .[129]

De Lattes frames the publishing of the Zohar within the context of apocalyptic immediacy, based on the kabbalistic notion of cosmic cycles.[130] He underlines the special urgency of the times, stirring the reader to embrace the knowledge that the mystical dimensions of Judaism can offer not only theoretically but also in enriching and providing meaning for the ritual expressions of Jewish life.

In Jewish historiography the causes that precipitated the printing of the Zohar in Mantua and Cremona, have received extensive treatment.[131] Heinrich Graetz, the German historian of the *Wissenschaft des Judentums*, saw the burning of the Talmud, which took place in several Italian cities in the 1550s, as a pivotal event that left behind a major religious and cultural vacuum, which could only be filled by an equally, if not more, authoritative and ancient source of knowledge, the Kabbalah. R. Immanuel of Benevento, who was closely associated with the printing of the Zohar, expressed his anxiety over what might happen to Judaism if the Kabbalah suffered the same fate as the Talmud. There is a clear assumption in his words that the emergence of Jewish mystical literature had become a source of hope for Jews in their struggle for survival and continuity against the draconian cultural and religious measures introduced by the Inquisition to force Jews closer to the babtismal font: "If we should lose this too, what would the man whose Torah is his way of life do in his desolation? From what book could he come to know the Glory of God?"[132] Graetz also argued that while the Catholic Church suppressed and proscribed the Talmud, it actively promoted the printing of Kabbalah, which it regarded as more conducive to the Christianization of Jews.[133]

The historian, Isaiah Sonne, attributed the printing of the Zohar to the emergence of a new group of wandering rabbis sympathetic to the humanist discourse, who were more liberal and flexible than their institutionalized counterparts to the idea of popularizing Jewish mysticism and saw its printing as a good source of income. Thus, for Sonne, rabbis who were involved in the printing of the Zohar were motivated first and foremost by the commercial opportunities inherent in the enterprise. Isaiah

Tishby, in contrast to Graetz and Sonne, marginalized and downplayed the role of external factors and amplified the significance of internal spiritual developments that culminated in the eventual printing of the Zohar. Boaz Huss, as we have seen, stressed the process of canonization through which the final printed version of the text became set and standardized.[134] Moshe Idel, argued that printing of the Zohar emerged against the background of two conflicting approaches to Kabbalah: one, represented by Yohanan Alemanno, which was more inclined toward philosophy, magic, and making Kabbalah more exoteric, and another position, which took a more conservative stance against printing and called for the preservation of the Zohar's exclusivity.[135]

Opposition against printing the Zohar in Italy was based on the notion, shared by prominent members of the rabbinic elite, that the wide dissemination of kabbalistic material would not only disrupt the traditional modes of transmission of this lore but would also dramatically alter certain cultural patterns in Jewish society.[136] The sudden transformation of esoteric knowledge into an exoteric discipline that can be purchased, read, and studied by any Jew without undergoing necessary preparatory steps elicited virulent criticism from leading rabbinical authorities.[137] The rabbis understood that printing of Kabbalah would fundamentally alter the relationship between popular and elite culture, open up the possibility for even unlearned Jews to apply their own intellect and cognitive faculties to understanding Jewish esoteric wisdom, which in turn would displace authoritative masters, who in previous centuries controlled the mode, level, and pace of learning and transmission. Rabbi Jacob Finzi, himself a kabbalist and one of the chief opponents of printing Kabbalah, articulated his position against the wide dispersion of this lore: "By way of printing, a person will come to study Kabbalah by himself, without a partner. And even young people, and children, and people who are not respectable [will engage in this], which is not according to the rule, 'one should not study without a partner,' he should be middle aged, modest, and respectable."[138]

When the prominent Italian rabbi and persistent opponent of the uncontrolled dissemination of Kabbalah, Leon da Modena decided to pen an attack against the broad circulation of kabbalistic works, he framed his own polemic by citing a passage by his predecessor, the great luminary of Polish Jewry, Rabbi Moses Isserles. In *Sefer Torat ha-Olah* (Prague, 1569), Isserles expressed strong opposition against the popularization of Kabbalah among the unlearned and uninitiated strata of Jewish society.

In this book, *Torat ha-Olah*, part three chapter four [Isserles wrote], "Many people among the masses leap up to study this matter of Kabbalah because it is a delight to behold. This is especially in the words of the recent ones who explicitly revealed their matters in their books. All the more so in these times when the books of Kabbalah have been printed, the *Zohar*, Recanati, and *Sha'arei Orah*,[139] which anyone can examine. Everything will be explained according to his understanding even though their words will not be understood by way of truth, since it is no longer transmitted from one recipient of the tradition to another. Not only this, that the enlightened ones should understand it, but even the common folk who do not know the difference between their right and their left, who walk in darkness, who do not know how to explicate the weekly potion or the portion with Rashi's commentary, even they leap up to study Kabbalah."[140]

Isserles here objects not to the study of Kabbalah, which he acknowledges to be a "delight," but rather to the improper transmission of this lore qua printing in place of the traditional oral model of exposition from master to disciple. A second tangent of Isserles's criticism is directed at the cultural and educational consequences of printing, which he saw as fundamentally corrosive to the traditional Jewish educational curriculum, which followed a hierarchical ordering of various sources of knowledge. Based on principles articulated in Maimonides's *Mishneh Torah*,[141] Jewish education was predicated on three foundational pillars—Bible, Mishnah, and Gemara.[142] Whereas the acquisition of knowledge in rabbinic academies was carefully controlled and monitored, the democratic access to Kabbalah by the nonelite strata of society threatened to undermine and profoundly alter the elite cultural monopoly. The new nonelite consumer became empowered to define and shape their own curriculum, which according to Isserles, could easily lead to confusion, error, and even heresy.[143]

One way of understanding the rise of internal censorship within Jewish communities is to realize the profound anxiety the spread of Kabbalah elicited among the rabbinical elite. News about the democratization of Kabbalah in Italy provoked a ban among the mystics of Safed, who instituted a moratorium on publishing the works of these kabbalists for a certain period of time.[144] The acerbic reaction of Moses Cordovero, one of the most erudite kabbalists of his generation, is clearly directed against the

upsurge among Christians to access and absorb Jewish esoteric teachings
fresh off the Italian presses.

> Just as foxes damaged the vineyard of God, the Lord of Hosts,
> today in the land of Italy the priests study the science of Kab-
> balah and they divert it to heresy, because of our sins, and the
> ark of the covenant of the Lord, the very science of kabbalah
> has hidden itself. But blessed is He who gave it to us, because
> neither they [priests] nor the gentiles distinguish between right
> and left, but are similar to animals because ultimately they did
> not fathom the inner [essence of the lore].[145]

The strong stance of the Italian rabbinate for securing the approval
(*haskhamah*) of three rabbis in good standing on every newly published
book, after 1554, reflects both a response to increased censorial pressure
coming from the Inquisition as well as internal measures of dealing with
the unbridled dissemination of the secrets of Torah. The successive threats
of excommunications and bans issued by various Italian rabbis, were
informed by an effort to disenfranchise Jews motivated to print Kabbalah
because of financial considerations. Rabbi Jacob Finzi waged a sharp
attack against Jews who promoted the printing of the recondite layers of
the Torah under the false pretense of bringing light to the masses, when
all they really cared about was lining their own pockets.[146]

By contrast Moses Basola, a contemporary of Finzi, argued that
printing in itself did not constitute a breach against revealing the mysteries
of the Torah. He maintained that since the Torah itself was comprised of
various layers, the Zohar's commentary to it also functioned at multiple
levels. The uneducated would be nourished by reading its plain meaning,
the marvelous stories, which would reveal to them new interpretations
of Scriptures. For those, however, who belonged to the inner circle and
already received initiation into kabbalistic doctrines, the Zohar would
open new horizons and expand their comprehension of the divine realm.

> For ultimately, when [the Zohar] discusses the essence of the
> divine and [the doctrine] of the emanations, it will do so in a
> veiled manner, and none will understand it except, one who
> is wise, understanding, and knowledgeable about the ways of
> Kabbalah. Therefore, I say that, considering everything, it is
> appropriate for the uneducated to learn the literal meaning of

the passages, by way of truth, which are sweeter than honey and the honeycomb . . . and when a person comes to the pure marble stones, "the lame will leap like a hart,"[147] for they will seem to him as the words of a sealed book and he will say, 'I cannot understand it, for these words are hidden and sealed." Those who are filled with knowledge, who have drunk from the well of living waters, will quench their thirst with its words [the Zohar], and paths of wisdom will be illuminated for them.[148]

The publishing of the *Tikkunei ha-Zohar* in 1557, in Mantua, by Meir ben Ephraim of Padua and Jacob ben Naphtali ha-Kohen of Gazolo marked the first appearance of *zoharic* literature in print. At this point, the printers did not hint at the possibility of a complete edition planned for a later release, which could raise the question whether the Mantua edition of the Zohar became crystallized only after it was revealed that preparations were underway at the Cremona press.[149] When the Cremona edition of the Zohar was released from the workshop of the Christian printer, Vincenzo Conti in 1558, it encompassed a single large volume, bearing the approval of the Inquisition but lacking a rabbinic *haskhamah* and a preface. Subsequent to the burning of the Talmud in Rome, in 1553, and the rise in ecclesiastical control of printed material, a rabbinic synod was convened in Ferrara in 1554, which instituted a decree that required the approval of three ordained rabbis to approve the printing of a new book.[150] The absence of rabbinic approval in the original Cremona Zohar is indicative of a general unease with which the rabbinic leadership greeted this edition, which became popularly known as the "Christian version." The fact that the publisher adopted the square type and not the Rashi script, which was generally employed for the printing of commentaries and rabbinic literature, served to elevate the status of the Zohar to a canonical text equal in stature only to the Torah. The editorial decision to upgrade the Zohar's status came at a time when the rabbis were painfully aware of the Christian mission to expunge the Talmud and replace it with the Zohar and therefore regarded this move as particularly callous. The textual inclusions and the typeface selected for the printing, revealed the tendentious predisposition of the Cremona editors and elicited the disapproval of rabbinic authorities who sought to regulate the printing of kabbalistic matter: "no one has permission to print any kabbalistic work, without permission of three rabbis from three different kingdoms, supported by truth and righteousness as is the custom."[151] When the Inquisition raided

the Conti workshop in 1559 to remove indexed books, they found 2,000
unsold copies of the total print-run, which allegedly numbered 3,000
copies.[152] This implies that within two years the press sold 1,000 copies of
the Zohar and underscores that in the early modern period the printing
of kabbalistic books constituted a financially lucrative enterprise.

To redress the shortcomings of the Cremona version, the printers
of the *Tikkunei ha-Zohar*, Meir ben Ephraim of Padua and Yaakov ben
Naphtali ha-Kohen of Gazolo, issued a new edition of the Zohar in the
Mantua workshop of Tommaso Ruffinelli, printed in the more appropriate Rashi typeface and comprised of three handy volumes released in
successive years between 1558 and 1560.[153] The Mantua editors claimed
to have relied on ten manuscripts in compiling their version, in contrast
to their colleagues in Cremona who used six manuscripts, two of which
were regarded as benchmarks, one from Egypt and another from the
land of Israel.[154]

Perhaps in response to criticism from Jewish circles, which aligned
themselves more closely with the Mantua edition, the publishers felt
that the Cremona Zohar had to be updated to make it more marketable
among Jewish customers. Consequently, the copies that were still held at
the press received an editorial facelift and were reissued as the second
Cremona edition between 1559 and 1560. A notable improvement in the
new version was the inclusion of an introduction, which served to upend
the Mantua, and attract customers to the Cremona version of the Zohar.
In his foreword, the publisher Vittorio Eliano, took pains to emphasize
the key selling features of his edition by castigating two major limitations
of the Mantua variant: the Rashi typeface, which according to him did
not befit the sanctity of the text and the omission of important kabbalistic sources, such as *Midrash Ruth*, *Ra'aya Mehemna*, and the *Hidushei
ha-Bahir*. It is interesting to note that Zvi ben Avraham Kalonimos Yaffe,
the first printer of the Zohar in Eastern Europe (Lublin, 1623), adopted
the Cremona edition as his benchmark with some minor but ubiquitous
concessions to its critiques, the clever choice of the Rashi over the square
typeface and the appropriation of the decorative frame of the Mantua
edition for the title page.

Once kabbalistic books were printed,[155] the genie was out of the
bottle, and while the polemic about what was appropriate to be printed
continued for some time among the Jewish elite, various cultural indicators
affirmed that by the end of the sixteenth century, Kabbalah had become
widely dispersed and "owned by many."[156] First, references to kabbalistic

texts and ideas multiplied in this period due in large to the profusion of kabbalistic classics in print, including the Zohar, the *Ma'arekhet ha-Elohut*, and the works of Menaḥem Recanati, Joseph Gikatilla, Yehudah Ḥayyat, and Meir ibn Gabbai. Second, access to the printed literature of Kabbalah produced variegated responses within the different strata of Jewish society. Among Ashkenazi rabbinic elites, the study of the Zohar became part of the educational curriculum and citing *zoharic* excerpts in new compositions at this time became a marker of intellectual sophistication and cultural prestige.[157] Third, Kabbalah constituted the fifth most printed literary genre in the period 1540–1640, comprising 459 books, which represented 8.2 percent of the total books printed. During the same period, the most printed genre was liturgy (1,062 books, 18.8%), followed by Bible and its commentaries (1,031, 18.3%), *halakhah* or Jewish legal texts (714, 12.7%), and, finally, rabbinic literature, Mishnah, Talmud, and their commentaries (602, 10.7%). It is interesting to note that at this time, philosophy as a literary genre enjoyed considerably less popularity than Kabbalah with 206 books comprising only 3.7 percent of printed compositions.[158]

Conclusion

Christian and Jewish circles were equally impacted by the emergence of printing in the fifteenth century, which both initiated and amplified a fundamental reorientation of religious life for the followers of these traditions. As novel areas of religious knowledge became disclosed through print, a new social stratum emerged to eagerly grasp what was available of a thereto closed body of knowledge. While the Christian Menocchio was enthusiastically immersed in the conceptualization of a counternarrative to the Bible's traditional creation account, his Jewish contemporary was engaged in learning about Kabbalah and hearing about the wondrous midrashim of the Zohar. Both of them lived at a time when a person's freedom to define the contours of one's spiritual world had to be carefully negotiated with the representatives and guardians of religious authority. The technological possibilities, engendered by the spread of print technology, were tempered in the early modern period by the growth of institutional control that shaped the boundaries of both literature and culture in European society. At the same time, new intellectual directions, the promotion of humanism, and a corollary return to ancient sources, created an indelible nexus between Jewish and Christian scholars who sought to harmonize rather than localize diverse religious and ideational systems. Christian demand for kabbalistic books, motivated largely by intellectual or missionary zeal, coupled with the gradual percolation of kabbalistic ideas into the traditional spheres of Jewish life, such as legal codes, liturgy, sermons and commentaries, resulted in a sustained disclosure of mystical texts and doctrines to new audiences. Exposure, however, did not guarantee comprehension. Thus, within a few decades after the Zohar's appearance in print, demand for abridgments, study aids, and anthologies provoked creative literary responses that aimed to ease both the linguistic and the theological complexities of these texts. In the coming chapters, especially in chapters 3 to 6, I will explore the unique ways in which kabbalistic study aids reorganized and represented knowledge to facilitate learning and comprehension.

Chapter 2

Cultural Agency and Printing
in Early Modern Ashkenaz

> [W]hen they come home tired and worn out from the effort of making
> a living, each one can take a book home with him and read it, and if
> he is baffled by the meaning of some text, or by some difficult word,
> he can jot it down on paper, even in [Yiddish] and he may send it
> to the *bet midrash*.[1]

The Rise of New Agents of Culture
in Early Modern Ashkenaz

R. Yissakhar Baer's literary activity marks a critical moment in the cultural
formation of Jewish communities in Ashkenazi lands. His works appeared
in print between 1609 and 1610, at a time when kabbalistic works both
from Italy and from Safed had already penetrated and deeply impacted
the spiritual world of all segments of Ashkenazi society. Printing of kabbalistic texts in Askenazi lands had begun already in the sixteenth century,
with Meir ibn Gabbai's, *Derekh Emunah* (1557) and *Tolaʾat Yaʾaqov* (1581)
appearing in Krakow followed by Moses Cordovero's *Pardes Rimonim*
(1592, Krakow/Nowy Dvor) and Mordechai Yaffe's *Levush Even ha-Yekarah*
(1595, Lublin), a supercommentary on Menaḥem Recanati's kabbalistic
exegesis on the Torah. In fact, Kabbalah came to constitute the fourth most
frequently printed literary genre both in Bohemia and Poland between
1540 and 1640. In Bohemia, 51 books of Kabbalah were printed within

this century, only marginally behind halakhic works, which comprised 64 books, and the Bible with its commentaries, 71 compositions. Indicative of the general demand for kabbalistic texts in Bohemia is the fact that it far outperformed in print copies the more traditional genre of Mishnah and Talmud, which comprised only 21 books. In Poland, by contrast, books on Mishnah and Talmud (203), represented the most frequently printed genre, followed by halakhah (182), liturgy (152), Kabbalah (86), while the Bible and its commentaries were printed less at 68 books *in toto*.[2]

Alongside printed works, Kabbalah was transmitted through the agency of peregrinating individuals, some of whom were from among the social elites while others belonged to the group of secondary elites. Elites generally filled major rabbinic positions, assumed the leadership of *yeshivot* (*rosh yeshivah*), and played a prominent role as legal decisors in the life of Jewish communities, either by composing halakhic treatises, by acting as head of the rabbinic court (*av beit din*),[3] or at times doing both. Wealth was instrumental for rabbinic elites who wished to pursue educational leadership positions, as financial stability contributed to the sustenance of the *yeshivot*. Rabbi Isaiah Horowitz, the scion of one of the most prominent Ashkenazi families relied on his wife's dowry to support his students.[4] However, while high economic status of a *yeshivah* principal enhanced the financial stability of his educational institution, it was by no means a prerequisite for scholarly status and authority. When the *rosh yeshivah* lacked the funds to support himself and his students, the community became responsible for ensuring their well-being. Wealthy patrons proudly undertook sponsoring both Torah scholars and educational institutions. A wealthy rabbi of Posen, for instance, bequeathed his considerable estate to scholars in financial need at the end of the sixteenth century, and the estate was still in use seventeen years later.[5] As educators, elites embraced oral forms of communication, which emphasized, on the one hand, the authority, expertise, and pedagogic method of the transmitter, while at the same time guaranteed control over the content that was transmitted. While some *yeshivah* heads resisted committing their teachings to writing, students valued the inscription of their master's thoughts and copied them into notebooks that aided the mental retention of the material they received orally.[6] In addition, the use of notebooks allowed students to build "their basic working library of texts" by copying various manuscripts they encountered during their studies.[7]

Social mobility, a possibility open to those with educational and intellectual prowess within Christian society, did not exist for Ashkenazi

Jewry. Those without the means to become *yeshivah* principals, heads of a rabbinic court, or communal rabbis had to leave the educational system after marriage in order to earn a living, unless they married into a family that could guarantee the continuity of their studies by providing financial support.[8] Thus, a class of secondary elites emerged alongside the elites and aristocracy of Ashkenazi Jewry, who joined professions, such as grammarians (*medaqdeqim*), preachers (*darshanim*), scribes (*sofrim*), teachers (*melamedim*), and other learned but not academic positions. They continued to fill an educational function within society but in contrast to the elites they turned to imparting more the practical and less the theoretical dimensions of knowledge. Preachers for instance, an important group of secondary elites, deployed their proficiency in the textual sources of the Jewish canon, including Bible, rabbinic literature, and Hebrew grammar, combined with rhetorical skills, to guide the less learned masses toward moral conduct and righteous behavior.[9] The secondary elite was poised to gain considerable social prestige and economic benefit from the diffusion of printed books and from the accessibility of certain areas of knowledge. For them, books constituted a cultural product that made independent learning suddenly possible and thus effectively broadened the intellectual horizons of the laity. Print also exposed new layers of the Jewish literary heritage as medieval works and authors, restricted in the age of manuscript production to the study halls and bookshelves of a few scholars, were set down permanently and enjoyed wider circulation through printed editions. The great medieval masters of the Sephardic intellectual world, Maimonides, Nachmanides, Don Isaac Abrabanel, Rabbi Abraham ibn Ezra, Rabbi Bahyah ibn Pakuda, Rabbi David Qimḥi, and others, became accessible for wider consumption by new reading communities in the lands of Ashkenaz.[10]

The availability of books, the medium of the printed word, the accessibility of new bodies of knowledge, such as Kabbalah, and a general realignment of elite and popular culture created novel opportunities for the secondary elites. Since this segment of society worked primarily as educators, their strategies of disseminating newly available texts, ideas, and learning were reflected in the innovative pedagogical tools they adopted to facilitate the movement of information. Three strategies became particularly salient in this period for popularizing new ideas to the public: oral, using the medium of sermons; literary, by way of creating or reemploying genres that reorganized past knowledge in more accessible ways; and institutional, through establishing libraries and study halls outside the elite academies for educating those not typically associated with book culture, such as businessmen, craftsmen, women, and children.

David Darshan unifies in one person all three strategies. He received formal rabbinic training from the *yeshivah* of Rabbi Moses Isserles in Krakow, one of the most prestigious rabbinic institutions in Poland at the time. Against his will, he was not permitted to complete his studies and thus had to abandon the hope of securing a permanent rabbinical posting. He nonetheless acquired a profound regard for books, which he began to collect at the age of nineteen and of which he proudly accumulated more than 400 by the end of his life.[11] His profession as an itinerant preacher enabled him to connect not only with new lands but also with new intellectual ideas, products, and institutions. With a keen eye for new educational opportunities he conceived of opening a *bet midrash* in 1571, in his native Krakow, which may have been modeled on a similar institution he was in charge of in Ferrara, Italy.[12] Darshan's *bet midrash* was conceptualized to rest on three basic pillars: complete accessibility for the general public; the focus on books as a source of knowledge; and last, his role as an educational resource to be consulted by the student when necessary.

In serving the "simple folk," David clearly recognizes the universal drive of his generation for more knowledge than what the traditional Ashkenazi model of learning was prepared to offer to the nonelite masses: "And there is not time [for a person] to be engaged in the study of Torah, in order to know the commandments thoroughly. On some occasion he has the time but no book; on others he has the book, but no understanding. Thus, when he enters the *bet midrash* his deficiency, whatever it may be, will be supplied."[13] In offering his 400 books as primary resource in the *bet midrash*, David proposes to elevate the status of the printed book, which unlike a teacher in an elite *yeshivah* can be freely and directly consulted by the reader. Fully aware of the time limitations his potential audience would face due to their work schedules and commitments, he devises new ways of bringing learning to them: "[W]hen they come home tired and worn out from their effort to make a living, each one can take a book home with him and read it, and if he is baffled by the meaning of some text, or by some difficult word, he can jot it down on paper, even in [Yiddish] and he may send it to the bet midrash."[14] In envisioning his own role, he was prepared to offer his own knowledge and religious expertise as a secondary resource to anyone who needed it when the books in themselves did not provide sufficient clarity. In contrast to the great yeshiva heads, whose authority authenticated the content of their teachings, David dismissed the traditional educational hierarchy and saw the role of a teacher as sometimes interchangeable with that of the student: "And if he understands better than I do, I shall not be ashamed to learn from him. And if there be something too difficult both for the one who asks and for me, I shall take the trouble to consult the great scholars."[15]

Anxious to secure enough dowry to marry off his daughters and wary of shuttling from place to place to earn a living, David Darshan's ambition to open a liberal institution of learning open to all segments of Ashkenazi society was presumably not only a philanthropic utopia but also a financially viable enterprise. Engaging the medium of writing and authorship, he composed *Shir ha-Ma'alot le-David* as a literary vehicle to advertise his numerous talents and skills. As a prolific author, he composed works with an explicit pedagogical objective including a guide for writing letters and a textbook to aid the memorization of the 613 commandments of the Torah. Lacking sufficient funds to print works, he included a sample of them in *Shir ha-Ma'alot*.[16] David was a cultural revolutionary, who understood his role in the technological transformation that was unfolding in the society around him and decided to respond creatively by proposing concrete practical strategies to bring learning to those who did not have the means to pursue education in adulthood. His failure to secure a wealthy supporter for his educational reforms illustrates the resistance secondary elites faced in Ashkenazi society as their popularizing strategies ultimately came up against the cultural, institutional, and economic hegemony of ruling rabbinic elites.[17]

Rabbi Yissakhar Baer ben Petahyah Moshe epitomizes the cultural agent among Ashkenazi secondary elites who embraced the literary strategy as the primary vehicle for the diffusion of a newly accessible body of knowledge, Kabbalah. The contribution of Yissakhar Baer and his works to the general development of Kabbalah in Ashkenazi lands in the early decades of the seventeenth century, before the onset of the Sabbatean movement in middle of that century, is a story untold.[18] Yet, as I argue, this time period is critical for understanding the geographical and cultural factors that facilitated the vertical penetration of Kabbalah into the middle and lower strata of Ashkenazi society contributing to new cultural formations at socially more popular levels.

Therefore, Scholem's strong dismissal of Polish Kabbalah as marginal to the development of Jewish religious thought needs to be reexamined anew.[19] While it is true that the majority of Polish kabbalists in the sixteenth and seventeenth centuries failed to innovate in the speculative and mythical realms of Jewish mysticism, their literary output needs to be appreciated not for its theoretical but for its methodological contribution to the development of Kabbalah. Authors who wrote kabbalistic treatises in this era, Yissakhar Baer ben Petaḥya Moshe, Eleazar Altschul, Shabbtai Sheftel Horowitz,[20] Isaiah Horowitz, Aharon Zeilig, and a few decades earlier, Yissakhar Baer of Szczebrzeszyn,[21] were remarkable synthesizers. They excelled at interpreting and reconciling the mystical systems they received, either orally or via books and manuscripts, which they represented in conceptually new ways, targeting primarily the nonelite reader. Their style is characterized by literary hybridity, which they often achieved by mixing traditional rabbinic genres such as midrash, halakhah, and Biblical commentary with one or more systems of kabbalistic thought, including medieval texts, such as the Zohar, and both medieval and early modern authors, like Joseph Gikatilla, Menaḥem Recanati, Moses Cordovero, and Isaac Luria.

A common genre adopted by a number of Ashkenazi authors for the presentation of kabbalistic content was the anthology, which proved effective for displaying different, at times even contradictory, systems of thought in one unified volume.[22] Eleazar ben Abraham Hanokh Perles-Altschul typifies an emerging anthologizer, who from a very early age on assiduously collected and recorded kabbalistic teachings into a notebook and printed them in a collection titled, *Sefer ha-Qaneh*, in 1610 in the city of Prague. He presents himself as an author fulfilling and harmonizing various functions, editor-commentator-corrector, for the sake of producing a unique product, the printed book, with the aim of popularizing the secrets of Kabbalah.[23] He locates the authenticity of his collection not in its theosophical and speculative originality, but rather in his own efforts and dedication to collecting the books and teachings of the acclaimed kabbalists of either his own generation or one just before it. He reveals his awareness of the new cultural paradigm of his age that ascribes authority to the inscribed word.

> Now that we have been found worthy and there have been discovered books of Kabbalah that were hidden and concealed until our generation . . . For it is now a little more than fifteen years ago that I copied the holy book, *Qaneh* . . . And since the day this holy book came into my hands . . . I have bought myself many books of Kabbalah and collected and gathered

the keys of Kabbalah, many innovations, some from authors and some from books, of which some are published and some are not.[24]

Rabbi Yissakhar Baer's Biography

Yissakhar Baer's life and literary activity can be located at the precise intersection of three geographical tangents, Italy, Safed, and Ashkenaz; competing kabbalistic systems, the one advocated by Rabbi Moses Cordovero versus the school of Rabbi Isaac Luria Ashkenazi (the ARI); and transition in the medium of transmission, the printed book against oral disclosure and manuscript culture. Researching the life of a member of the secondary elite almost necessarily runs into a major methodological obstacle: because authors like Yissakhar Baer were not among the well-known leaders of Jewish communities, there is scant primary, and even less secondary, information available about their lives and personal circumstances. While this limits my ability to accurately reconstruct details of his life and immediate surroundings, there are a number of original sources that provide some, albeit limited, biographical information about him. First, his compositions have a number of well-known approbators from Italy, the land of Israel, and Ashkenaz. Second, the printers themselves provide valuable information about the author, his work, and the conditions of publishing. At times, on the colophon, sometimes on the title pages, we find short texts by the printers indicating the time it took to complete the project, and on occasion special issues and personal circumstances in the life of the authors that may have affected the publishing process.

A list of approbations (*haskamot*) printed at the end of his work *Meqor Ḥokhmah* (1610) provides us with a reliable picture regarding the presence of a network of kabbalists who created intellectual pathways that ensured the constant flow of books, individuals, and ideas between Safed, Italy, and Ashkenaz. Rabbi Menaḥem Azariah da Fano (1548–1620), the preeminent Kabbalist from Italy, relates that he received a pamphlet from Krakow, which contained "two or three passages from the *Zohar* with fine commentary by a person from Kremnitz."[25] He extols the author for following Rabbi Moses Cordovero's kabbalistic system, "in which [the author] neither errs nor stumbles," and therefore it represents, according to Fano, an authentic effort for the sake of Heaven.[26] The year of his

approbation is indicated as 1609.[27] It is noteworthy that two different
names are given at the top and the bottom of the *haskhamah*: the name
Immanuel is used above and the name Menahem Azariah is marked
on the bottom. Abraham Kahanah explains that authors in this period
sometimes differentiated between their Hebrew and their secular names
and Immanuel or Manuello represents Fano's secular name.[28]

The great halakhist and rabbinic luminary of Poland, R Mordekhai
Yaffe (1530–1612),[29] writes the second approbation, which reflects a much
more intimate tone than either Fano, who does not even mention the
author by name, or any of the other approbators. Yaffe begins by praising
the author in rhythmic verse.

> Yissakhar, knowing understanding (*yod'ei binah*)
>> filled with wisdom and intelligence
>>> with splendor adorned
>>> with a crown crowned—
>>> an honorable man.[30]

Yaffe's approbation is not book or content-specific, he refrains from men-
tioning any of Yissakhar Baer's works by title, except a hint to the author's
unpublished Zohar commentary, *Yod'ei Binah*. It seems from his remarks
that he had already received two pamphlets from the author and his
approbation is directed at encouraging him to express his ideas, which are
all correct, and to actualize his intellectual abilities.[31] It is noteworthy that
Yaffe's words were completed just before Shavuot in 1603, which places this
approbation significantly earlier than that of Fano. His words of endear-
ment at the end of the approbation (*ahavat Mordekhai*) and the general
tenor of his *haskhamah* suggest that he knew Yissakhar Baer well and
may have acted as a teacher or mentor to the young man. As mentioned
earlier, Yaffe spent time both in Prague and Kremnitz in the last decade
of the sixteenth century, and it is conceivable that he became acquainted
with Yissakhar Baer during those years.

It is only the approbation, written by Rabbi Isaiah Horowitz,[32] that is
explicitly based on the book *Meqor Hokhmah*, which he recommends for
publication because "its words are true and correct, the words of the Living
God."[33] While there is no specific date associated with Isaiah Horowitz's
haskhamah, it is undersigned by him as head of the rabbinic court and
yeshivah (*av bet din* and *resh-metivta*) of Austria, posts which he occupied
only from 1603 to 1606.[34] Therefore, as in the case of Mordechai Yaffe, it is

likely that he also wrote his approbation several years before the work was published. General accolades are provided by less known rabbinic figures, two of whom served as head of the rabbinic court and *yeshivah in* Lutsk and Ludmir, respectively, Rabbi Moses ben Judah Katz, and Yehudah Leib ben Ḥanokh and another rabbi Judah ben Natan Halevi from Kremnitz.

It is instructive that Gedalyah Cordovero's endorsement of *Meqor Ḥokhmah* is conditioned by the fact that Yissakhar Baer is a close follower of his father, Moses Cordovero's kabbalistic system and not the rival school, that of R. Isaac Luria.

> He brings to light all hidden things, expert in all wisdom, revealer of the concealed,[35] the consummate Sage . . . Since I saw that your words were based on "sockets of fine gold,"[36] the preliminary works of my esteemed master, my Father and Teacher, may the memory of the righteous be a blessing, in the book *Pardes* [*Pardes Rimonim*], I attest that it is apparent from this treatise that all your words are true and righteous, 'Giving an honest answer is like giving a kiss.'[37] I pray for the well-being of the Master and of all those who take refuge in his shadow.[38] My soul desires your well-being.[39]

In addition to Gedalyah Cordovero, we have one other approbation sent from the land of Israel, written by Israel Luria Ashkenazi. While Elbaum notes that he could not identify this particular sage,[40] in the Warsaw edition of *Meqor Ḥokhmah* (1899) the editors provide additional clues, saying that this rabbi was none other than the teacher of R. Meir Poppers, an important kabbalist in the seventeenth century. It therefore seems likely that this mysterious approbator was none other than R. Israel Sarug Ashkenazi, the transmitter of Lurianic Kabbalah and the father-in-law of R. Solomon Shlomiel Dresnitz, whose correspondence with Yissakhar Baer will be discussed below.[41] It is to be noted that the tone of Israel Luria Ashkenazi's endorsement is markedly reserved as he offers only a terse comment on Yissakhar Baer, saying that authority and support for his words stem from the stature of his father, who it seems, was also a kabbalist. At the end of the list of *haskhamot*, the printers mention "seven pillars of Egypt," who came to recommend the book; however, only one of them is mentioned by name, Joseph ibn Tabul,[42] a close disciple of R. Isaac Luria's.

The fact that the printers mention ibn Tabul only by name, without receiving an actual approbation from him, and that Israel Luria

Ashkenazi's *haskhamah* appears more like a concession rather than an enthusiastic endorsement, may suggest that the close disciples of Isaac Luria were not too willing to endorse Cordovero's rival system at this time. For the printers, however, having at least one of Luria's disciples recommend the work at hand likely meant a more lucrative future for the distribution of the book. It is clear that the list of approbators served as a clever marketing tool deployed by the printers for securing financial advantage. Their words added at the end of the *haskhamot* express this sentiment, "[A]nd what is well known needs no proof, and one who sees all these [names] come forward, how can he also not come forward [to purchase this book]?"[43] The conspicuous lack of enthusiastic voice coming from the Lurianic camp of kabbalists to support the publication of Yissakhar Baer's book suggests a deep division between the followers of the two regnant schools of Kabbalah in Safed, the Cordoverean, and the Lurianic that vied for intellectual prominence in the first half of the seventeenth century.

The tension that characterized the reception history and diffusion of these two paradigmatic approaches to Kabbalah left an indelible mark not only on the printing of Yissakhar Baer's works but also on the general formation of kabbalistic ritual and thought in the centuries to come. Within the academic study of Kabbalah, scholars are divided into two camps: on the one hand, Isaiah Tishby and Elliot Wolfson emphasize the predominance of Lurianic symbolism and thought; on the other hand, Moshe Idel and Zeev Gries underscore the influence of Moses Cordovero and his more systematic approach to Kabbalah as reflected in the works of Ashkenazi authors.[44] Yet, shortly after the demise of these great kabbalists, at the very heart of Rabbi Menahem Azariah da Fano's esoteric world, these two mystical systems meet and get reorganized into a unique hierarchy. In his introduction to *Pelah ha-Rimon*, R. Azariah constructs a fascinating multitiered system of three types of knowledge represented by David Qimhi, Moses Cordovero, and Isaac Luria. For Fano, David Qimhi, the medieval grammarian and Bible commentator represents "the opening of the gates of understanding, the simple meaning [of Scripture], which never lies, although it may contain hidden matters (*nistar*)."[45] David Qimhi, with his emphasis on understanding Hebrew grammar and the simple meaning of Scripture, represents the elementary but essential step in the learning process. He continues to expand on the difference among these three distinct curricula.

> This matter is similar, for the Sage [Moses Cordovero] opened
> for us the wondrous gates within true wisdom . . . However,
> just as the pathways of the *Pardes* [*Rimonim*] are higher than
> Qimḥi, similarly the pathways of the Ari [Isaac Luria], of blessed
> memory, ascend higher than the pathways of this book [*Pardes*
> *Rimonim*] . . . and do not be surprised, for both in the *Book*
> *Elimah* by this Sage [Cordovero], of blessed memory, and in
> the works of the Ari, there will be pathways one deeper than
> the other . . . and the measure [of difference] will be according
> to the *shekel hakodesh* as it is explained in Tractate *Hagigah*,
> in its chapters regarding the Holy Creatures in the [heavenly]
> chariot, [saying] that the height between one creature and the
> other was exactly the height between itself and the one below
> it. And so, just as it is forbidden to mingle and intermix the
> plain meaning of Qimḥi with the *Pardes* . . . so it is to mingle
> and mix, the wisdom of the Ari, either all or parts of it, with
> this book [*Pardes Rimonim*], or any like it. . . . For the Ari,
> sought out the foundations of the *Idra* and the *Sifra di-Zni'uta*,[46]
> which deal with the divine world itself and the pattern above,
> and enough has been said about this.[47]

This ladder-like conceptualization of knowledge that Fano envisions, in
which Qimḥi occupies the lowest, Cordovero, the middle, and Luria the
highest rung of mystical gnosis, became one of the earliest explicit statements that sought to establish a clear hierarchy between the kabbalistic
systems of Isaac Luria, and his colleague and teacher, Moses Cordovero.
In my opinion, Fano's statement here is critical for the development of
Kabbalah, as it sets the parameters for the ideal curriculum for future
generations of kabbalists. From here on, the popularity of Cordovero's
Kabbalah and authors who follow his paradigm, become permanently
eclipsed by a demand for Lurianic teachings and compositions, which
are seen as inherently superior and mystically more refined than their
Cordoverean counterparts.[48]

Rabbi Yissakhar Baer as an emerging author and authority in the
field of Kabbalah was pulled into this debate in spite of his own inten-
tions. The paucity of information available about his life comes to us from
a series of letters, one addressed to him directly, written by Solomon
Shlomel Dresnitz, a Jew born in 1574 in Moravia, who vividly depicts his

own efforts grappling to find the right books, methods, and teachers for understanding Kabbalah as a young man in his native land.[49] He recounts the great joy he felt upon encountering Cordovero's *Pardes Rimonim*, which became available in print through its 1592 edition in Krakow, and the great pains he took to study it. It is evident from his account that the *Pardes* constituted a foundational text in his development that prepared him for the more complex studies he would undertake later in his life.

> And when [the book], *Pardes Rimonim* was revealed to me, I felt elated . . . and I labored with great pain to acquire the simple meaning (*peshat*) [of Kabbalah] and to explain passages of the Zohar using the clear and lucid arguments and dialectics (*pilpul*) that arose from the premises (*haqdamot*) of the kabbalist, the Sage, Moses Cordovero . . . And thus, I began to sail in the sea of wisdom, according my ability, to read the Zohar, the *Tikkunim*, and the *Zohar Ḥadash*, [all] with the help of his premises.[50]

Far from learning Kabbalah only through the medium of books, he turned with all his efforts to self-mortification and ascetic practices through, "fasting, weeping, wailing, donning sackcloth, and ashes, . . . I stood before God weeping like this for more than four years."[51] He displays an astute awareness of the limitation of books as sources of divine knowledge, while he derives hope of receiving more direct mystical illumination, especially regarding the hidden meaning of the commandments, from his own commitment to a life of asceticism.

That Rabbi Azaria da Fano's cultural agency in shaping the reception history of the two mystical systems that emanated from Safed was germane to subsequent generations of kabbalists is strongly supported by R. Solomon Shlomiel Dresnitz's letter. In his search for enlightenment, R. Solomon Shlomiel, encounters a transformative moment upon reading Fano's introduction to *Pelaḥ ha-Rimon*, an experience that changes his life forever. Fano's work was printed in Venice in 1600, and R. Solomon Shlomiel left Moravia for Safed in 1602, which implies that the appearance of *Pelaḥ ha-Rimon* in Ashkenazi lands was relatively timely. It was one short sentence from Fano's long introduction that particularly touched the young R. Solomon Shlomiel's heart: "if Israel Sarug, of blessed memory had not come to our lands [Italy] and revealed to us a small portion of those complete mysteries that the Ari of blessed memory revealed, we would have never attained the light of Torah."[52] Anxious to immerse himself in Lurianic teachings, he wastes no time to depart for Safed "empty and naked," having left behind in Moravia a wife, an eight-year-old daughter, his clothes, and books.

R. Solomon Shlomiel's fascinating journey for the sake of acquiring the Lurianic system of Kabbalah embodies a form of pilgrimage that parallels strongly the *"peregrinatio academica,"* defined by David Ruderman as one of the important cultural expressions of the early modern period.[53] However, while Ruderman invokes this term to designate the general mobility of Europeans, Jews and non-Jews, to large metropolitan centers or university towns "in quest of learning," within Kabbalah studies, the term, *peregrinatio kabbalistica*, encapsulates more directly the neophyte's quest for the purpose of acquiring a particular type of knowledge, which in this case, is esoteric by nature. Accessing Lurianic teachings outside the land of Israel became a particularly acute challenge at the turn of the seventeenth century, exacerbated by a strict ban imposed on its dissemination by the Ari's close disciples.[54] These restrictions motivated kabbalists from all over the Jewish world, Italy, Ashkenaz, and even North Africa to move to Safed and learn from the "lion cubs" as Luria's disciples were often called.[55] It was only after 1600, following the printing of Pelaḥ ha-Rimon that Israel Sarug and others began to travel first to Italy and later to Poland, in an effort to circulate the Ari's teachings outside the land of Israel.[56]

We encounter Yissakhar Baer in one of Shlomel Dresnitz's four letters printed for the first time in Joseph Delmedigo's *Ta'alumot Ḥokhmah* in Basle, 1629–1631. The letters are included in a section of the book titled, "Documents of Praise, Tribute, and Prominence of the Ari z"l." It is the third of four letters, printed on folios 41a to 49b, that addresses specifically Yissakhar Baer. The date indicated in the letter, twenty-fifth of Ḥeshvan 1606, is likely incorrect as noted by Benayahu, as that particular day fell not on a Thursday, but on a Tuesday that year. It is therefore more likely the letter was penned in 1608 and not in 1606.[57]

According to R. Solomon Shlomiel, Yissakhar Baer, whom he knew from Moravia, sent a letter asking him to secure approbations from the Kabbalists of Safed for the works he was about to publish. In his reply, R. Shlomiel explains that he endeavored to show his work to all the Kabbalists in the land of Israel, with the exception of Hayyim Vital, as he lived in Damascus at the time. Nonetheless, he manages to show what Yissakhar Baer sent him to two kabbalists, to Masood Sagi Nahor, R. Shlomiel's teacher, and to Suleiman ben Ohana.[58] It seems that Yissakhar Baer sent R. Shlomiel a sample chapter on *Parashat Teẓaveh*,[59] which he took from his major commentary on the Zohar, titled *Yod'ei Binah*. In the kabbalistic composition, *'Amudei Shevah*, printed in Krakow in 1635, Aharon Zeilig from Zolkiev incorporated two passages from a manuscript copy of *Yod'ei Binah* into two sections of the work: a longer commentary on the *Zohar* from *Parashat Shoftim* (fol. 19b) and another section from *Parashat Va-yehi* (fol. 8a).[60] This composition, which Yissakhar Baer mentions by title in his introduction to *Yesh Sakhar*, was ostensibly never printed, nor do we have it in manuscript form:[61]

> And because of the enormity of the expenses required of me at this time for printing (*Yesh Sakhar*) I have withdrawn, for the time being, from publishing my commentary on the Zohar, which I called by the title, *Yod'ei Binah*,[62] as is known, until the time that God expands my means for behold I have "learned the lesson,"[63] distress has taught me, and found my aid against the foe.[64]

R. Shlomiel's response to Yissakhar Baer's sample chapter is measured enthusiasm: on the one hand, he praises the author for constructing his exegesis on Moses Cordovero's kabbalistic system and the framework set up by him; at the same time, reliance on the Cordovean system constitutes the gravest flaw in the composition. With great sadness he informs Yissakhar Baer that the Sages of Safed did not agree to provide him with their *haskhamot*, "because they had already heard and ate from the Tree of Life, the premises of the Ari," and would not endorse a work that was built on Cordovean teachings.[65] In consoling his friend, he exclaims, "for I have surely seen that God is with you and desires the success of your hand; and since God desires you, if only He had not shown you all this. To compose a work so comprehensive as this [*Yod'ei Binah*], a commentary on the entire Zohar, yet to be left without the approval [of the Safed Kabbalists]." R. Solomon Shlomiel offers only one solution to his friend, "[G]ird your loins as a warrior and run [all] the way; arise and ascend to the place and to the land that is God's inheritance, and stand before the sage R. Ḥayyim [Vital] and inquire from him regarding the *urim* and the *thumim*."[66] R. Solomon Shlomiel urges Yissakhar Baer to settle in Safed for two reasons: first, Ḥayyim Vital is already old and needs to transmit his wisdom, and second, R. Solomon Shlomiel knows in his heart with certainty that Yissakhar Baer "is the Sage regarding whom our teacher the great sage, R. Ḥayyim Vital, said that he is the reincarnation of the Ari."[67]

R. Solomon Shlomiel's letter does not disclose much detail about Yissakhar Baer's life but we do get a colorful depiction of what it was like to live in Safed at the turn of the seventeenth century, at a time when its glory had begun to fade. R. Solomon Shlomiel offers us a glimpse into the darker side of Safed politics, where a junior scholar was denied support if he represented the wrong mystical ideology. In spite of the political machinations of the kabbalistic elites in Safed, who unanimously endorsed the Ari's Kabbalah as the authoritative tradition, the fact that Yissakhar Baer's four works found willing printers in Prague to publish them suggests that they believed the books had the potential to turn a profit among Ashkenazi readers.

Before I move to the next section, which will discuss the printers of Yissakhar Baer and those in Poland, let me summarize here what little information we have about Yissakhar Baer's life.[68] He must have died sometime before 1635, as he is mentioned among the dead in 'Amudei Sheva, written by Aharon Zeilig and printed later that year.[69] The printers refer to him as young at the time when his books were published, which means he must have been in his late twenties or early thirties at the time. In addition, according to the published genealogical booklet of the Rivlin family, Yissakhar Baer's father Rabbi Petaḥyah [Moses?] son of Joseph Hazan Sofer Stam is identified as the *parnas* and trustee (*ne'eman*) of the Prague community, who died in 1599.[70] In another place Petaḥyah, son of Joseph Sofer who died in 1599 in Prague, is discussed by Alexandr Putik as one of the putative authors of the *Anonymous Chronicle from Prague*, discovered and published by Abraham David.[71] David ben Aryeh Leib of Lidda, a rabbi in the Amsterdam Jewish community and author of *Sefer Sod ha-Shem* mentions him as his uncle, "the light of my glory, the divine kabbalist, our teacher the Sage, Rabbi Yissakhar Baer, of blessed memory."[72]

The Printers—The Gersonides Dynasty of Prague

Yissakhar Baer's four extant works were published by two different printing houses in the first decade of seventeenth century, both of which belonged to the dominant Gersonides dynasty of Prague. The first two compositions, *Pitḥei Yah* and *Yesh Sakhar*, were printed in 1609 by Gershom ben Beẓalel Katz, while the other two works, *Imrei Binah* and *Meqor Ḥokmah*, were published by Moses ben Beẓalel Katz in 1610 and 1611, respectively. Of the two printers, Moses ben Beẓalel was by far the more productive according to extant records.

In addition to the two 1609 titles by Yissakhar Baer, the works listed by Heller as products of the press of Gershom ben Beẓalel are the following: *Berit Avraham* by Abraham ben Ephraim Niederlander; *Yosef Daʾat* by Joseph ben Yissakhar Baer of Prague; and *Keneh Binah*, attributed to Kanah Aben Gador. In contrast to the works that were printed by Moses ben Beẓalel, these publications were much more modest in terms of their presentation. None of them display the kind of elaborate ornamentation that characterizes the Gersonides family of printers in general and more importantly none of them show on the title page the two hands of the Kohen, which had become by then the signature printer's mark of the dynasty. In terms of their thematic scope, the six works cover three areas: Kabbalah (*Qeneh Binah, Yesh Sakhar,* and *Pith ei Yah*); mathematics (*Berit Avraham*), and Biblical supercommentary (*Yosef Daʾat*). It is worth noting that none of these works was authored by a leading rabbinic authority of the day, which, as we shall see, was an important difference between these works and those printed by the other Gersonides press of the time.

Perhaps the best known among the authors of the above works was Abraham ben Ephraim Niederlander, also known as Abraham Sofer because he served as the scribe for the Maharal.[73] *Berit Avraham* was his only published work; it is a short book on mathematics providing problems and solution on the basis of earlier Jewish and non-Jewish mathematical works. Although there is no indication of the exact date of publication, the title page shows Gershom ben Beẓalel as the printer. The place of publication is also not mentioned on the title page, however, it does appear later in the text. There is a brief description of the content and the organization of the volume on the title page that was provided by the printer: "Arranged for minors and adults, elderly, young, and children. Comprehensive in its scope of five gates (*sheʾarim*) that include all the calculations. Small in size but great in value. Therefore, come hither, hasten, and acquire for a low price these collections by Gershom ben Beẓalel Katz, the printer."[74]

Joseph ben Yissakhar Baer of Prague, the author of *Yosef Daʾat*, is less known but he is said to have studied with three major scholars of the time, the Rabbi Judah Loew ben Beẓalel (Maharal), Rabbi Mordechai Yaffe (*Levush*), and also Rabbi Ephraim Luntshits.[75] Like *Berit Avraham*, Yissakhar Baer's *Yosef Daʾat* was also a work designed, at least in part, for educational purposes. Although the main objective of the volume was to correct errors in Rashi's Torah commentary by taking an early manuscript as the basis, the book contains a number of vivid illustrations and maps that rendered it a helpful teaching tool. In the following pages I will reproduce these illustrations as examples of the kind of visual aids that Early Modern

Hebrew printers and authors applied. Similarly to *Berit Avraham*, the text of *Yosef Da'at* is also printed in a single column with notes printed on both the left- and right-hand margins, with the exception of pages 2 to 4, which contain extensive approbations that are printed in two columns.

The text of *Yosef Da'at* follows the order of the Biblical books: *Sefer Bereshit, Sefer Shemot, Sefer Vayikra, Sefer Bamidbar,* and *Sefer Devarim.* The book does not have a separate colophon page, the last page of the book, and indicates one more time the name of the printer. An interesting feature of the introductory section of this book is an entire page dedicated to a short verse, the initial letters of which form an acrostic of the author's name: Yosef bar Yissakhar of Prague. The purpose of work is clearly summarized on the title page, which also indicates the name of the author.

> The heart of the prudent acquires knowledge and the ear of
> the wise seeks knowledge (Proverbs 18:15). One who has a
> heart to understand enigmas by himself and does not require
> another's assistance, he is prudent, expressed in the singular,
> and it says heart and acquires, in the masculine. However,
> one who is in the likeness of the feminine and receives from
> others, this wisdom is in the plural. It says ear and seeks in
> the feminine. All the distortions and errors are due to the
> printers from old, 'without knowledge" (Job 38:2, 42:3) to the
> commentary of the great light, Rashi, on *Hamishah Homshei
> Torah, Nevi'im, Ketuvim,* and *Hamesh Megillot,* in all the printed
> editions before us, new and old, for it says, 'he taught the
> people knowledge: for he weighed, and sought out, and set
> in order' (Ecclesiastes 12:9) from the Torah sage, Joseph ben
> Issakhar Baer of Prague.[76]

In contrast to the other works, *Sefer Qeneh Binah* was not an original work.[77] It was a kabbalistic composition written in the Middle Ages, presumably, by Qanah Aben Gedor, and copied in the late 1500s by Eleazar Abraham Hanokh Perles Altschul, who was born and lived most of his life in Prague.[78] Altschul, as a member of the emerging "secondary elite," played an active role in divulging thereto closed and unrevealed mystical secrets by copying and collecting unpublished kabbalistic manuscripts and eventually publishing some of them. Some twenty years after he had copied the text of *Qeneh Binah,* between 1609 and 1611, he edited and arranged for the publication of a larger work *Qeneh Ḥokhmah Qeneh Binah*, of which *Qeneh Binah* was the first part.[79]

The title page features an unusually long text that explains in kabbalistic terms the meaning of the title of this book and gives the date 26 Kislev as the start of the work. However, neither the author nor the printer is identified in the same clear fashion that characterized that other works mentioned earlier. The colophon indicates that the publication was completed in 1611, by which time Gershom ben Bezalel Katz was no longer printing. Thus, it is possible that the printing of this work was started by one printer but was completed by another. The text of *Qeneh Binah* is printed in a single column, except for four pages midway through where a double column is used. The printer applied rabbinic font except for the headers and the first words of each new section throughout the work, which are printed in larger square letters.

The second Gersonides printer who would publish works at this time in Prague, including Yissakhar Baer's *Imrei Binah* and *Meqor Ḥokmah*, was Moses ben Bezalel Katz, sometimes appearing as Moses ben Josef Bezalel Katz. There is no indication that they would be different individuals or printers. The number of titles associated with Moses Katz is far greater than those printed by Gershom Katz and it is also clear that he was active in business for far longer than Gershom. Moses in fact was active from 1592 to 1648, and printed for the first time in 1592–1594 with his uncle Solomon, the famous chronicle *Zemah David* (1592), the Maharal's sermon on the Torah (1593) and *Pesak al-Agunah* (1594). Later on, in the early decades of the seventeenth century he continued on his own, and in 1635 printed *Tefillah shel Rosh Ḥodesh* and in 1648 *Minhagim*.[80] In 1610, the year in which he printed two of Yissakhar Baer's works, Moses Katz also published '*Even ha-Ezer* by Eliezer ben Nathan of Mainz (Raban), *Ḥamisha Ḥomshei Torah*, and *Siftei Da'at* by Solomon Ephraim ben Aaron Luntshits.

'*Even ha-Ezer* was originally composed some 500 years before it would be printed in Prague for the first time in 1610. It constitutes a collection of the Raban's halakhic responsa but it also "provides the reasons for customs, explains prayers, and interprets aggadah."[81] As with all of the other works printed by Moses Katz at this time, the title page is nicely ornamented, featuring a rich display of images and a frame. The Gersonides mark, the spread-out hands of the High Priest, is shown on both sides of the frame. The page is dated the New Moon of the month of Nissan in 1610. The text of the work is printed in two columns using square letters rather than rabbinic type. The organization of the content is also quite a bit different from what we saw in the publications by Gershom Katz. Here, the verso of the title page contains the author's introduction followed by approbations from ten major rabbis of the time. Next we find an introduction from the printer and an index of subject headings to assist the reader. Similarly to 'Even ha-Ezer, Hamisha Homshei Torah is not an original work; it is a Yiddish translation of the Torah, including Kizur Rashi (An Abridgment of Rashi).[82]

Siftei Da'at by Solomon Luntshits was written as a compendium to the author's earlier major publication Keli Yakar, printed in 1602 by the press of Kalonymous Jaffe in Lublin.[83] This book contains 372 homilies from the authors' festival and Shabbat sermons. The title page is ornamental with frames running all along and it is dated the New Moon of the month of Elul in 1610. Along each of the four sides of the frame we find a verse quoted. The colophon dates the completion of the work on 2 Kislev, the same year. Similarly to 'Even ha-Ezer, the author's introduction begins on the verso of the title page and runs for three pages. At the bottom of the third page we find the standard Gersonides mark of the Kohen's hands. It is interesting to note that the mark is not shown on the title page, which was certainly the norm of the Gersonides printers at the time. The last four pages of the work contain an index to point the reader to the specific homilies indicated by their short theme and page number. The text is printed in two columns using square letters.

In conclusion, the early modern period gave rise to a new stratum of cultural agents, the secondary elites, who usually did not occupy positions of juridical and religious authority communal organizations, yet successfully embraced new opportunities to participate in cultural creativity. Increased mobility, the rise of transregional networks, and most importantly the technological, logistical, and economic perspectives that the printing press opened up enabled this new group of authors to produce novel literary genres that responded to the educational demands of new readers. Each of Yissakhar Baer's four works constituted a unique pedagogic contribution to the development of the early modern library, where the printed classics of Kabbalah were complemented by the appropriate study guide meant to mediate primary mystical sources to less learned community of readers.

Chapter 3

Kabbalistic Abridgments and Their Cultural Impact

[He] gathers together in one short volume the opinions . . . so that the seeker need not consult an abundance of books [because] the brevity of the extracts assembled offers, effortlessly, what he is looking for.[1]

The Use and Impact of Christian Reference Aids

An important cornerstone of Renaissance pedagogy in Christian circles was to encourage students to avoid accessing the requisite literary classics of their curriculum without the aid of reference tools. Experts were charged to compile digests and summaries with the explicit purpose to process and repackage large quantities of information, and sometimes intellectually challenging texts, into more accessible and manageable units for the neophyte reader. Abridgments of ancient classics, composed by humanist teachers or novice scholars, served multiple didactic functions. First, as an educational tool, a précis enabled young aristocrats and clerics to navigate the often voluminous and conceptually complex works of venerable masters with clarity and comprehension. Second, the preparation of digests stimulated the formation of collaborative scholarly networks between apprentice scholars, responsible for compiling them, and pupils, who imbibed them, adumbrating the social rather than the solitary dimensions of reading. Third, these summaries provided the theoretical and structural framework to be engaged by the student later on in life, when he was left to his own devices to navigate new texts and process novel information. Finally, the printing of these abbreviated study aids in the sixteenth century set down and formalized innovative and original methods of reading classical texts for an ever-broadening market of new readers.[1]

The appearance of a variety of new reference genres, including abridgments, anthologies, florilegia,[2] concordances, encyclopedias, and indexes, originate from the Middle Ages. As textual intermediaries, these valuable intellectual tools were developed at large European universities and libraries as cognitive shortcuts in the management of information load and the organization of complex ideas.[3] As reference aids, digests proved to be particularly expedient for university students, who could avert spending long hours poring over volumes of unintelligible material. Rather than consulting directly the original works, students saved time by reading abridged summaries that highlighted and explained key concepts and representative passages from the source material making learning and memorization more effective. As material objects, digested works were far easier to carry and handle than original classics, which facilitated more frequent consultation.[4] Conceptually, concise summaries served to introduce a classical author's intellectual and ideational world by excerpting key doctrines and passages, and simplifying complex arguments in the original work.[5]

The use of digests became so pervasive at universities throughout Europe that students and professors gradually abandoned the consultation of the original works and relied more on secondary summaries. In some classrooms, the abridgment displaced the classic as the core textbook in the curriculum.[6] While some derided working aids as unoriginal, "sterile,"[7] and secondary, the shift from monastic- to university-based knowledge processing necessitated a utilitarian approach to employing resources. The tripartite learning structure of monastic learning, reading-meditation-contemplation, was supplanted by three new stages, commentary-discussion-spiritual dimension, with discussion (*disputare*) emerging as the ideal form of learning in the educational program of universities.[8] Form follows function, and as the classroom required students to acquire knowledge quickly and use texts and ideas effectively in their disputations and discussions, slow and deep reading of original texts was eventually relinquished. Abridgments and other types of reference aids, which emerged originally to ease the processing of lengthy, difficult, and conceptually sophisticated classical texts, became dominant literary genres in their own right and continue to remain indispensable staples in the educational curriculum to our day.

Reference aids proved to be instrumental not only within the educational sector, but also at the level of censorship and literary canon formation. The compilers of reference tools filtered the material they processed for the reader frequently omitting passages and ideas that did not fit in with their religious, ideological, or doctrinal orientation. Certain Christian orders, in fact, took advantage of the popularity and broad diffusion of abridged works and encouraged their circulation. Whereas classical texts, on occasion, presented doctrines contradictory to normative Christian tenets, reference works came under the direct control of the Church and quickly became the preferred medium for the communication and interpretation of ancient texts and ideas.[9] Beyond their utility in censorship and doctrinal control, study aids proved effective in reinforcing the canonical status of already well-known and recognized compositions, while at the same time diffusing selections and ideas from relatively little-known authors.[10]

Reference compilations were praised for their concise organizational format, relative ease of consultation, and simplified mode of presentation, which allowed them to offer "something for everyone."[11] Preachers constituted one of the most enthusiastic consumers of reference tools, as these contained useful quotations, excerpts, exemplars, and encyclopedic material that they could weave into their sermons. As authoritative sources, intellectual aids played an important role in printers' workshops where they served to amend and verify information in other works.[12] Yet, in spite of some recognition of their varied utility, not everyone embraced excerpts and summaries as unequivocally valuable intellectual working tools.

One sustained criticism leveled at reference books maintained that such a genre obfuscated the meaning and context of original compositions, leading to misrepresentation of ideas, and ultimately to errors and confusion by the reader. More importantly, however, at the core of the complaints was a tacit unease by the elites with the cultural and educational transformation they bore witness to and the attendant democratization of knowledge that clearly impacted the types of written works produced.[13] In other words, compilations that sought to present classics in a simplified and more accessible manner were perceived to threaten the exclusivity of learning and radically redefine the educational curriculum. A strong voice against this equalizing tendency is expressed by the Anglican bishop, Richard Montagu: "The abridgments that have beene made long since, and of late, are held to be one of the chiefe plagues of learning, and learned men. It maketh men idle, and yet opinionative, and well conceited of themselves."[14] Montagu's lament echoes the depreciation of the ideal model of learning and the subsequent deposition of its guardians. Knowledge, which in centuries past had to be acquired with painstaking laboriousness from expert masters and in the Latin language, became with the diffusion of print, readily available in vernacular languages, disseminated to a much broader public, who for the first time had the opportunity to access areas of learning that had been previously closed to them. The repackaging of ancient learning and timeworn classics in the form of intellectual study guides served to commercialize knowledge through mass printing and distribution and address a new nonelite consumer, for whom book learning offered the possibility for social mobility and cultural empowerment.

A Jewish Response to Printing: The Emergence of Shortcuts

Christian efforts to address a growing demand for new literary reference tools by producing intellectual aids in the form of anthologies, florilegia, and digests found parallel expression in various areas of Jewish learning in the early modern period. One attempt to assist novice readers with the processing of new texts was to compose study aids in the form of digests and abbreviated treatises. Medieval works, especially in the realm of halakhah, tended to be voluminous and hindered quick and easy referencing. Shem Tov ben Judah Sidiqaro in the late fifteenth century composed a thirty-two-folio digest that functioned as a table of contents to the legal responsa of the medieval Spanish rabbinic leader and halakhist, R. Solomon ibn Adret. While Sidiqaro was reticent about his own enterprise, nonetheless, he recognized the pressing need for such an aid in managing knowledge and information in the face of adverse conditions that ameliorate effective learning.

> Our ancestor's [sinful] deeds caused the destruction of our
> Temple, and we continue to stray from the path. Our houses
> have been destroyed, our bones have been broken, our joy has
> turned into mourning, our song to dirge and lamentation. We
> wander to and fro among those who seek to kill us, we seek
> out our livelihood among them and we cannot earn even our
> daily bread. All of this darkens our eyes and distracts our
> minds. Only a few remain among us who understand the
> books of our teachings. The gateways of our hearts are closed.

The slightest distraction makes us lose our train of thought. That is why I, Shem-Tov, have summarized this book, with every section on its own: its laws are put in order, where originally they were all mixed up and spread about. Now the reader will run through them like water pouring downhill [2 Samuel 14:14], to find what he is seeking, like a happy man singing a song. Many asked questions of Rabbi Solomon ibn Adret (of blessed memory), and he answered each and every one. I . . . have organized these laws and concerns, and placed them where they belong.[15]

Potential consumers of halakhic abridgments included rabbis, who used these digests as tools for teaching halakhah; preachers and teachers, many of whom were errant and therefore appreciated the concise format of these works; and lay individuals who, received a good educational foundation but whose daily work precluded them from finding time for regular study and thus welcomed halakhic summaries, which lent themselves to quick consultation.[16] The distinction between the halakhic compilation that was studied by the specialist and the more popular halakhic manual that was read by the nonspecialist became especially pronounced in the age of print. Joseph Qaro's literary production in the area of halakhah illustrates this point. In composing his comprehensive and erudite legal code the *Beit Yosef*, Qaro clearly targeted the expert, who would benefit from his work because it presented the opinion of preeminent medieval decisors with clarity and set down the principles that promised consistency in the halakhic decision-making process.[17] At the same time, he was cognizant that he will attract only a limited audience for the *Beit Yosef* due to its length and highly scholastic style.

Therefore, in order to bring halakhah into the daily study program of a broader segment of Jewish society, he needed to compose a more concise and simplified code, that could be printed and reprinted inexpensively, and would function as a quick reference guide to halakhah, benefiting the scholar, the layperson, and young students. His own conceptualization regarding the distinguishing features of the Shulḥan Arukh compared to the Beit Yosef is instructive about the pedagogical aim of the two works.

the great work, which I composed on the *Arba'ah Turim*, and called it *Beit Yosef*. In it, I have included all the laws found in the works of both contemporary and past authorities together

with their source: their courtyards and castles—the Babylonian and Jerusalem Talmuds, the *Tosefta*, the *Sifra*, *Sifrei*, and
Mekhilta, the words of the commentators, the rabbinic decisors,
and the authors of responsa both new and old. Every law is
properly explained therein . . .

However, I saw it fit in my heart to collect the flowers
and jewels of its words in a concise way, in a clear language
including all that is fine and proper, so that God's Torah would
be complete and eloquent upon the lips of everyone in Israel.
[In this way] when a scholar is asked a legal question, he will
not stammer concerning it, but rather will "say to wisdom, you
are my sister."[18] At the same time, knowing [the halakhah] that
his sister is forbidden to him,[19] thus all the laws, concerning
which there was a practical halakhic query will be clarified
for him as he learns this book, [a tower] built with armory,[20]
a promontory to which all turn. [The book] can be divided
into sections of thirty for daily study and thus each month a
person will return to its study, saying 'happy is the person who
can return here and direct one's own study.'

Furthermore, young students will practice it regularly,
learning the text by heart, and imbibing the practical matters
of halakhah from their childhood and a young age, and thus
even as they get older, they will not depart from it.[21]

The instant popularity of Joseph Qaro's *Shulḥan Arukh*, which made it
one of the most frequently printed texts in the Jewish literary canon,[22]
was due in no small part to its ability to offer a concise practical guide
to daily halakhic observance. The *Shulḥan Arukh* became an authoritative
guide to religious life in most Jewish communities drawing the criticism
of some rabbis who saw their position and power undermined by the
wide diffusion of Qaro's code as expressed by a lay Jew in Leon Modena's
circle: "When I have the *Shulḥan Arukh* underneath the joints of my arms
I do not need a single one of you rabbis."[23]

Abridgments to Works of Kabbalah

Within the field of Kabbalah, the two works that generated the largest
number of abridgments in the sixteenth and early seventeenth centuries

were Elijah de Vidas's *Reshit Ḥokhmah* (*The Beginning of Wisdom*) printed in Venice in 1579 and Moses Cordovero's *Pardes Rimonim* (*Garden of Pomegranates*), which appeared in print in 1592 in Krakow. De Vidas, a prominent disciple of Moses Cordovero, having come to the conclusion that his own *Reshit Ḥokhmah* was too dense and expansive for certain readers, prepared a more condensed summary to it, titled *Toẓa'ot Hayyim* (*Life and Its Consequences*), which was published in Korogashmi in 1597.[24] In 1580, the Italian scholar Jacob Poyetto prepared *Reshit Ḥokhmah ha-Kazar*, printed in Venice only two decades later, in 1600.[25] De Vidas saw his work as complementing his teacher's encyclopedic compendium, the *Pardes Rimonim*, the primary focus of which was the systematic exposition of the theoretical concepts and symbolism of Kabbalah, whereas de Vidas sought to place ethical imperatives and the refinement of the human character at the center of his composition.[26]

Toward the end of the sixteenth and in the first half of the seventeenth century, the *Pardes* came to stimulate many more authors to seek new ways for re-presenting its comprehensive kabbalistic theology. It is instructive that a number of authors who produced abridgments to the *Pardes* came from either Cordovero's circle of disciples or that of Menaḥem Azariah da Fano, which may suggest that the digest as a literary genre functioned much like a notebook and study guide, which enabled a student to record key points from the original text, facilitating learning and memorization. At the same time, once a novice completed his studies, the digest could be used as an effective teaching tool in the transmission of esoteric concepts and ideas.[27]

The transmission history of the *Pardes* reveals that authors of these abridgments become creative cultural mediators refracting the original work they edit through their own particular aesthetic, ideational, intellectual, and theological prisms. In addition, the number of textual witnesses in manuscript,[28] print, and some cited but no longer extant, demonstrate that the *Pardes* generated intense literary activity by copyists and abridgers alike. Arguing that as a literary genre, abridgments belong to the category of anthologies, we may posit invoking David Stern's conceptualization of anthologies, that the preparation of digests to the *Pardes* served a function of canonization, that is "authorizing, sacralizing, and legitimating" its presentation of what constituted Kabbalistic knowledge and "marginalizing, delegitimating and anathemizing" other competing sources.[29] Alternatively, the reframing of the *Pardes Rimonim* in the form of abridgments can best be recognized and appreciated as an expression of literary performance.

Thus, these manuscripts and printed variants become important textual evidence that help us reconstruct the goal and agenda of the editor-author. As Thomas Tanselle notes, a "textual artifact deserves our attention as each extant source of a particular work represents significant moments of its performance as responses to some original intent."[30]

The first two printed abridgments of the *Pardes* appeared in Venice in 1600 and 1601. *Pelaḥ ha-Rimon* was penned by the Italian rabbi and kabbalist of great renown, Menaḥem Azariah da Fano, who invested his intellectual acumen and his considerable wealth to acquire first Cordovero's and later in his life Luria's mystical system.[31] In 1601, the Venetian printer, Daniel Zanetti, decided to print another précis of the *Pardes*, which incorporated Samuel Gallico's original work with Mordechai Dato's glosses added in the margins.[32] In 1708 these two works the *Pelaḥ* and the *Assis* appeared in a new edition in Amsterdam by the title, *Sefer Pa'amon ve-Rimon* (*The Book of Bell and Pomegranate*) printed by Moshe Daish, in which these two sources were printed side by side for the first time and became a template for subsequent editions of the *Pardes*. The authors, Gallico and Dato, journeyed at different times in the sixteenth century from Italy to Safed to pursue kabbalistic studies with Cordovero, and by the time *Assis Rimonim* was printed, they were no longer alive to offer any input into the editorial arrangement of their works. The final product was so replete with errors and inconsistencies that R. Menaḥem Azariah da Fano resolved to impose on himself the role of emendator as he undertook to correct the 1601 edition, which was reprinted in Mantua in 1623.

It is worth citing Fano's introduction to the Mantua edition of the *Pelaḥ Ha-Rimon* in its entirety, as it poignantly illustrates several important points. First, his self-awareness as an emerging editor/corrector who set himself a "heroic task" of clearing all textual obstructions that would impede the reader's comprehension. Second, this excerpt illustrates some of the shortcomings associated with the print industry that, on occasion, forfeited textual and intellectual integrity for the sake of commercial profit. Third, he provides useful feedback concerning the relatively slow circulation of the *Assis Rimonim* at the time, which could be attributed to the competition of this work with Fano's own digest, which was likely to have been the version he promoted among his many students who came to study with him from all over Europe.

The great sage, the author of *Pardes Rimonim*, included lengthy expositions of hidden wisdom in his book according to the breadth of his intellect. Later on, to substantially abridge the *Pardes* he added delightful [new] chapters to make that wisdom beloved in the eyes and teach the children of Israel the greatness of its benefit. He called this work *Or Ne'erav* [which stands], in addition to his many other great and extensive compositions. When the pious Rabbi Samuel Gallico, R. Cordovero's student, realized that not many will acquire that wisdom because of its [the *Pardes*'s] great length "a measure longer than the Earth,"[33] and especially not by way of the shorter version [the *Or Ne'erav*], he first set out to complete this abridgement in a sagacious way and called it *Assis Rimonim*. Then came his friend the great sage, R. Mordechai Dato, also a disciple of R. Cordovero,[34] who added to the abridgment of the *Pardes* and thus doubled the learning. In fact, he [R. Mordechai Dato] wrote his additional comments separately in the margins to avoid changing the [original] meaning of his friend, the first abridger [R. Gallico], until scholars came without erudition, wise only in their own eyes, who transcribed the notes into the body of the text. And it was not enough that they inserted many of them in the wrong place, worst yet, they added and subtracted, and confounded the meaning of the book itself. Furthermore, within the appended material they altered the meaning and made its comprehension more difficult for the reader. In the end, that abridgment was published without any mention of [R. Dato] the author of the appended comments, and nothing is known regarding who assembled them. In addition, the work is replete with a great many errors and much confusion and the Sages "toiled in vain to find the entrance;"[35] nothing can be worse for a beginner.[36] Given that the Sages have only just begun to use this work, I saw it fitting to correct it with an attentive eye with [the aid of] the first version [of the text]—the properly edited manuscript—that I loved with the love of my soul,[37] in order to educate and improve. I examined it now, after it was printed by someone else, and saw it wallowing in confusion[38] and deficiency. [Therefore], I clasped it and did not desist until I cleared the stones off the path that ascends to the House of God (*Beit El*) arranging all the precepts and directives in the appropriate manner—a path [well] paved—producing a proper abridgment that will appeal to the reader, will be easy to comprehend, and as difficult to part with as one's wallet. Therefore take note to discern between the *Assis Rimonim* that has been corrected and the one that was not. If I omitted certain teachings, I replaced them with new and valuable ones, may the heart of those who seek God, rejoice. At last, the book *Pardes*, which until now was lacking, has become complete. May God in his mercy bestow [upon us] from His own mouth, wisdom, knowledge, and understanding.[39]

This excerpt vividly illustrates that shorter is not always better; the transfer of knowledge from a more fluid manuscript format to a standardized printed text may entail the loss of important details and the proliferation of errors. The passage highlights another important notion that editors, who prepare other authors' works for publication, need to display a certain level of familiarity with the subject matter. In other words, the editor's function needs to include that of the corrector to ensure that the printed text communicates accurate information to readers.

One important abridgment to the *Pardes Rimonim* that remains in manuscript is *ha-Netzo ha-Rimonim*, extant in two versions and both copied in Italy.[40] The copyist introduced his work in the original manuscript with the following incipit:

> This is the day when I begin my work [the abridgment] of the content of the *Pardes* and I have corrected [the errors] with additional clarification in several places. To the Heavens I raise my hands [to purify me in the study] and completion of His Torah . . . today Monday (*yom bet*) [missing month] in the year, 1604.[41] I am 24 years old today, may God grant me to correct the mistakes and may the spirit of generosity give me support to perceive the loveliness of the secrets of our Torah to learn, to teach and to keep His Torah.[42]

The author provides interesting autobiographical details, which reveal valuable information about the study of Kabbalah in Italy at the beginning of the seventeenth century. He thus, narrates at length the formative years he spent learning from an esteemed Rabbi Moshe, whose last name is illegible in the manuscript, with whom he studied not only halakhah but also the general principles of Kabbalah even though he was younger than eighteen years old at the time. Dramatic events unfold in his life as he gets married at age eighteen but in the same year loses his beloved rabbi. After some time, he moves to Reggio in order to learn Kabbalah from R. Menaḥem Azariah de Fano, who imparts him some introductory teachings to Kabbalah by studying the first Gate of *Pardes Rimonim*. Benayahu contends that the rabbi the author initially studied with may have been Moshe Basola, who was a friend of Cordovero's son, Gedalyah and supported the printing of his father's books in Italy. Be that as it may, let us look more closely at the author's intention to write an abridgment to the *Pardes*.

It should be noted, that the author is fully aware of the two printed abridgments to the *Pardes*, the *Assis* and the *Pelaḥ*, nevertheless he engages in the task of composing a new one, which according to him offers superior organization and easier access to the reader than the competing works. He deems the previous digests to be too long and difficult for readers. He markets his own product by offering a new method of presentation one, which faithfully reproduces the content of each chapter of the *Pardes* and adds his own notes of clarification only selectively "here and there."[43] He also takes pain to simplify some of the difficult chapters in order to facilitate the comprehension of the reader: "It is good to ease comprehension so that the Torah would not be forgotten in Israel."[44] The title of the book is a reminder of his mission: not to alter the original but "to let a flower bring forth a flower and a blossom a bloom."[45]

> My intention was to copy the language of the author and to include the content of each chapter more concisely so that it would help the reader's retention. In addition, the reader thus will have the proper order to all the indexes of the Zohar so that when they hear them, they would be [easily] recognized. I have however, omitted certain obvious references from the Zohar so that the *Pardes* would be presented in a succinct manner, and grasping a little will go a long way.[46]

This author's strategy was to limit the number of *zoharic* citations so as not to burden the reader with too many locator indexes that might aid a scholar but would be too diverting for the beginner in the study of Kabbalah. I propose to attribute the reason that this digest remained in manuscript to the deeply entrenched authority of Rabbi Menaḥem Azariah de Fano in Italy, who saw himself and was broadly conceived as the primary interpreter and disseminator of authentic Safedian Kabbalah at the time. This conjecture is evinced by the fact that the only two printed digests to the *Pardes* produced in Italy to this day are the *Pelaḥ* authored by Fano and the *Assis*, emended and edited by him.

Pitḥei Yah: A Digest to Cordovero's *Pardes Rimonim*

R. Yissakhar Baer's first work, *Pitḥei Yah* (*The Portals of God*), was printed by Gershom ben Beẓalel in Prague in 1609. The format of the work is in quarto written in rabbinic script and comprised of sixteen folios. There is no decorative front page and the printer's information appears on the colophon.

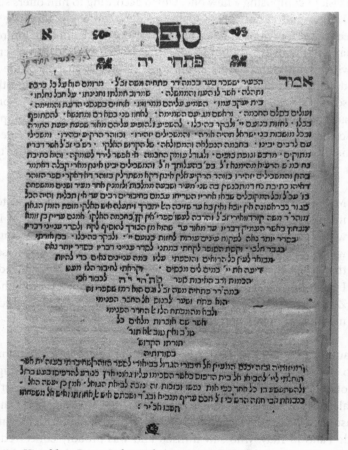

Figure 3.1. Yissakhar Baer, *Pitḥei Yah* (Prague, 1609), fol. 1a, from the (Scholem Collection, National Library of Israel).

The work is conceptually divided into ten gates (she'arim), which allude to the total number of the Sefirot. Structurally, he departs from Cordovero's Pardes, which is divided into thirty-two gates and 278 chapters (peraqim). Yissakhar Baer's thematic organization notably leaves out the subdivision by chapters which appears in the original work, due presumably to his considerably abridged version of the Pardes, in which the ten gates could comfortably accommodate the kabbalistic content he wished to present to the reader. By contrast, the abridgments produced by Samuel Gallico, Assis Rimonim, and Menahem Azariah da Fano's Pelah ha-Rimon, printed almost a decade before the appearance of Pithei Yah, exhibit a much closer thematic and structural analogy to the Cordoverean masterpiece. Gallico's Assis Rimonim faithfully reproduces the original division of thirty-two gates but omits the chapter divisions, while Fano's Pelah ha-Rimon reorganizes the original into twenty-two gates corresponding to the twenty-two letters of the Hebrew alphabet, "the foundation with which the Torah was built" and 100 chapters (peraqim) corresponding to "the sockets of the Tabernacle (adnei ha-mishkhan), reflecting the one hundred prayers that a person [offers] each day to God (nora alilah)."[47]

Yissakhar Baer constructs part of the introduction in rhymed prose praising God and extolling R. Shim'on bar Yohai, the second-century rabbi and sage to whom the Zohar is traditionally ascribed.

> Exulted is He [God] beyond all blessing and admiration
>   to whom belong power and dominion,
> Who from His abundant mercy and compassion,
>   for Jacob's house, His people, and his allotted portion
> Harkened to them from His lofty place . . .
> To shine upon them and emanate
> A spark of Torah, delightful and abundant
>   And in Israel's dwelling light will be attendant
> And the enlightened will shine, like the radiance of the sky,
> they will sparkle[48]
> And the wise, will turn multitudes to understand[49]
>   the wisdom, adorned and marvelous, of the divinely holy Rashbi,
> Whose words are sweeter than honeycomb and honey;
>   To the great depth of [this] wisdom descend you cannot
> For it is an abyss like Noah's Ark.[50]

The allusion to the parallel between the Zohar and Noah's ark is based on a passage in Ra'ayah Mehemnah on the Torah portion "Be-Ha'alotekha"[51] that Yissakhar Baer cites in his introduction. In this *zoharic* segment, the enlightened (*maskhilim*) are defined as individuals who endeavor to study the Zohar, which like Noah's Ark, is inaccessible save for the persistent few, "two from a town and seven from a kingdom; but at times, only one from a town and two from a clan."[52] Yissakhar Baer further explains that in spite of the effort of authors to compose countless treatises following the appearance of the Zohar, such attempts were nonetheless in vain because Kabbalah continued to remain inaccessible and closed, as it was before. The copious writings of Rabbi Moses Cordovero offered a glimmer of hope but failed to promise a complete solution to making Kabbalah more accessible: "and yet, ben Zoma is still outside, because his [Cordovero's] words are impenetrable to such an extent that his works require additional clarification and a better organization of his topics."[53]

Yissakhar Baer here refers to Talmud Yerushalmi *Hagigah*, chapter 2:9, where various rabbinic personalities discuss aspects of two of the most recondite topics in Jewish religious literature, the Works of the Heavenly Chariot and the Works of Creation (*ma'asei merkavah* and *ma'asei bereshit*). In this context, Rabbi Joshua encounters ben Zoma, who seems to be engaged in a monologue on the relationship between the upper and lower waters. When R. Joshua sees him in such a state he states, "See, ben Zoma is outside"; a few days later, the Talmud tells us, ben Zoma died. In addition, ben Zoma was one of the four rabbis who merited entrance into Pardes, the heavenly place where gnosis could be attained regarding esoteric matters.[54] Ben Zoma's inability to take only a measured amount of the heavenly knowledge damaged his mental faculties and ultimately resulted in the loss of his sanity. Yissakhar Baer's use of the idiom, "Ben Zoma is outside," signifies that just as ben Zoma's knowledge was inaccessible for everyone, save for himself, Cordovero's works are also incomprehensible without the aid of proper explanatory tools. His implicit stance concerning the popularization of Kabbalah is to use new literary genres for the mediation of divine knowledge that dilute and temper its potentially explosive potency.

Yissakhar Baer's assessment of Cordovero's *Pardes Rimonim* led him to three important conclusions: (1) that in its current form the *Pardes* was unsuitable for broad consumption;[55] (2) that the source material was profoundly innovative and, with the right intellectual tools and conceptual framework, deserved to be repackaged in a more accessible format; and (3) that as an editor, he had a unique opportunity to shape and create a new product and through that process redress the conceptual limitations inherent in the original work. In sketching his authorial program, Yissakhar Baer's primary motivation was not the presentation of innovative ideas based on original conceptualization of kabbalistic mythology and speculation; instead, he saw his creative calling in the processing of information and representation of old ideas in new frameworks. In this, he reflects a general tendency espoused by his Ashkenazi contemporaries, "who preferred to comment on existing works rather than create works of independent thought."[56]

The title of the book, Yissakhar Baer explains, reflects his desire to dedicate the work to the memory of his father, Petaḥya Moshe, while at the same time, it also reveals his pedagogic program. Like Moses Cordovero, who wrote an educational primer to his *Pardes Rimonim*, titled *Or Ne'erav* (Venice, 1587), so that the kabbalistic novice would receive some preparatory guidance in this lore before embarking on the study of his scholastic treatise, here also Yissakhar Baer expresses a similar sentiment in composing *Pitḥei Yah*.

> And I called this composition, short in length but great in substance, *Pitḥei Yah*, in honor of my father, the great Sage R. Petaḥyah Moshe, of blessed memory. At the same time, it is also an allusion that my book constitutes a portal and a gateway to enter into the inner court, and to move from these preliminary [chapters] to the inner room, where the treasures are, filled with good (*tov*), and there is no goodness like Torah. His [God's] Torah is holy in all its mysteries and allusions, [all of] which the reader will be able to access with the help of my large composition, my commentary to the *Book Zohar* (*Sefer ha-Zohar*), that I wrote with the help of God, may He be blessed, and trusted in God to be able to bring it to press, as the Sages of the Land [of Israel] had already approved it, as is well known,[57] that it should be printed with an iron pen, so that each person could delight in it according to the desire of his soul, and through this may we merit the coming of the Messiah.[58]

This passage displays the author's intention to present a clear educational curriculum. Pedagogically, both Cordovero and Yissakhar Baer emphasize the need for gradual initiation into the mysteries of the Torah. In the textual transmission of these secrets, the teacher's voice is encoded in the literary framework of their composition.[59] Thus, the literary strategies adopted for the presentation of Kabbalah in these various books is adjusted to the reader's level of preparation and prior knowledge. The brief, simple, and introductory style of *Pithei Yah* like Cordovero's *Or Ne'erav* is meant to ease the novice's entry into the unfamiliar and potentially perplexing world of Kabbalah, while *Yod'ei Binah* is addressed to a more advanced reader in keeping with the intended audience of Cordovero's *Pardes Rimonim*. This carefully stratified educational program was meant to guard the reader against theological confusion that might give rise to antinomian views and beliefs, especially at the preliminary stages of study. Introductory texts, such as *Pithei Yah* and Cordovero's *Or Ne'erav*, displaced the necessity for a teacher and promoted independent self-study, which allowed a person to advance at a pace appropriate to the one's prior preparation and knowledge. Yissakhar Baer regarded the popularization and dissemination of this lore not only as "signs" and precursors to the Messianic era but also as instruments that contribute to the spiritual preparation and perfection of the generation,[60] as he makes this sentiment evident in the preface to *Yesh Sakhar*, printed in the same year as *Pithei Yah*.

> One who comes to be purified and hasten the End, they assist him[61] to the fullest extent without limitation. God will protect him for His sake; He will widen his stride[62] so that he may be prepared and established.[63] For the sign has come to understand and teach the way of Torah 'and they shall serve as lights in the firmament,'[64] in the lofty spheres of thought, to circumcise the heart and 'to return the heart of parents to children and the heart of children to their parents.'[65] May they unite to inspire the ears to learn, 'for the land shall be filled with the knowledge of the Lord.'[66]

As for the organization of content, Yissakhar Baer displays no familiarity with either Fano's *Pelah ha-Rimon* or Gallico's *Assis Rimonim*, which exhibit much closer thematic and structural resemblance to Cordovero's original. Citing a short passage from the *Sefer Yezirah* as prooftext, the *Pardes* and its Italian abridgments, open with problematizing the actual number of the *Sefirot* or divine potencies: "They are ten *Sefirot* without substance (*beli'mah*), as the number of fingers; five against five."[67] Yissakhar Baer, by contrast, adopts a more philosophical approach and begins his treatise with the dictum that emphasizes the perfect unity of God and

dismisses the admissibility of notions of corporeality, limitation, or trans-
mutation in describing Him. This is an interesting opening for the author
since, unlike Cordovero, and his Italian abridgers, who immediately launch
into a theoretical discussion about the *Sefirot*, Yissakhar Baer treats correct
theological principles as the foundation to Kabbalah studies and therefore
places the subject of the incorporeality of God at the incipit of his composition.[68] It is not coincidental that *Ma'arekhet ha-Elohut*, an anonymous
kabbalistic composition written in the Middle Ages, opens not with a
mystical topic, but first, by delineating the necessity to believe in God,
and second, by disputing the corporeal depiction of the Divine.[69] Since the
Ma'arekhet was printed twice in Italy in 1558 (Ferrara/Mantua) it is likely
that Yissakhar Baer had some exposure to the work. In fact, we know
from *Imrei Binah*, based on the author's admission, that the *Ma'arekhet*
constitutes one of his primary sources in explaining the foreign terms of
the Zohar. The source informing both compositions is undoubtedly Moses
Maimonides, who devotes considerable discussion in his *Guide of the
Perplexed* to finding a rational justification for the Torah's deployment of
anthropomorphic images and terminology in depicting God.[70] Maimonides'
unequivocal refutation of ascribing any finite and material representation
to the Infinite is reflected in Yissakhar Baer's opening lines.

> Here is the hedge of truth and the tradition of the Covenant,
> that everything the Torah relates with respect to above [the
> Divine], such as "the hand of God," "the eyes of God," and
> similar things, that are depictions of physical limbs, attributes,
> characteristics, and actions are corporeal, separate, accidental,
> and subject to change, but the Divine Being is neither a corpus
> nor a physical force and know [therefore] that these expressions
> can never in any way serve [to describe] Him or the unity of
> the *Sefirot*, in whose midst He conceals Himself.[71]

Yissakhar Baer's hermeneutic method to invoke a major theological
debate centered on the corporeal depiction of God in Scripture that kept
Jewish philosophers occupied in the post-Maimonides period needs to be
contextualized within the intellectual milieu of early modern Ashkenaz.
We have established already in the previous chapter that it is reasonable
to assume that the young Yissakhar Baer was acquainted with Rabbi Mordechai Yaffe and probably studied with him either during Yaffe's years in
Prague or during his stay in Kremenets, Poland. Yaffe's eclectic style as a

writer is informed by extensive studies in all major fields of the Jewish secular and traditional religious curriculum. With Rabbi Moses Isserles,[72] he studied Jewish law, rabbinic literature, Scripture, and philosophy, while with Matityahu ben Solomon Delacrut[73] he studied Kabbalah. During a decade-long stay in Venice he sharpened his knowledge of the sciences, mathematics, and astronomy, and deepened his study of Jewish mysticism, enjoying direct access to the newly printed kabbalistic works produced by the Italian print shops. In his magnum opus, the *Levush Malkhuth* (*The Garment of Royalty*), he synthesized these discrete branches of knowledge into ten gates, conspicuously the number of gates that Yissakhar Baer adopts for presenting his digest of the *Pardes* in *Pithei Yah*.[74]

Yaffe's pedagogical conceptualization invokes Fano's use of the image of a ladder to describe the ascent of the student through various fields of knowledge that are hierarchically arranged. However, whereas Fano distinguishes three levels of knowledge, David Qimhi, Moses Cordovero, and Isaac Luria, and applies this stratification primarily to the field of Kabbalah, Yaffe's theoretical system evinces greater variegation. Thus, for Yaffe the ten gates represent the ten *Sefirot*, the ten archetypes of wisdom, which move from the most mundane categories of inquiry to the most recondite register, "the science of kabbalah."[75] By acquiring each rung, the Jew unifies knowledge of the sciences, "the sublunar world," astronomy "the intermediate world" with the rabbinic curriculum, including both halakhic and meta-halakhic subjects "and will enter into the Pardes of wisdom onto the road that leads straight away into the house of the Lord [*Bet El*]."[76] In clothing oneself in the ten garments, a person acquires the totality of knowledge that the Creator made available for the created being and attains the gnosis with which God clothes and wraps Himself.[77]

Yaffe's integrated approach to knowledge, in which philosophy, science, Kabbalah, and Torah are complementary rather than contradictory disciplines, is invoked in three sections in *Pithei Yah*, although Yissakhar Baer's tone toward secular science is markedly less conciliatory than the one adopted by Yaffe. I already discussed the unusual opening of the work, which deviates considerably from Cordovero's original and follows more closely Maimonides's discussion in the *Guide*, on the one hand, and the *Ma'arekhet ha-Elohut*, on the other. In discussing the nature of the *Sefirot*, Yissakhar Baer first establishes that there can be no division among the *Sefirot* and therefore polemicizes against those who argue that every *Sefirah* contains some portion of another *Sefirah*. Instead he poses a question to further clarify the nature of the *Sefirot*: if one rejects the notion that division can exist among the *Sefirot*, then can we assume that they are completely equal without any separation? In answering this query he cites Maimonides' *Mishneh Torah, Hilkhot Yesodei Torah*, to state that just as the four elements, fire, water, air, and earth, all comprise a dominant property or characteristic differentiating it from another element, similarly each *Sefirah* is associated with a characteristic distinctive to it and not present to the same intensity in other *Sefirot*. It is therefore the dominant characteristic present in a *Sefirah* that assigns it its name and primary function.[78] In an earlier chapter, explaining the reason for the emanation of the *Sefirot*, Yissakhar Baer, follows Cordovero's original more acerbic polemic against the scientists, who reject the kabbalistic view according to which the *sefirotic* emanation continued until the lowest, deepest, point of our planet, and therefore "even in this heavy and rough earth, [deep] within its navel are seven rungs of earth"[79] While these references to philosophy and science are not central to the work as a whole, they influence and frame the author's discourse.[80]

The ten gates (*sha'ar*) of *Pithei Yah* are arranged in descending rather than the ascending order that Yaffe adopts. A major pedagogical focus for Yissakhar Baer in Gate 1 is to delineate the relationship between God, the *Sefirot*, and human beings, and in this manner to harmonize kabbalistic principles with the tenets of normative Judaism. A general argument against the popularization of Kabbalah among the masses was motivated by an anxiety that the concept of multiplicity that characterize the world of the *Sefirot*, Divine names, and attributes, may in reality lead the uninitiated into religious heresy and antinomian beliefs. The audience that Yissakhar Baer addresses is fundamentally different from the readers of the *Pardes*. While Cordovero could take it for granted that those who pick up his book will have had some basic preparation not only in the principles of Kabbalah, but also in the traditional facets of the rabbinic curriculum, Torah, Talmud, and halakhah. For Cordovero and his learned audience, the doctrine of the *Sefirot* posed no potential challenge to the principle of the unity of God and therefore he devotes only a short discussion to this question and only toward the end of Gate 1.[81] Much more endemic to his scholarly inquiry is to reconcile certain theories of Kabbalah already in circulation, which at times presented contradictory interpretations and theories to the advanced reader.

However, what was axiomatic for Cordovero was not so for Yissakhar Baer. Writing to a nonspecialist audience, he was acutely aware that *Pithei Yah* might constitute the only encounter his readers might have with

Kabbalah and therefore, the fundamental tenets and principles of this lore needed to be carefully articulated for his readership. Consequently, after establishing the unity of God he focuses his teaching on delineating the characteristics of the *Sefirot* advancing a short discourse on the dynamic relationship between their hidden, spiritual, and revealed, physical aspects. At the beginning of the treatise, he emphasizes that the *Sefirot* are not separate entities but vessels whose main function is to channel the Divine will and energy. He further delineates that since the *Sefirot* are interconnected, on the one hand, with each other and, on the other, with the Emanator (*ma'azil*) and the rest of the created world, they are in constant flux and their names and function change according to the primary activity that they assume in a given moment.[82]

The unique role and responsibility of each human being are important topics for Yissakhar Baer not only at the outset of his digest but also in his subsequent publication, *Yesh Sakhar*, in which he turns to the enumeration of the mystical meaning of the commandments collected from various sections of the Zohar. Following preliminary observations regarding the basic nature of the *Sefirot*, he turns to delineating the theurgical potential of the human being in general, and more particularly, of the individual Jew. Accordingly, just as the *Sefirot* are linked to and reflect the Divine will, the human soul, and material form, are also structurally linked to metaphysical forces and potencies in the upper world.

> All the limbs and organs of the human being constitute palaces and garments for spiritual entities and supernal forces, which cleave to these and become intertwined with them through the extension of their roots, and due to this interdependence [it is up] to a human being's power and preparation to become a vessel (*merkhavah*) to a particular *Sefirah*, because each person who purifies oneself from all manner of sin and becomes rigorous about one of the commandments—pursuing it more than all the others and cleaving to it—such a person becomes a vessel to the essence of the *Sefirah*, which that commandment denotes.[83]

The conceptualization of the Biblical commandments as a rope that pulls human beings closer to the Divine and thereby reconnects the microcosm with the macrocosm, forms an important pillar in Yissakhar Baer's teaching. As a secondary elite, in touch with broader strata of the Jewish community, it was an important educational imperative for him to emphasize the ethical dimensions of kabbalistic theories. Notably, while Yissakhar Baer opts to underscore the profound consequences of human actions on the divine world in the first chapter of his composition, Cordovero in the *Pardes* treats this topic at the conclusion of the book, in Gate 31 from chapters 8 to 11, which expound the mystical meaning of the human body, its organs and various parts, and in Gate 32, which delineates the theurgical efficacy of concentration (*khavanah*) during prayer.

The *Sefer Yeẓirah*'s statement regarding the "ten *Sefirot* without substance (*beli'mah*)," so pivotal for structuring Cordovero's initial discourse on clarifying alternative theories and establishing that the number ten is the only correct numerical representation for the *Sefirot*, receives a lengthy treatment in the second part of the introductory chapter in *Pitḥei Yah*. Cordovero's methodology in presenting his theoretical conclusions rests on the fundamentals of dialectical reasoning, in which an original statement is elucidated through the careful juxtaposition of contradictory arguments, which are systematically refuted by the author. This process allows the writer to refine the reader's comprehension of the question at hand and add new information or highlight an alternative perspective at every stage of the process. Thus, Cordovero's learned and highly scholastic deliberation on determining the correct numerical value of the *Sefirot*, engages a variety of sources, some taken from zoharic literature, such as the main part of the Zohar, *Tikkunei ha-Zohar*, *Idra*, and *Ra'ayah Meḥemnah*, while others derive from other medieval sources, *The Bahir*, a responsum by Hai Gaon, and a tradition attributed to Shimon the Righteous and recorded by Hamay Gaon in his book, *Sefer ha-Iyyun* (*The Book of Contemplation*).[84] In contrast to Cordovero's editorial decision to include multiple sources when explaining a problem, in the case of Hai Gaon both the original query directed at the Gaon and his subsequent response are provided, Yissakhar Baer includes only a short reference to the Gaon's words. The lack of explicit references to other works or debates in his abridgement sets it apart from both the *Pardes* and the Italian abridgments.

Another technical and conceptual feature of the *Pardes* is the inclusion of kabbalistic diagrams, which appear interspersed throughout the work for the purpose of providing visual illustration regarding certain kabbalistic concepts and processes. Yissakhar Baer's summary includes one visual aid only, a schematic diagram representing the ten *Sefirot*.[85] What is interesting, however, is that the 1592 Krakow edition of the *Pardes* does not contain this diagram. Cordovero includes a similar *sefirotic* tree in

Gate 7, devoted to the explication of "channels," which function as con-
duits connecting the *Sefirot* and directing the divine emanation from one
Sefirah to the next, yet, this diagram is markedly different from the one
Yissakhar Baer is using. Azariah da Fano's abridgment *Pelaḥ ha-Rimon*
includes absolutely no kabbalistic diagrams, while Samuel Gallico's *Assis
Rimonim*, does reproduce a number of illustrations from the *Pardes*. In
fact, Yissakhar Baer's depiction of the *Sefirot* displays a striking similar-
ity with Gallico's *sefirotic* diagram as shown on the following pages. It is
worth noting that Fano's stance against the use of visual depictions of the
Sefirot and divine processes remains consistent so that the 1623 version
of the *Assis* edited by him omits all the diagrams included in its original
1601 edition.

Such variance in the creative reproduction of texts and images
demonstrates the porousness of intellectual boundaries that characterized
the early modern world in which Yissakhar Baer lived and worked. As
I discussed earlier, an important feature of this period was the mobility
of individuals and ideas facilitated by the emergence of transregional
networks. In contrast to local communities, whose lives and boundaries,
both real and intellectual, were regulated by communal institutions led by
the establishment elite, transregional networks were, by definition, much
less regulated and as such they provided an excellent opportunity for the
secondary elites, such as Yissakhar Baer, to develop their authorial individuality. At the same time, the variant presentation of the Cordoverean
diagram may also point to the absence or delay in the development of
a consistent and unified body of theoretical knowledge of Cordoverean
Kabbalah. Alternatively, Yissakhar Baer may have based his abridgement
on a manuscript copy of the *Pardes*, for unlike in *Yesh Sakhar*, where
he openly discloses that he consults the Cremona edition of the Zohar,
here he provides no indication of his source. Whatever the actual reason
is, the variation in the re-presentation of this important diagram across
multiple texts suggests that at this critical moment in the history of
knowledge transfer in the early modern period, the printed book had not
yet replaced but rather still coexisted and competed with other media of
communication and transmission, such as manuscripts and oral discourse.

In conclusion, Yissakhar Baer deploys his own unique strategy to
manage the kabbalistic information overload that Cordovero provides in
the *Pardes Rimonim*. His focused treatment of the four worlds in Gates
1–4 and the ten *Sefirot* in Gates 5–10, enables him to eliminate topics,
original sources, and polemical debates that are useful in a scholastic or

academic setting, which characterized Cordovero's world and audience, but which offered no spiritual meaning or practical benefit for the Jew with little or no kabbalistic education, whom Yissakhar Baer addressed. In composing *Pithei Yah*, Yissakhar Baer offered new intellectual horizons to Jewish readers, who could pick up his pocket-sized book with ease and immerse themselves in its clear language and succinct conceptual presentation. At the beginning of the seventeenth century, Yissakhar Baer put forward a genre that in the twenty-first century would sell millions of copies: *Kabbalah for Dummies*.

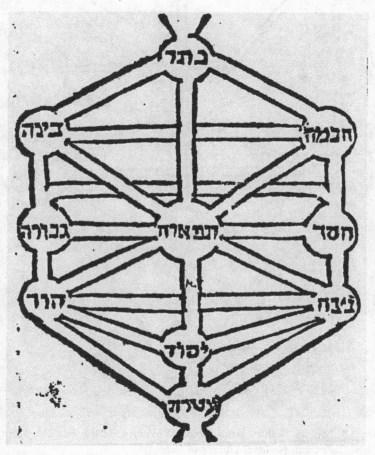

Figure 3.2. Yissakhar Baer, *Pithei Yah* (Prague, 1609), fol. 14b, from the Scholem Collection, National Library of Israel.

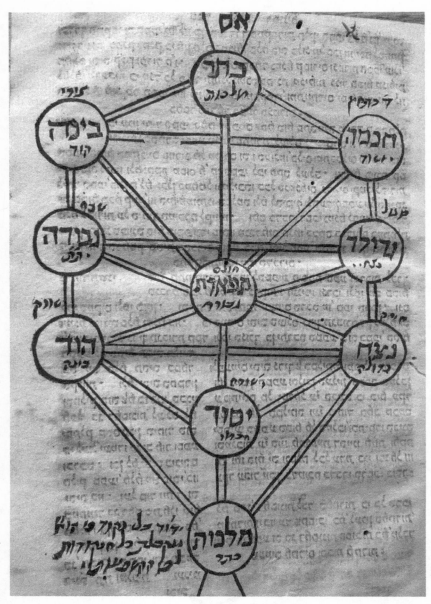

Figure 3.3. Samuel Gallico, *Assis Rimonim* (Venice, 1601), fol. 23a, from the Scholem Collection, National Library of Israel.

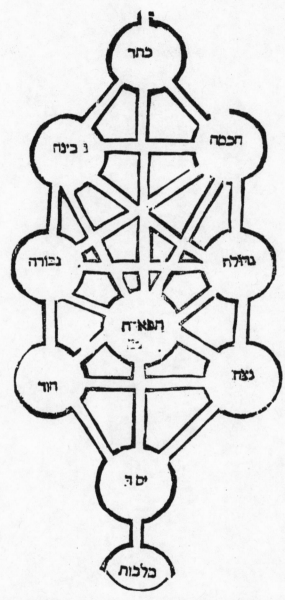

Figure 3.4. Moses Cordovero, *Pardes Rimonim* (Krakow, 1592), fol. 39b, from the Scholem Collection, National Library of Israel.

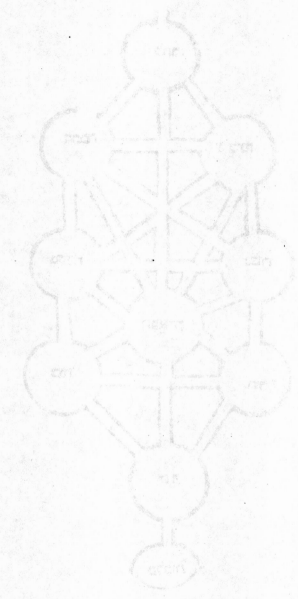

Chapter 4

Zoharic Customs in a Halakhic Framework[1]

I order you to learn the wisdom of Kabbalah because a man who
does not learn this wisdom is not God-fearing . . . *Sefer ha-Pardes*
should be for you like the *Shulhan Arukh*.[2]

Halakhah and Kabbalah: Issues and Developments

In a number of important studies on Kabbalah and halakhah, Jacob Katz
delineates the inherent complexities that characterize the relationship
between these two foundational pillars of Medieval Jewish consciousness.[3]
Katz argues that from the rabbinic period on, Jewish religious inquiry and
preoccupation can be divided into two essentially different but at times
imbricated systems: halakhah and aggadah.[4] Halakhah denotes Jewish law
and jurisprudence focused on prescribing the ways in which the divinely
ordained commandments of the Torah should be executed and performed.
At the fulcrum of the halakhic position is to define and regulate proper
ritual conduct. Aggadah, by contrast, encompasses the realm of interpretation, a way of infusing religious action with meaning.[5] Aggadah formed
an integral part of the classical rabbinic textual repertoire, including the
Talmud and various midrashic compositions, and by the Middle Ages
comprised two new fields of inquiry, Jewish mysticism and the Kabbalah,
on the one hand, and Jewish philosophy and rationalism, on the other.[6]
While legal compendia and codes continued to be produced throughout
the medieval period,[7] halakhah was primarily perceived as a "closed
system" with its endemic rules and postulates that made it impervious
to the incursions of extrinsic influences of philosophy and Kabbalah.[8]

Nonetheless, as scholars have repeatedly shown metalegal considerations often informed the deliberations of juridical authorities.[9]

Throughout the medieval period philosophy and Kabbalah constituted rival interpretive systems competing for authority and legitimacy in the realm of Jewish belief and praxis.[10] A major difference between philosophy and Kabbalah was that while the former was viewed by many as an essentially exogenous system to Judaism communicated via Greek, Christian, and Arabic sources, the latter was presented as the most recondite layer of the Sinaitic Revelation and therefore endogenous to the Jewish tradition.[11] It is not surprising, therefore, that when the printing press revolutionized European intellectual and material culture, Kabbalah and not philosophy was destined to challenge halakhah and vie for religious and ideological primacy. The appearance of the printing press ushered in a gradual process of transition in the medium of knowledge presentation, and transmission, from the manuscript to the printed book. Among others, this process was also characterized by the precipitation of new literary genres, which allowed the proponents of Kabbalah to engage halakhah in novel ways.

The proliferation of the printing press fundamentally transformed the organization of Jewish knowledge in the sixteenth century and impacted the development of halakhah and Kabbalah in analogous ways.[12] David Ruderman notes that the transmission of rabbinic knowledge prior to the age of printing was largely orally based and unfolded through gradual addition of glosses (hagahot) that were appended to the margins of classical rabbinic sources, which by way of copying became eventually fully integrated into the text.[13] Such binary systems, partially oral and in part written, furnished the rabbinic commentator with a degree of freedom and flexibility in halakhic deliberations that allowed for the selective incorporation of local customs (minhag ha-maqom) and for the admissibility of other considerations.[14] By contrast, the composition of legal codes in sixteenth-century Europe became such a prominent enterprise that it impacted Jewish legal activity as well.[15] Rabbi Joseph Qaro's comprehensive legal code the Shulḥan Arukh (Venice, 1565), written from the perspective of the Sephardic tradition, and expanded in its printed form with the adaptations of R. Moses Isserles, which facilitated its acceptance in Ashkenazi lands, ensured the creation of a unified legal voice and reduced the elasticity of individual rabbinic authority.[16] Thus, as David Ruderman observes, "the text—not the teacher—became the ultimate word, and thus diminished the teacher's authoritative capacity for interpreting the law."[17]

In the centuries that followed the appearance of the Zohar, kabbalistic approaches to halakhah became widespread in both Ashkenazi and

Sephardic communities.[18] The theological disposition of the Zohar exerted lasting influence on the writings of one of the major codifiers of Jewish law, R. Joseph Qaro. Zwi Werblowsky's penetrating analysis of Qaro's life and works portrays a man who moved with equal confidence from halakhic deliberations to questions of Kabbalah.[19] In his major legal compendium, the *Beit Yosef*,[20] Qaro undertook to codify and harmonize the works of three medieval legal masters, Alfasi, Maimonides, and Asher ben Yehiel, with the explicit goal of presenting an all-encompassing reference tool that would serve as the standard guide to all future halakhic decisors, in both Sephardi and Ashkenazi communities. Notwithstanding Qaro's achievements in the field of halakhah, his truly original contribution to Jewish thought can be found in the creative incorporation of *zoharic* ideas and passages into the fabric of a legal code. Qaro's contribution to the harmonization of halakhah and Kabbalah was threefold. First, he clearly acknowledged the use of the Zohar as a resource. Second, he accepted the Zohar's legal stance as more normative than any of his predecessors. Third, he incorporated more passages from the Zohar than anyone else had done before him.[21] In composing the *Beit Yosef* he was driven by a fundamental objective to deliver not only a synthesis of the major authoritative sources of halakhah, but also to expand the scope of the work by using the "teachings of the Zohar" to elucidate the meaning of the commandments, as he explains in the introduction to the *Oraḥ Ḥayyim* section of the *Beit Yosef.*

> Thus, whoever has this work before him will have the Talmud's teachings arranged in front of him with Rashi's commentary, *tosafot,* and Rabbenu Nissim; the rulings of R. Isaac Alfasi and R. Asher ben Jehiel, *Mordechai,* Maimonides and the *haggahot* thereon; *Maggid Mishneh, Rabbenu Yeruham, Sefer ha-Terumah, Sefer ha-Terumot, Shibbolei ha-Leket, Rokeah, Sha'arei Dura, Tashbez, Sefer ha-Ittur, Nimmukei Yosef, Sefer Mizvot Gadol* and *Sefer Mizvot Katan, Orhot Hayyim, Torat ha-Bayit, Haggahot Asheri, Sefer ha-Manhig, Agur, Ba'alei ha-Nefesh* by R. Abraham ben David [of Posquières]; the response of R. Asher ben Jehiel and R. Solomon ibn Adret; as well as R. Joseph bar Sheshet, R. Simeon ben Zemah, R Joseph Colon and the *Terumat ha-Deshen.* All of their teachings have been elucidated and in some places [I have cited] teachings of the *Zohar* . . .[22]

The inclusion of the Zohar and its kabbalistic rulings in the *Beit Yosef* alongside, and in the company of, the principal literary representatives of medieval halakhic activity, conferred a degree of authority on the Zohar from the perspective of Jewish law. Qaro, unlike the majority of his contemporaries and predecessors, took a decidedly interdisciplinary stance and rather than compartmentalizing discrete areas of Jewish learning, he viewed them as organically connected, forming a unified whole. In this he acted both as a lawyer and as a kabbalist; thus, just as one of the main tasks of a kabbalist was to unify the ten functionally diverse *Sefirot*, which comprise the *sefirotic* tree in Kabbalah, here, too, Qaro set himself the task of connecting and interweaving various branches of rabbinic knowledge. In his mystical diary, *Maggid Mesharim*, Qaro revealed that his methodology was strongly influenced by the instructions of his heavenly mentor (*maggid*), who enjoined him daily to "engage regularly in the study of halakhah, Gemara, Kabbalah, Mishnah, Tosafot and Rashi," as much as he could, for by so doing he would be able to " 'join them and combine one with another, 'inserting the clasps into the loops.' "[23] In other words, the methodological imperative of the *maggid* became legislated into Qaro's code as a new theoretical approach to halakhah that emphasizes the holistic nature of Torah, in which legal precepts were seen not as independent of, but rather intimately connected to, meta-halakhic considerations.[24] At the same time, he was aware of his own limitations as a legist to allow the inclusion of precepts into halakhic practice that were based entirely on metaphysical considerations, which at times ostensibly contradicted accepted norms. Thus, for instance, he refused to accede to the *maggid*'s repeated appeal to fast on the day of the New Year, *Rosh Hashanah*, in spite of the angelic informant's appeal that had he done so even once he would have averted many calamities in his life.[25] Nevertheless, Qaro's selective admission of the Zohar into the *Beit Yosef* paved the way to works such as Yissakhar Baer's *Yesh Sakhar*, where the kabbalistic rationale of the commandments is presented in an ostensibly halakhic framework.[26]

As a jurist, Qaro was notably vigilant concerning the proper alignment of literary form and content. In writing the *Beit Yosef*, he addressed the elite rabbinic reader, the halakhic specialist, who had already received extensive training in all branches of the rabbinic curriculum and therefore could discern when and how to engage the kabbalistic dimensions of his work. When he turned to bringing Jewish law into the household of every Jew, by composing the *Shulḥan Arukh*, he conspicuously left out divergent legal deliberations as well as nonnormative, kabbalistic references.[27] Taking advantage of print technology, Qaro realized the need for a standard halakhic code that when printed in a pocket-sized format would provide both the scholar and the lay Jew with an accessible reference tool that readily lent itself to quick and easy consultation.[28] Reflecting his consideration to popularize the *Shulḥan Arukh*, Qaro ordered rabbinic law in a concise and descriptive manner. His objective was to provide standardized halakhic praxis to a large and diverse audience and therefore he was interested in setting down what to do without registering the attendant historical precedents and legal deliberations. The *Shulḥan Arukh*, which followed the topical organization of the medieval *Arba'ah Turim*, domesticated halakhic performance, which had previously belonged to the restricted domain of learned specialists, and enabled Jews to connect with the ritual aspects of daily life without the direct involvement of a rabbi. To be sure, the *Shulḥan Arukh* did not completely displace the rabbi, whose legal expertise was decisive in more complicated halakhic cases and litigation, nonetheless, Qaro's code proved successful in providing heterogeneous Jewish communities with a unified guide to practical observance. Textual standardization, an important technical consequence of print technology, therefore, clearly impacted the organization of knowledge in the field of halakhah and reshaped the Jewish tradition and collectivity in new ways.[29]

Ritual Observance and the Sustenance of the Divine World: Yesh Sakhar

The first edition of *Yesh Sakhar* published by the printing house of Gershom ben Betsalel Katz in 1609 bears a number of features that are worth noting.

First, the pagination follows the folio format that was common practice among printers since the incunabula period. Second, the title page contains a simple decorative border but lacks the elaborate design characteristic of other works printed in Prague and elsewhere at this time, including Yissakhar Baer's last two works, *Meqor Ḥokhmah* and *Imrei Binah*, which I will discuss in the next chapters. In addition to its simplicity, the title page draws attention to the cultural agency of the printer as the arbiter and transmitter of knowledge. Whereas the name of the author is barely visible toward the middle of the page and is clearly relegated to the background, the name of the publisher and the place of publication are prominently displayed using a font that is almost the same size as the title of the work itself. Always cognizant of the need to market and promote the commercial product, the printers included a short synopsis of the book directly below the title, which served to situate the work in relation to the kabbalistic classic, the Zohar, and Qaro's halakhic best-seller,

Figure 4.1. *Yesh Sakhar*, Title Page (Prague, 1609), from the Scholem Collection, National Library of Israel.

the *Shulḥan Arukh*.[30] The ostensible association between Yissakhar Baer's composition and these authoritative literary sources acted as a powerful tool to advertise and legitimate his work even before the reader opened its first page.

The first page contains the author's introduction, which provides
a wealth of detail and information regarding reasons that prompted his
composition, adverse economic conditions that he encountered in printing his other composition, *Yod'ei Binah*, and the cultural resources he
consulted and engaged for completing his literary mission. It is therefore
worth citing the author's introduction in full.

> Yissakhar Baer, son of my master and my most exalted father,
> our great teacher, the Sage, Petahya Moshe, may his righteous
> memory be a blessing, said: I saw and my heart and even my
> soul stirred within me, 'as I was in the days of my youth,'[31] with
> my lips and heart [unified] as one, to explore divine knowl-
> edge: 'and I saw after He saw me,'[32] for it is good in the eyes
> of God and [other] people to go forth in the battle of Torah as
> warriors, 'the smallest shall become as a thousand,'[33] to over-
> come and shatter the 'jagged mountains'[34] 'with great power'[35]
> and 'vigor'[36] 'come what may upon me,'[37] 'and let me run,'[38]
> and arrive. Barely anything, yet already something; through
> contemplation of the principles and 'depths of wisdom'[39] may
> my heart live forever 'to bask in the light of [eternal] life,'[40]
> 'that is sevenfold, like the radiance of the Sun,'[41] before the
> awesome and terrible God. Today I shall come to the fountain,
> to *Ein Mishpat* which is *Qadesh*, supernal holiness, to enter the
> innermost sanctuary, and complete a delightful composition
> consisting of all the laws found in the Zohar by the holy and
> saintly man, R. Shimon bar Yohai, and [add] a commentary
> that is pleasant, 'how sweet is the light, what a delight for the
> eyes'[42] for those who look upon it, the enlightened ones will
> read it, behold it, and they 'will shine like the radiance of the
> firmament.'[43]
>
> Because of the enormity of the expenses required of me
> at this time [to undertake] the printing (of this manuscript),
> I have withdrawn, for the time being, from publishing my
> commentary on the Zohar that I called, *Yod'ei Binah*,[44] as is
> known, until such time that God expands my means for behold
> I have 'learned the lesson,'[45] distress has taught me and found
> my aid against the foe.[46] . . . One who comes to be purified and
> hasten the end, they assist him[47] to the fullest extent without
> limitation. God will protect him for His sake; He will widen
> his stride[48] so that he may be prepared and established.[49] For

the sign has come to understand and teach the way of Torah
'and they shall serve as lights in the firmament,'[50] in the lofty
spheres of thought, to circumcise the heart and 'to return the
heart of parents to children and the heart of children to their
parents.'[51] May they unite to inspire the ears to learn, 'for the
land shall be filled with the devotion to the Lord.'[52] Amen. So
shall be His will.

This shall serve as a preface to all who read my book that
wherever I placed a reference it will indicate the source of that
law and its appropriate page in the Zohar using the pagination
of the large Cremona edition, for it is more accurate in most
of its rendition than the small Venice edition, even though it
is [still] riddled with many errors. Another argument in favor
of the larger [Cremona] version is that it is more widespread
in our lands.

Furthermore, I have omitted those laws that we are
not accustomed to following for the reason that there is no
agreement regarding their validity. Also, at times when I refer
to issues cited in the interpretation of the *Gemara* or another
place, my intention was not so much to bring up that problem,
but rather to explain the secret of the matter together with its
hidden reason and profundity. Let God, may He be blessed,
teach us the true path 'to bask in the light of [eternal] life.'[53]

The introduction is written in classic rabbinic style using a rich
repertoire of Biblical tropes and allusions. As I mentioned earlier, the
author was forced by economic considerations to give up printing his
extensive commentary on the Zohar, *Yod'ei Binah*, and dedicate his efforts
to publishing first his technically more innovative and in regard to literary genre less conventional treatments of the Zohar, in the hope that
publishing these will afford him the necessary financial resources to print
Yod'ei Binah at a later time. From the publisher's point of view, *zoharic*
commentaries, such as *Yod'ei Binah*, represented an established and widely
diffused genre in kabbalistic texts and therefore did not constitute novelty that would immediately draw a large readership. In fact, one of the
earliest printed kabbalistic texts was Menahem Recanati's *Commentary on
the Torah*, printed in Venice in 1523, which was regarded as a standard
and authoritative rendition of the Zohar even among Ashkenazi rabbis.[54]
By contrast, all three of Yissakhar Baer's works on the Zohar constituted

potentially innovative literary genres, which if they had existed already,[55] did not enjoy broad circulation, and therefore, the printers hoped to attract potential customers by offering a new product. An alternative consideration that may have influenced the printer's decision could have been the size of the publication. The three works on the Zohar that they decided to print, Yesh Sakhar, Meqor Ḥokhmah, and Imrei Binah, were relatively short in size, whereas Yissakhar Baer repeatedly refers to Yod'ei Binah as an extensive and most likely lengthy composition, which may have deterred the printers, who wanted some guarantee on their investment.

The author's declaration and identification of the Cremona edition of the Zohar as the basis of his referencing system, is instructive regarding the knowledge transmission from Italy to Eastern Europe. Yissakhar Baer is not the only author who notes the greater availability of the Cremona Zohar in the Jewish communities of Ashkenazi lands. A number of other authors writing a few decades before and after Yissakhar Baer reveal in their introductions their reliance on the Cremona version as the one more frequently owned and consulted by Central and Eastern European Jews. Thus, for instance Yissakhar Baer ben Naftali ha-Kohen from Szczebrzeszyn, notes in the introduction to his book, Mar'eh Kohen, that the Cremona and not the Mantua Zohar is the prevalent edition extant "here in our lands."[56] The Venice edition that R. Yissakhar Baer mentions poses an interesting conundrum in the history of Zohar printing. To date, there are only two extant sixteenth-century editions of the Zohar from Italy and these are the Cremona and the Mantua versions as I discussed extensively in chapter 1. Yet, Zeev Gries posits that there is sufficient evidence to suggest that there was a pirated Venice edition of the work, which authors like Yissakhar Baer either saw or were aware of, copies of which, however, did not survive. The Venice Zohar, apparently was small in format contained many errors and most likely used a stolen copy of the Mantua Zohar as its base text.[57] At a time, when copyrights were still selectively negotiated, printers felt at liberty to try their own fortune by illicitly acquiring financially promising publications.

Yissakhar Baer's presentation of the halakhic portions of the Zohar, together with his interpretation of these passages, is embedded in the organizational framework of Asher ben Yeḥiel's medieval code, the Arba'ah Turim, which formed the basis of Joseph Qaro's Shulḥan Arukh as well. The main feature that contributed to the popularity of the Tur was its accessible style of presentation, which organized the halakhic content in a systematic and orderly manner that made it "superior to any earlier work."[58] While in the introduction Yissakhar Baer does not mention either the *Tur* or the *Shulḥan Arukh*, in a postscript on the concluding page of the composition he firmly aligns his work with the *Tur*: "blessed is God who guided me on the true path to bring to light the laws of the Torah found in [the Zohar], which I organized in the order of the *Arba'ah Turim* produced by the Sages, of blessed memory."[59] The association with the *Tur* and the *Shulḥan Arukh* conferred religious authority and legitimacy to Yissakhar Baer's composition, an approval that he consciously cultivated by stating both in his introduction and again in the postscript that he refrained from commenting on *zoharic* laws that contradicted accepted halakhic practice. As an author, he underlines his efforts to exercise self-censorship to neutralize antinomian tendencies that the innovative combination of halakhah and Kabbalah in *Yesh Sakhar* could potentially generate.

At the same time, Yissakhar Baer took great pains to emphasize the kabbalistic dimensions of his work, which distinguished it from other purely legal compendia. His purpose in composing *Yesh Sakhar* was to provide readers with a practical guide that resembled the *Shulḥan Arukh* in its apodictic statements, but offered Jews, who had little or only basic knowledge of kabbalistic teachings, the secret meaning of the commandments and laws of the Torah, so that they could imbue their practice with more meaning. An important literary precedent to *Yesh Sakhar* was no doubt Moses Galante's *Mafteaḥ ha-Zohar* (Venice, 1566), in which the author dedicates a separate section to organize the commandments found in the Zohar into twelve topically arranged categories reflecting the enumeration of the tribes of Israel: (1) prayer (weekdays, Shabbat, and festivals); (2) Torah study; (3) afterlife/death, reward/punishment; (4) charity and good deeds; (5) repentance (*teshuvah*); (6) the exulted status of the righteous; (7) deeds that cause a person's soul to merit the Garden of Eden or *Gehinom*; (8) destruction of the Temple, its rebuilding, four expulsions, the in-gathering, coming of the Messiah, and resurrection; (9) holiness of Shabbat, festivals, and new moon, what the upper beings do on the festival, and what is appropriate to do for those below; (10) bride- and bridegroom, procreation, circumcision; (11) the sublime status of the Land of Israel and of the one who merits to die in it; and (12) rabbinic sayings and other matters.[60] These topics do not receive detailed treatment as they do in *Yesh Sakhar*, however, here the purpose is to organize the content of the Zohar that relates to the daily ritual and ethical life of a Jew and provide pagination reference for easy location of source material in the original text. Nevertheless, Galante's approach to collate those passages of the Zohar that deal directly with ritual praxis and ethical demeanor prefigures the rise of a prominent literary genre in the seventeenth and eighteenth centuries—conduct literature (*sifrut ha-hanhagot*)—that infused *halakhah* with kabbalistic rationale to propagate the proper mode of conduct in both earthly and divine matters.[61] It was the turn toward strengthening Jewish observance that motivated Rabbi Yissakhar Baer to compile a work more expansive, self-referential, and user-friendly than the one offered by Galante.

Among the organizational features of the book we find two functionally different referencing systems: one followed by the author and the other most likely by the printer. Yissakhar Baer specifies already in his introduction that he will provide the reader with pagination references to the Cremona edition of the Zohar that will be included with each *zoharic* passage. Although he does not justify why he considers the adoption of this device important, he may have anticipated the need of his future audience to contextualize a particular law within its original literary setting. At the same time, the inclusion of *zoharic* page numbers establishes the author's integrity and methodological rigor as a scholar.

The subject index included at the conclusion of the main text and before the colophon page references each law in order of the four main sections of the text (*Oraḥ Ḥayyim*; *Yoreh De'ah*; *Even ha-Ezer*, and *Ḥoshen Mishpat*). The laws in each section are assigned a letter of the Hebrew alphabet but folio identifiers are not provided. The work nonetheless exhibits an excellent referencing system, which functions in the following way: the body of the text identifies only the major legal categories under consideration at the top of the page, while subcategories are marked not by a header but by indented paragraphs, which are assigned Hebrew letters. The same letter then references the main text, the corresponding commentary (*peirush*) by Yissakhar Baer, and the brief summary of the *mizvah* indicated in the Index. This system establishes *Yesh Sakhar* as a convenient and handy reference guide where content is explicitly organized to facilitate the user's interest. The reader thus can decide the amount and depth of reading he wants to pursue; the index gives a brief practical summary of what to do, while the commentary and the main text provide layered meaning.

Thematically, *Yesh Sakhar* is organized into four sections of unequal length, each named after, and corresponding to, the main parts of the

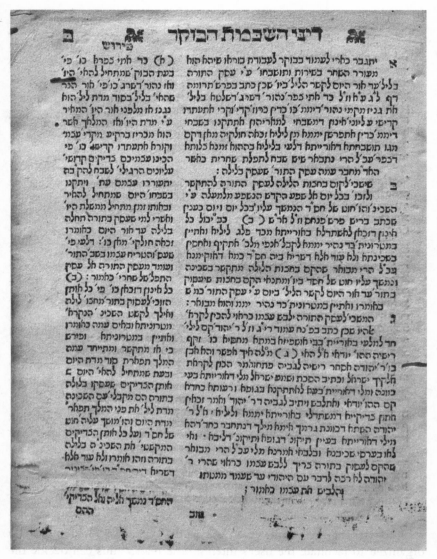

Figure 4.2. *Yesh Sakhar* (Prague, 1609), fol. 2a. "Laws of Rising in the Morning," from the Scholem Collection, National Library of Israel.

Tur and Joseph Qaro's *Shulḥan Arukh*: *Oraḥ Ḥayyim, Yoreh De'ah, Even ha-Ezer,* and *Ḥoshen Mishpat.* As in the case of the *Shulḥan Arukh,* by far the longest section with the greatest number of halakhot is *Oraḥ Ḥayyim,* which deals with daily prayer, rituals, and festivals. The area that receives the least amount of mystical treatment in *Yesh Sakhar* is bound up with judicial matters, which reflects a general tendency in conduct literature to omit discussion of topics related to torts and legal disputes, which pertain more to regulating interpersonal interactions.[62] It is of note that Yissakhar

Figure 4.3. Index of Laws, *Yesh Sakhar* (Prague, 1609), fol. 78a, from the Scholem Collection, National Library of Israel.

Baer addresses this issue directly in his postscript to the work: "And I could not find more laws [in the Zohar] concerning *Hoshen Mishpat* even though there are such matters, as when a person speaks ill of his fellow and similar things [that could be considered here]. I will, with God's help, present these issues in a separate work, which will also comment on other [positive] character traits such as righteousness, asceticism, and piety."

Yissakhar Baer laments the Zohar's sporadic treatment of issues that relate to the moral refinement of human beings and of precepts that could promote ethical conduct among individuals, and discloses his intention to fill this gap by writing a book devoted to desirable character traits and virtuous conduct. As far as we know this work has never been published. However, this statement clearly indicates his objective to compose yet another work that would follow in the footsteps of Moses Cordovero, whose work *Tomer Devorah* (*The Palm Tree of Devorah*), printed in Venice in 1588, exerted a strong influence on the burgeoning *musar* literature in Eastern Europe.

Yesh Sakhar retains a uniform structure and the presentation of each commandment is broken down into three parts: (1) a brief summary statement of a mitzvah; (2) a textual citation from the Zohar, which serves as the base text for Yissakhar Baer's explication of the commandment; and (3) a commentary that simplifies the Zohar or at times amplifies the mystical significance of the mizvah in question. It is the latter part that reveals Yissakhar Baer's creative genius as he intersperses often very distant and disconnected *zoharic* passages with other meta-halakhic explanations in an effort to arrive at halakhic statements. A set of three passages will illustrate this dynamic.

Pesaḥ

Commandment (*Mizvah*)

Great is eating maẓa during Pesaḥ for it expels demons. Thus it is written in *Parashat Pinchas* in the *Zohar*.[63]

ZOHAR

One who eats *ḥameẓ* during Pesaḥ brings death close to oneself, both in this world and in the world to come as it is

written: '[for whoever eats leavened bread from the first day
to the seventh] that soul will be cut off [from Israel]' (Exodus
12:15). Why *maza* [what is the reason for eating *maza*]? For
thus we have learned, *Shaddai*, that is, He said to His world
'*dai*, enough!' and also said concerning our suffering, 'enough!'
Maza functions as a similar expression, for it [*maza*] removes
all evil and stirs up dispute. Just as the Divine Name, *Shaddai*,
on the mezuzah removes evil spirits and demons that are at the
entrance, here also the *maza* removes them from all sanctified
dwellings and rouses dispute and quarrel among them as it is
written, 'trouble and quarrel (*masah u-meribah*).'[64]

Commentary (*Peirush*)

For the *hamez* (leaven) is in the mystery of the power of the
demonic (*kelipah*), the aspect of death which is the leaven in
the dough. By eating leaven at this time [during Passover],
one brings upon oneself death by drawing this demonic force
upon the self. Even after one's death in this world, the soul
will also be cut off (*karet*) from the domain of Holiness in a
way that the demonic will plunder one's soul and a person will
not merit to enter inside the curtain [*pargod*],[65] which is the
essence of being cut off (*karet*), may the Merciful One save us.
Therefore a person should be careful not to eat leaven during
Passover for there is no repair for it either in this world or in
the world to come. Now to explain the word *maza* (unleavened
flatbread) the Zohar asks, 'why *maza*?' Why is it called *maza*?
And the answer is 'for thus we have learned,' that is to say
that the [Divine name] *Shaddai* removes the demons from the
entrance of a house and says concerning our suffering 'enough'
('*dai*). Here also, *maza* constitutes an expression of dispute from
the phrase 'in their quarrel against God' (Numbers 26:9).[66]
The eating of *maza* causes the removal of the demonic, the
leaven, from Holiness and stirs up quarrel and discord among
the demonic forces (*kelipot*) themselves. Therefore the Zohar
explains 'just as the Divine Name, *Shaddai*.' The reference to
this matter in Scripture is the verse, '*masa umeribah*,' where
the letter *samekh* changes into *zade* because the source [of
these two letters] is the same as they are dental letters (*zayin*,

samekh, shin, resh, ẓade)[67] and thus the verse seems to imply
that the leaven (*maẓa*) itself causes the dispute within the
demonic (*kelipot*).[68]

This tripartite presentation enables Yissakhar Baer to reorganize knowledge
in novel ways. The brief summary at once fuses Torah law with its efficacy
against metaphysical or demonic forces focusing on the positive command
to eat *maẓa* during the seven days of Passover (Exodus 12:15). It is of note
that the *zoharic* prooftext he quotes does just the opposite, as it begins with
enumerating the dire consequences of one who violates the negative Torah
command, which admonishes against the consumption of leaven during
Passover (Exodus12:15). Yissakhar Baer's organization, in fact, follows more
closely the thematic order in the Torah where the positive command to eat
maẓa precedes the negative imperative, not to eat leaven. In his commentary
(*peirush*), he sets himself two concurrent tasks: (1) to translate the main
ideas in the *zoharic* passage from Aramaic to Hebrew and (2) to provide
enough additional mystical rationale to render the metaphysical source of
the law lucid. It is important to emphasize here that by assuming the role of
translator, Yissakhar Baer anticipates the potential difficulties his readers will
experience in deciphering the Zohar's uniquely complex Aramaic parlance
and responds to this challenge with the technical adjustment, translation. As
we will see in the next chapter, he will devote an entire book to elucidating
the difficult words of the Zohar, in *Imrei Binah*.[69]

In regard to content, this passage focuses on the dynamic interplay
between the demonic and sacred elements imbedded in the rituals associated with the festival of Passover. The negative commandment found in
the Biblical text against eating leavened bread and the positive injunction
to eat *maẓa* or unleavened bread during Passover receive a unique mythological reading that emphasizes the power of divine commandments to
proscribe the influence of demonic forces at work in the world. The tools
to successfully defeat demonic powers stem from the latent spiritual potencies buried in the orthographic character of the Hebrew language. Thus,
while the word, *shed* (*shin, dalet*) displayed on the *mezuzah*, found on
the doorposts of Jewish homes, signifies demon, the addition of the letter
yud at the end of the word transforms it into the divine name *Shadday*,
which obviates the activities of demonic side and displaces it outside of
the domain of human habitation.

Similarly, with the words, *maẓah* and *masah*, because *ẓade* and
samekh are guttural letters, formed in the same area of the mouth, they

share certain ontological commonalities. Therefore the *zade* in the word *mazah* ostensibly neutralizes the forces of the *kelipot* or evil—denoted by the word *masah*—that are particularly empowered at the time of Passover. Thus, according to the Zohar's theology of evil, the letters of the Hebrew language, serve as the basic building blocks of sustaining demonic powers but at the same time also offer the antidote against them based on their inherent potential embedded in the ontological characteristics of the language.

Understanding the source and nature of evil was a persistent preoccupation of kabbalists beginning with the Middle Ages. The *Zohar*, the classic source of kabbalistic speculation, devotes much attention to the question of evil focusing on the unique interplay between the Biblical commandments and their latent spiritual potential to effectively defeat demonic forces through their performative dimension.[70] In this, the Zohar's conceptualization of evil espouses a fundamentally different view than more philosophically inclined kabbalistic works, such as the early fourteenth-century annyomous composition, *Ma'arekhet ha-Elohut*. According to the Zohar's "positive" theology, evil assumes a real and separate existence from the Holiness of God and the world of the *Sefirot*.[71] By contrast, the *Ma'arekhet ha-Elohut* treats evil based on the philosophical conceptualization that emphasizes the "relative" nature of evil, as the absence of holiness but not as an ontologically independent domain.[72]

The Zohar's mythological approach to the commandments accommodates a dualistic conceptualization of the world, in which the forces of good and evil are in constant battle and where the outcome of this battle depends on the theurgical actions and pious intention of each Jewish devotee.[73] In this worldview, the performance of rituals as diverse as the observance of festivals and proper conduct in sexual matters become the battleground between the forces of evil and the sacred. The Biblical commandments become transfigured into weapons which when wielded properly can effectively contain evil and its negative influence. Jewish philosophers such as the great medieval thinker and theologian, Moses Maimonides, have struggled greatly to ascribe reason and rational understanding to the Biblical commandments in his *Guide of the Perplexed*.[74] While he was successful in arguing that most of the commandments have a rational basis because they contribute to the ethical and moral perfection of human beings and thus produce a better society, he failed to explain all the commandments on such grounds. In the end he conceded that certain *mizvot* were beyond logic and reason. Yissakhar Baer's work appearing in the early seventeenth century in East Central Europe constitutes an important guide to Jewish piety that predates the large-scale commitment to these ideals by Hassidic masters and their followers a century later.[75]

The following two textual selections illustrate another important characteristic of *Yesh Sakhar*, namely, the author's manifest interest in providing lengthier analysis on certain subjects. His decision to do so may be attributed to the greater availability of secondary source material on those topics that he could engage for his *peirush*. Alternatively, it may reflect the author's deeper personal interest in the matter or his recognition that some laws are more difficult to grasp and require therefore more detailed esoteric explanation. Whatever the actual reason may have been, the lack of uniformity in the treatment of the *zoharic* precepts points to the high degree of discretion and authorial autonomy that was available to a secondary elite, who disseminated its teachings through the medium of the printed book.

Counting of the *Omer*

Commandment (*Mizvah*)

The counting of the *omer* needs to be completed standing only and its mystical meaning is elucidated in *Parashat Emor* in the Zohar.

ZOHAR

'And you shall count for yourselves from the day after the Shabbat . . . seven weeks' (Leviticus 23:15) and this is the commandment to count the *omer*, as we have already learned. Based on this even though Israel has purified itself sufficiently to perform the Pesaḥ sacrifice and has gone forth from her impurity, they have not yet become complete and purified in the proper way. For this reason, complete Hallel is not recited on the days of Pesaḥ because until, now (that is *Shavuot*) Israel has not become sufficiently perfected, thus Israel is like a woman who goes forth from her impurity and when she moves from there forward 'she shall count off for herself [seven days]' (Leviticus 15:28). Here also when Israel went forth from Egypt, it went forth from her impurity and then performed Pesaḥ to eat at the table of their Father, and from then onwards they [Israel] will complete the counting [of the *omer*] to bring close the bride to her husband. Now, since these days [of the counting] are associated with the masculine world, therefore this counting was not given to the women but to the men only, and this is the reason that the counting is done standing but the matters of the lower world are done sitting and not standing and this is the mystery of the two prayers, the sitting and the standing ones. And what is the reason for the 50 days? These are the totality of the facets of the Torah for this day is in the mystery of the Torah only and these are those 50 days in which we have the Sabbatical [every seven years] and the Jubilee years [every 50 years]. Thus it is explained that the essence of the counting is the standing, and we learn other laws from this.

Commentary (*Peirush*)

Thus we have explained that the *sefirah* (counting of the *omer*) is entirely about the purification of Israel and enabling them to stand a higher level even though they have already taken up the eating of the *maza* and the performance of Passover properly, nevertheless they have not yet attained the requisite level of purity from the *kelipot*,[76] that had already [surrounded them] in Egypt and so they have not attained the perfection appropriate from them. Now just a woman who is impure from her *niddah* has to count her days of purity [when she has no impure flow or discharge], here also Israel, because it has gone forth from her impurity which is the *kelipah*, has to count the days of purity towards supernal holiness. Thus, these 49 days that we count out they are meant to purify with supernal holiness of the 49 gates of *Binah* that shine forth from her, and she [that is *Binah*] is associated with the masculine world, who emanates constantly [to the lower worlds], therefore, everything that comes from the masculine world has to be done standing and by men and not by women like, as for example, the *Amidah* prayer. By contrast, the sitting-down prayer is the mystery of the restoration of the lower world, the *Sefirah* of *Ateret/Malkhut* with all her aspects and therefore it is done sitting. The essence

of the 50 days is found in the supernal branches that extend
from the 50 gates of *Binah* that shine forth into *Ateret/Malkhut*,
for she is the aspect of the Sabbatical year. To explain the matter
more succinctly, I am telling you that when Israel went forth
from Egypt they have not yet been thoroughly cleansed and
purified from the filth of the serpent, and without the help of
the heavens that supported Israel in Egypt, they would have
sunk into the mire of the mud into the power of the impure
kelipah, which overpowered and ruled over them until they
entered into it [into this impure world of the [*kelipot*] up to
the 49th gate and all the levels contained therein. For just
as there are 49 aspects of purity there are also 49 aspects of
impurity, and if the 49 aspects of purity have not ben aroused
upon them, we, our children and all the generations would
still be under their [the *kelipot*] authority. That is the reason
why they left in haste so they would not enter the 50th grade
of impurity, however, they were not yet joined to the level of
the masculine world and the impurity has not ceased from
Israel until they stood at Sinai, for had they become purified
during their leaving of Egypt, they would have received the
Torah then. However, when they left Egypt, only their days of
impurity were removed and afterwards they had to count 7
weeks like the counting [of a woman] 'and she shall count for
herself 7 days" for the 7 weeks correspond to the 7 white/clean
days that a woman counts to become purified from her flow.
The reason [for counting the *omer*] is that Israel should enter
into the 49 gates of Holiness and so that their entry should
be through the 50 gates that in *Ateret/Malkhut* is the aspect
of the days, and since the days derive from their source, the
years, from which they are illuminated and obtain all their
activity from their power, therefore the days are associated
with the years and we bless over the counting of the *omer*.
The *omer* alludes to the *Shekhinah* [Divine Presence] and
the word *sefirah* [counting] comes from the expression *sapir*
or *sapphire* to indicate that we adorn *Ateret/Malkhut*, which
is illuminated by the supernal gates that are in *Binah* all the
days that are found in *Ateret/Malkhut*. That is why we have
to specify [every day] that it is such and such a day, for it is

the gate [corresponding to that specific day] that will become revealed and thus we need to join it to the previous days, so that all their illumination should become one. We also need to count the weeks, which thus comprise all the gates to each *Sefirah* in order to unify the branch with its root.

Shavuot

Commandment (*Mizvah*)

A great mitzvah and elevated rank is allotted to a person who engages in Torah on the night of *Shavuot*, for thus it is written in *Parashat Emor*.

ZOHAR

One who arrives at this day purified, without losing the counting [of the *omer*], when he comes to this night [of *Shavuot*] he needs to study Torah, to join himself to Her [Torah] and also to preserve that supernal purity that he attained that night [*Shavuot*] when is purified. We have learned that the Torah that he should study on the night of *Shavuot* is the Oral Torah, so that they should be purified as one from the sources of the deep river, afterwards, during the day, the written Torah should follow, so that he should join himself to both of them and thus they will be in unity, through a single coupling above. Thus they will announce [the angels in the heavenly realm] concerning him saying: 'And this shall be My covenant with them, said the Lord: My spirits which is upon you, and the words which I placed I your mouth, they will not be removed from your mouth . . .' Because of this, the righteous masters of old, would not sleep on this night, and would study Torah saying: 'let us inherit the blessed heritage for ourselves and for our children in two worlds [this world and the world that I coming].' Further, on that night [*Shavuot*] the Congregation of Israel, *Knesset Israel,* is crowned on their account and she comes to be unified with the King, and the two of them are crowned upon the heads of those who merit it.

Commentary (*Peirush*)

When counting out the *omer* he should not forget the [proper] numbers so that he should not err in the counting of the number and thus should follow the proper counting and then he will be called a purified person. Given that he is pure, he needs to add additional holiness to the purity in a manner that he studies the Torah all night on *Shavuot* so that the next day, on the fiftieth, he unites with the *Shekhinah* [Divine Presence], and adorn her with the jewels of the heavenly lights. However, the order of the study should be such, that at night he should study the Oral Torah, which is the adornment of *Ateret/Malkhut*, for she is in the mystery of the Oral Torah the supernal *peh* or mouth of the Torah above. During the day, one should study the Written Torah, which is the adornment of *Tiferet* and thus one unites the two aspects, the aspect of the day and that of the night, as one. We have further learned that the Oral Torah should be studied on the night of *Shavuot* so that purification should come from the very sources of the deep river which is [the *Sefirah*] *Binah*, the place where purity flows through the supernal waters, the waters of *miqveh*, and thus a person merits to have children and grandchildren who study Torah until the end of all generations. Therefore, it is necessary to study all kinds of Scriptural readings in order to adorn the Bride, *Ateret*, with all Her ornaments to bring Her to enter the wedding canopy the next day, during the day. Happy is the share of one who merits all this glory for they will be counted as the retinue of the King's palace and as one of the companions of the Bride, the supernal *Shekinah*. If, however, sleep forces a person, one should rest one's head low but not lying down to prevent one from prolonging sleep and then one should rise with zeal to do one's work until the day shines forth and by rising early one gives thanks and praises in the Synagogue to the Master of all with songs and praises for the goodness that He has done to us, giving us a share in His Torah and selecting us for Himself as a beloved nation from amongst all the other nations. And how good is our portion and may He deem us righteous enough so that we may crown this day with the crown of the entire Torah.

In regard to content, *Yesh Sakhar* can be situated in the broader context of the *ta'amei ha-miẓvot* literature, a large body of mystical texts originating from the early Middle Ages, which sought to uncover the reasons and metaphysical foundations for the precepts of the Torah.[77] Elliot Wolfson identifies three distinct positions within the *ta'amei ha-miẓ vot* literature: a minimalist, an intermediate, and a maximalist. He arrives at this classification based on the degree to which a kabbalistic work is prepared to ascribe mystical significance to laws in the Torah. Minimalists argue that only few commandments are informed by esoteric considerations while maximalists posit that all commandments have an identifiable metaphysical layer. Yissakhar Baer's approach to halakhah is decidedly more closely aligned with the maximalist position, adopting the stance of the Zohar, which implies that for him all the commandments of the Torah encompass an esoteric layer, as demonstrated above.[78]

At the same time, Yissakhar Baer's conformist posture in including only those *zoharic* precepts that do not contradict normative praxis is attested to in his commentary to the priestly blessing.

> Since the priest is a man [associated with] the *Sefirah* of Grace (*Hesed*), he cannot become a chariot to *Ḥesed* except by way of the *Shekhinah*, the mystery of *Ateret*, as is known. Given that he is unmarried, he is blemished, and the *Shekhinah* does not rest upon him. And since the *Shekhinah* does not rest upon him how can he become a man of *Ḥesed*? Once he gets married, however, he becomes perfected and a cord of *Ḥesed* unites with him joined by the *Shekhinah* . . . And this is brought down by the *Beit Yosef* in section 128, in the name of the *Mordechai* and the *Shibolet ha-Leqet* in the name of Rabbi Yiẓhak bar Yehudah, that perhaps Rabbi Yiẓhak's intention was to hint at the secret discussed above, and all reflects the same conclusion.[79]

This passage discloses his familiarity and knowledge of halakhic sources. Accordingly, he is aware that there was division among the medieval halakhic decisors as to whether an unmarried priest was allowed by halakhah to raise his hands for the priestly benediction or not. The two rival sides were represented by the positions of the *Mordechai* and *Shibolet ha-Leqet*, against the opinion of Solomon ibn Adret (Rashba). Yissakhar Baer cites the *Beit* Yosef, but expands it by saying that R. Yiẓhak ben Yehudah, like other medieval decisors, may have known about the Zohar's ruling regarding the mystical meaning of the commandment even if they did not reveal this explicitly.[80]

Continuing his discussion of the priestly blessing in section 6, Yissakhar Baer states that the laws, which govern how the priest should separate their fingers during blessing "is not elucidated in the *Gemara* and even Maimonides does not cite it at all because it was never discussed in the *Gemara* anywhere."[81] R. Asher ben Yeḥiel's attempt to offer a technical solution for implementing the priestly blessing, by holding the fingers in such a way so as to peer forth from five crevices, is discounted by Yissakhar Baer based on the *Mordekhai* as an extraneous explanation (*drash*) not instituted by the Talmud itself.[82] It is interesting that neither the Zohar nor Yissakhar Baer offer any practical guidance as to how the priests should hold their fingers during the blessing, but instead emphasize the need to separate both the fingers of the hands and the syllables pronounced by the mouth so as not to confuse and intermingle divine potencies represented by the human limbs and verbal utterance.

That Yissakhar Baer relied on the *Beit Yosef* as his primary halakhic source and guide, which he embellished and expanded by adding kabbalistic customs and explanations, is substantiated by an interesting passage that Qaro writes concerning the custom that the Levite was required to pour water and wash the Kohen's hands before the priestly blessing.

> And thus I saw that the Jews of Ashkenaz, were used to wash their hands at the time of the priestly blessing even though they had already washed their hands in the morning. I have also heard that they used to follow the same custom in Sepharad that the Levites would pour water over their hands, and I did not know from where they got this [custom] until by God's grace I found it explained in the *midrash* of the *Zohar*, in *Parashat Naso*.[83]

In its literary structure, Yissakhar Baer adopts the genre of a legal code for the exposition of his conceptual content and not the more traditional format of Biblical commentary by *parashiyot* (chapter by chapter). By contrast, another composition, the *Shnei Luḥot ha-Berit* by Isaiah Horowitz,[84] penned in close geographical and temporal proximity to *Yesh Sakhar*, espouses a distinctly different structural framework. Horowitz merges three facets of Jewish lore in his popular composition:

Torah commentary, proper identification and understanding of the commandments, and finally, the advocacy of ethical conduct.[85] Arguably the
pedagogic program that motivated Horowitz was to advocate a curriculum
in which Torah, halakhah, and Kabbalah were studied in an integrated
and synchronic manner. Therefore, the point of departure for him is the
Biblical *parashah* into which he compresses his kabbalistic expositions of
the commandments and his ethical imperatives. Indeed, even a brief glance
back at the printed *zoharic* corpus displays a predilection for arrangement
of mystical-halakhic content according to Biblical chapters.

Conclusion

Yissakhar Baer's departure from the form-convention of the Zohar and
of other contemporary compositions, such as the *Shnei Luhot ha-Berit*,
lead to a number of conclusions. First, the adoption of the codificatory
format of the *Shulhan Arukh* legitimates kabbalistic inquiry and presents
it as equal in authority and stature to halakhah. Second, the strategic
inclusion of kabbalistic material within the framework of a legal code
breaks down the conventional literary boundaries that used to demarcate
between apodictic-legal and discursive-homiletic inquiries and obliterates
the attendant hierarchical disparity between these two disciplines.[86] Third,
in his introduction to *Yesh Sakhar*, Yissakhar Baer displays a measured
stance against *zoharic* customs and laws that explicitly contradict halakhic
norms of Ashkenazi communities of his time. By adopting such a stance,
he resists their admissibility into his code: "In addition, I have omitted
those laws that we are not accustomed to following for the reason that
there is no agreement regarding their validity."[87] Fourth, concerning the
relationship between Talmud and Kabbalah he affirms the superiority of
the latter by underlining that Talmudic references in his work are included
to support kabbalistic verities and not because they are authoritative in
their own right as law. On this position he sides with other medieval
kabbalists who read kabbalistic ideas into Talmudic passages.[88] The fact
that Yissakhar Baer adopts the codifying format of the *Shulhan Arukh*
implies that he shares Qaro's goal to address a wider audience by simplifying halakhic discourse. Arguably, Qaro's work was also directed at a
new audience that was no longer inclined toward an in-depth study of the
masters of Jewish jurisprudence but wished merely to receive a practical
guide to the observance of Jewish law. At the same time he goes beyond

Qaro's work by infusing discussion of halakhah with its corresponding kabbalistic explanation. By doing so he, as an author, shapes a new idea and ideal: Jewish mysticism cannot remain on the margins restricted to elite circles but, instead, needs to be made accessible to a wider audience. He achieves this goal in *Yesh Sakhar* by synthesizing the most fundamental realm of Judaism, halakhah, with its most esoteric one, Kabbalah.

Chapter 5

Constructing a *Zoharic* Lexicon

And I have called it [my book] *Imrei Binah*, according to the verse, "To know wisdom and the tradition, to comprehend the words of understanding"[1] for all who want to know the wisdom and the tradition, hidden in the words of the *Zohar*, first must understand, *Imrei Binah* . . .

—Yissakhar Baer, *Imreh Binah*

The Use of Lexical Aids among Humanist Scholars in Early Modern Europe

The making of dictionaries is often bound up with more than the simple aim of providing unequivocal meaning to a given word that a lexicographer retrieves from a different and often alien historical and cultural context. In fact, as John Considine notes, dictionaries "have sometimes been records of the emerging sense of identity of particular speech communities or reading communities, groups defined by use of a common spoken language or by commitment to the study of a common body of texts."[2] They do not merely transmit information, but exhibit also a performative dimension, which puts the reader in intimate contact with a past that the lexicon strives to recover and reappropriate, while at the same time, firmly embracing the goals of collection and conservation. While it is true that the deployment of particular languages can exclude certain communities of readers and speakers—especially those that over time lost a speech community, such as Latin in the Christian, and Aramaic in the

131

European Jewish literate populations—dictionaries, nevertheless, retain the functional advantage to "search" for new communities and reestablish contact between past and present.[3]

The organization, translation, and adaptation of foreign words into lexicons and dictionaries by European authors, Jewish and Christian alike, was animated by a greater intellectual objective of creating intellectual bridges to an idealized place and time that could be accessed and acquired with greater ease. Dictionaries thus opened up new gateways not only to extinct languages but also to new epistemological fields spurred by the availability of printed matter. Along the recovery of a number of ancient disciplines by humanists, such as Greek mathematics, the Kabbalah also gained prominence that coincided with growing interests in this field by a broader Jewish readership. It is indicative of the far-reaching impact of Kabbalah on Christian scholastic circles in the early modern period that the Encyclopedia (1630) of Johann Heinrich Alsted includes the field of cabbala.[4] In the transmission history of Jewish mysticism, early-modern lexicons and dictionaries to the Zohar became indispensable didactic tools that stimulated better mastery of this new area of study for Jews and non-Jews alike.

That the task of the lexicographer was a heroic or even Herculean undertaking (Herculei Labores) was emphasized by Erasmus, the humanist scholar and theologian, who in the early sixteenth century likened his project of composing a dictionary of ancient Greek and Latin culture to the efforts of the legendary demigod of ancient Greek mythology. According to Erasmus, "[I]f any human toils deserved to be awarded the epithet of 'Herculean' it seems to belong to in the highest degree to those at least who devote their efforts to restoring the monuments of ancient and true literature."[5] Erasmus explicitly establishes the compiler of dictionaries as a larger-than-life figure who puts his intellectual acumen in the service of conserving and reviving the vast intellectual resources of the past for the benefit of others. He pays tribute to the humanist ideal, which classified ancient knowledge and texts as the true unadulterated sources of wisdom to be recovered by the thorough philological and linguistic removal of layers of textual corruptions like Hercules' "purging of Augean's stables from its filth."[6] Philological diligence through textual emendations was to constitute the primary tool for clearing the way to classical learning. Therefore, the scholarly agendas of a great many humanists were stimulated by intense lexicographic activity to imitate and reformulate classical texts and learning.

For the serious student of Greek, Giovanni Crastone's dictionary, *Lexicon Graeco-Latinum*, was an indispensable tool to acquire the requisite skills for the study of ancient Greek sources. It was a comprehensive attempt of 520 folio pages printed in 1476 with approximately 18,000 entries of mostly single-word glosses, which were occasionally supplemented by lists of two or three word variants.[7] Another notable example of a serious scholarly effort to judiciously emend the philological deficiencies of earlier generations is Johann Reuchlin's *Rudimenta Hebraica*, a comprehensive handbook of Hebrew grammar and a dictionary arranged in three volumes and printed in 1506. While the work appealed primarily to a specialist Christian readership and sold only 700 copies of the total print-run of 1,500, becoming a financial disaster for the author, the linguistic competence and meticulous presentation of the material established it as the handbook of choice for the eminent Christian theologians of the sixteenth century, Martin Luther and the Swiss Reformer, Huldrych Zwingli.[8] Finally, the best-selling Latin dictionary of the sixteenth century was produced by the Augustinian lexicographer, Ambrogio Calepino. It was reprinted 211 times between 1502 and 1779, and like the contemporary Webster dictionary became known proverbially as the *Calepinus*.[9] The arrangement of its content aimed to classify the vocabulary of printed Latin classics that have enjoyed wide circulation among early-modern Christian readers. Responding to a technical desideratum already identified by the eleventh-century philologist, Papius, Calepino incorporated illustrative citations from ancient authors, making it an appealing didactic feature of the book.[10] These three examples illustrate the preoccupation of Christian humanist scholars with philological analysis as the ground for reconnecting and reclaiming the cultural ideals and wisdom of Antiquity. From the beginning, therefore, dictionaries functioned with a dual purpose: as repositories of textual elements (artifacts) and as means to conserving and diffusing textual heritage.[11]

"Entrance" into the Words of the Zohar: Lexicographic Practice in Kabbalah

The Zohar's linguistic peculiarity, a preference for the use of Aramaic as opposed to Hebrew in its ostensibly medieval Iberian cultural context, elicited early scholarly notice and demanded serious inquiry. In the thirteenth century, while many theological works of the Jewish literary canon appeared in Hebrew, Judeo-Arabic was still frequently deployed for books on religious topics, alongside Arabic, which was the language of choice for subjects such as philosophy and science, especially among Jews in the Iberian Peninsula. Aramaic, an ancient Semitic language, once the vernacular of Jews living in distinct geographical locales of the Middle East, became textualized in Jewish religious literature through the Targumim and the Talmud, which was redacted over several centuries by generations of rabbis active in Babylonian academies of learning. As scholarly consensus ascribes the authorship of the Zohar to thirteenth-century Castillia, and hence rejects the pseudepigraphic claim of the work as the product of the second-century tanna, R. Shimʻon bar Yoḥai, the conundrum of the Zohar's unique style of Aramaic still fascinates readers and constitutes the subject of enduring academic discussions and debates.[12] What perplexes most researchers is that the Aramaic of the Zohar does not reflect the natural philological development of the language into Western and Eastern dialects and is more a product of textual accretion that incorporates layers derived from other languages, notably Hebrew, Arabic, Spanish, Latin, and Greek.[13] Gershom Scholem called the Aramaic of the Zohar an artificial idiom that borrowed from genuine Aramaic sources in order to manufacture a language that resembled the one it sought to imitate.[14] New attempts in the last decade have called into question Scholem's conclusions and advocated for more systematic philological analyses.[15]

Yehudah Liebes, in contrast to earlier scholars, has repeatedly celebrated the creative and playful appeal inherent in the Zohar's Aramaic and its literary potential for fomenting the formation of a reading community that share its mystical purpose and theological imperative.[16] Liebes therefore argues that the Zohar's Aramaic is an entirely natural construct and the only suitable vehicle for its narrative and theological articulation. Words, as "living and portable" entities from the past, can become compelling "mediators to embody a culture with particular fullness and meaning.[17] In this case, Aramaic is analogous to and derived from the world of evil, the *sitra aḥra*, and serves as a fitting linguistic antidote to its destructive potential. The poet, Haim Naḥman Bialik, depicts the enduring vitality and linguistic puissance of the Aramaic language to express hidden mysteries.

> Even at night, her [Aramaic's] heart did not sleep nor was her
> light extinguished. Through the classic book of the Kabbalah
> [the Zohar], this nocturnal vision of the Hebrew nation was
> created in her language and her spirit. The wonder of it is that

in the days of the *Zohar* the Aramaic language was already completely dead in the speech of the Jewish people. Perhaps for this reason it was appropriate for [expressing] the mysterious, like the pale light of the dead moon for the dreamer.[18]

Early modern kabbalists, such as Meir ibn Gabbai and Menaḥem Azariah da Fano, emphasized not so much the latent spiritual, but the effective magical capacity of the Aramaic language by prescribing the public recitation of the Zohar as a spiritual and magical panacea with the potential to reintegrate the forces of evil into the side of holiness.[19]

The translation of the Zohar from Aramaic to Hebrew had begun already in the thirteenth century as attested to by the works of the medieval kabbalists, Yosef Gikatilla and Moses de Leon, where select passages appear in Hebrew that correspond to Aramaic parallels in the Zoharic corpus.[20] While it is difficult to definitively conclude that these Kabbalists translated the Zohar from Aramaic into Hebrew, since it is conceivable that the authors of the Zohar translated Gikatilla and de Leon into Aramaic. Nevertheless these parallel passages attest to the efficacy of translation to mediate semantic elements of the text from one language to another. It is the Kabbalist David ben Yehudah he-Hassid who undertakes the first extensive translation of the Zohar into Hebrew at the beginning of the fourteenth century, without an explicit attribution of the translated sections to the Zohar.[21] Excerpted sections translated from Aramaic to Hebrew can be found in the fourteenth-century work, *Menorat ha-Maor*, written by Israel ibn Joseph Al-Nakawa of Toledo. In the last decade of the fifteenth century, the kabbalist, Rabbi Isaac Mor Hayyim assumed the translation of the *Idra Zuta* portion of the Zoharic corpus complete with his own commentary sent in an epistle to Rabbi Isaac of Pisa. Presumably the Italian Rabbi experienced some difficulty with deciphering the Aramaic original. The sixteenth century produced more Hebrew paraphrases or translations of the Zohar including, *Ẓror Hamor*, by Rabbi Avraham Saba,[22] another more comprehensive attempt by Rabbi Yehudah Masud in Egypt, and two other anonymous works both completed in Egypt.[23]

Kabbalists also generated their own dictionaries and lexicons to the Zohar, which much like their philosophical counterparts,[24] functioned as reference tools that readers could consult when they encountered kabbalistic concepts and terminology that were unfamiliar to them.[25] An early example of a *zoharic* lexicon is the anonymous composition, *Bi'ur ha-Milim ha-Zarot* (*Dictionary of Foreign Words*), which came to serve as the basis of many subsequent reference aids and anthologies to the Zohar.[26] Today it is extant in several manuscript variants[27] and two abridged, defective printed editions.[28] It is clear that Sim'on ibn Lavi and Abraham Azulay, the two foremost anthologists of the Zohar, both originally from North Africa, were not only familiar with the *Bi'ur* but also cited from it extensively in their own works.[29] Other works influenced by the *Bi'ur* include *Yesha Yah*, written by Isaiah ben Eleazar Ḥayyim of Nice (Venice, 1637)[30] and *Imrei Binah* by Yissakhar Baer ben Moses Petaḥyah, to be discussed in detail below.

The preparation of study guides, lexicons, anthologies, and interpretative manuals on the Zohar constituted major strategies for the exoterization of Kabbalah beginning with the fourteenth century. Many regarded the Zohar as the foremost repository of kabbalistic wisdom and therefore the reading and comprehension of the text was tantamount to acquiring its mystical content.[31] Owning textual fragments of the *zoharic* corpus and the ability to quote from and comment on the Zohar ascribed cultural power to those who pursued such activities.[32] Prior to the appearance of the Zohar in print, in the middle of the sixteenth century, the main hermeneutic activity associated with the Zohar was the admission of select textual fragments into the works of kabbalistic authors. Menaḥem Recanati's *Commentary on the Torah* incorporates the highest number and the longest passages from the Zohar and therefore constitutes an important medieval attempt to make Kabbalah available to a broader audience.[33] Recanati's literary achievement in synthesizing diverse areas of study, in part Biblical and in part kabbalistic commentary, facilitated the promotion of a new integrated study of Torah, in which the mystical layer became an essential and not a subsidiary facet of Jewish learning. The content arranged in the order of Biblical chapters (*parashiyot*) presented the esoteric material in a framework already familiar to the reader. It is not accidental, that Recanati's work constitutes one of the earliest printed texts of Kabbalah, published in Venice (1523) well before the appearance of the Zohar in print.[34]

The printing of the Zohar in 1558–1560, fixed the format of the text, standardized its content, and at the same time, amplified earlier perceptions that attributed a canonical and sacred status to this mystical literary corpus.[35] In the wake of the Zohar's diffusion in print, cultural power, thereto conferred on the owner of the *zoharic* manuscripts, became transferred on the exegete whose explicatory technique and depth of kabbalistic knowledge proved most effective in making the Zohar meaningful. A formidable obstacle that daunted the study and assimilation of the Zohar as a text stemmed partly from its language, Aramaic, which differed substantially from the Aramaic of the Talmud, and partly from its symbolic semantic layers, which demanded its own interpretive apparatus. Thus, as soon as it was printed, the textual complexities inherent in the Zohar demanded the mediation of both lexical and conceptual aids. Writing in the last decades of the sixteenth century, Yissakhar Baer ben Naftali ha-Kohen from Szczebrzeszyn articulates in his *Mar'eh Kohen* (Prague, 1589) the need for more accessible presentation of the Zohar to readers unfamiliar with kabbalistic lore, for whom this text presented a formidable intellectual obstacle.

> There is no entrance into the words [of the Zohar], save for certain exceptional individuals, a small number of extraordinary intellects; and yet, there is so much more [to the Zohar], things delightful and precious more than pearls, sweeter than honey, for the old and the young alike: plain meanings, allusions, homiletic interpretations, explications, and terrible admonitions, to rebuke (*mor'im be-ezbah*) saying, 'this is the way, walk in it, so that when a person performs his actions, through them, he would live two kinds of lives . . . and just because things like these are available to all souls, [nonetheless] they are gathered, hidden, [and] held among the [deep] secrets of the emanation among the mysteries facets of Kabbalah. . . . [T]hus I, young in age, saw it fit to collect the scattered passages for anyone who wants to come and take, and organized them into chapters (*she'arim*), a thing properly articulated.[36]

In this passage, Yissakhar Baer from Szczebrzeszyn unequivocally implies that printing was an important but not a sufficient medium for the popularization of the Zohar and states that without further conceptual, organizational, and linguistic aids, the Zohar, in its raw and unrefined textual state would remain accessible but to a select few. Yet, a reformulation of the material using translation and a reorganization of content by topics systematically arranged in relation to quotidian religious conduct would prove beneficial to ordinary Jews of all ages by providing them with a kabbalistically inspired practical guide to the performative aspects of daily life. His pedagogical strategy therefore aimed to include brief *zoharic* excerpts that reflected various topics in Jewish ritual and religious life organized into seventeen main chapters.[37] The number of chapters is an allusion to the Hebrew word *tov* (good), which using *gematria*[38] equals seventeen. It is interesting to note that Yissakhar Baer in his introduction to *Pitḥei Yah*, discussed in chapter 3, also invokes the kabbalistic connotation of the word *tov*, which suggests that he might have had a copy of *Mar'eh Kohen* in his library that inspired his work.[39] Furthermore, the overall ethical orientation of *Mar'eh Kohen*, organized into topical chapters related to daily conduct, could arguably constitute a precursor to Yissakhar Baer's *Yesh Sakhar*—examined more extensively in chapter 4—representing a more erudite and expanded version of Yissakhar Baer ben Naftali ha-Kohen's work. Be that as it may, the proliferation of *zoharic* study guides in the late sixteenth and early seventeenth centuries, offered alternative hermeneutic methodologies by way of focused topical treatments, in the form of lexicons, subject indexes, anthological collections, and glossaries, that enhanced the comprehension and absorption of the Zohar's more literal layers.

Offering *Words of Understanding*:
Yissakhar Baer's Lexicon to the Zohar

In penning his last two compositions, *Imrei Binah* and *Meqor Ḥokhmah*, Yissakhar Baer took up the challenge of proffering two powerful pedagogic tools, which promoted and aided the conceptual and linguistic processing of the Zohar. I will treat these works in two separate chapters here although it should be noted that the author himself regarded them, from their inception, as complementary compositions.[40] While both books follow the order of *parashiyot*, *Imrei Binah* assembles the difficult and foreign words of the Zohar into a lexicon, while *Meqor Ḥokhmah* undertakes to elucidate select words of the Torah by condensing the Zohar's narrative related to the word in question into brief explanatory paragraphs. Both works were printed in Prague by Moshe ben Beẓalel Katz in brief succession, *Imrei Binah* on December 14, 1610, and *Meqor Ḥokhmah* on December 30, 1610. The same elaborate decorative frame is employed on the front page of both books displaying prominently the Kohen's hands with outstretched fingers denoting the priestly provenance of the printer.

Figure 5.1. Yissakhar Baer, *Imrei Binah*, Title Page (Prague, 1610), from the Scholem Collection, National Library of Israel.

In *Imrei Binah*, Yissakhar Baer offers two types of learning aids to the Zohar. The main part of the book, organized into double columns, constitutes a *zoharic* dictionary, which functions simultaneously as a concordance that helps to locate difficult expressions and foreign terms (*milim zarot*) in the place of their original source within the *zoharic* texts, as well as offer cross-references to other compositions that mention and comment on these, such as Cordovero's *Pardes Rimonim*, Yehudah Ḥayyat's *Minḥat Yehudah*, and also Meir ibn Gabbai's *Derekh Emunah*. The author's postscript on the colophon summarizes the sources he engaged for the writing of the book.

> Blessed is the Lord, the God of Israel, who has aided me to bring to light the mysteries of the words of the Zohar, its foreign terms and multiple expressions together with the original source of these sayings in the *Tikkunim* and other compositions, such as the *Pardes* [*Rimonim*], the *Ma'arekhet ha-Elohut* with its commentary, the *Minḥat Yehudah*.[41]

By comparison, it should be noted that the anonymous *Bi'ur* turned more to classical rabbinic sources, such as the Aramaic Targumim to Scripture and rabbinic literature, especially the Tamud Bavli, to uncover the philological and etymological roots of the difficult expressions in the Zohar. In addition, the author of the *Bi'ur* deployed works by the medieval grammarian and commentator, R. David Qimḥi and the book, *Mashal ha-Kadmoni*.[42]

The second type of reference tool the author provides is inserted just before the colophon and assembles the homiletical material (*ma'asiyot*) of the Zohar and organizes these stories into a list adopting the format of two running columns that follow the order of Biblical chapters.[43] For *Parashat Tazria*, for example, Yissakhar Baer includes the following three stories:

> The story of Rabbi Hiyya and Rabbi Abba who saw a star battling three other stars at midnight. The story of Rabbi Yose and Rabbi Hiyya, who met a man that was covered in sores and had with him two sons. The story of Rabbi Yose, who entered a house that had a demon in it, but he was saved.[44]

The inclusion of a separate section, titled *Ma'asiyot* (*Stories*), a collection of brief summaries of semi-independent narrative units within the framework of the Zohar's overall literary space, at the end of *Imrei Binah*, constitutes the last thematic and structural feature of the book.

Here the author is singularly driven by a desire to provide an easily searchable catalog to the Zohar's aggadic material. Following the Biblical *parashiyot*, he identifies each *zoharic* tale, adds a brief synopsis, and provides the corresponding page numbers in the Cremona edition of

Figure 5.2. Catalog of *zoharic* stories in *Imrei Binah* (Prague 1610), fol. 33a, from the Scholem Collection, National Library of Israel.

the Zohar. These stories are centered mainly on the Zohar fellowship—a group of Rabbis headed by the revered second-century Sage, Rabbi Shimon bar Yohai—whose peregrinations and adventures in an imaginal Land of Israel provides the narrative backdrop to *zoharic* homiletics.[45] The stories do not comprise separate units in the printed versions of the

Zohar but are woven deftly into the particular Biblical exegesis under consideration. Supernatural tropes play a prominent role in these literary units embellishing the rhetoric with elements that emphasize the fluidity between the real and the imagined, the natural and the supernatural, the earthly and the heavenly spheres of existence. At the same time, these hagiographic stories disclose attitudes toward religious leadership, ethics, social values, and ritual ideals, as espoused by the authors of the text. Registering points of social and theological fault lines and conflicting approaches to piety, the zoharic story became a pivotal instrument for the textual editors to sanction their own version of normative spiritual conduct while undermining alternative approaches. This point is made particularly trenchant by comparative analyses of homiletic units that were textualized exclusively in limited manuscript witnesses but were never included in the printed versions of the Zohar. The religious dispute between Rabbi Yose and Abba, recorded in only one *zoharic* manuscript (Vatican 206)—over whether silence or dialogue serves God better when walking with a fellow on the way—is resolved in the printed editions of the Zohar by censoring out Rabbi Abba's quietistic doctrine of advocating silence as the higher spiritual ideal.[46] The presentation of a separate section with an ostensibly distinct thematic focus, at the end of *Imrei Binah*, constituted a particularly effective reference tool for preachers, who could conveniently locate these stories in the Zohar and incorporate them seamlessly into their sermon. As agents and markers of authoritative and sanctioned spiritual postures, they represented important sources for the propagation of righteous conduct and ethical imperatives for preachers as they disseminated Kabbalah more broadly in the Jewish communities of Central and Eastern Europe.[47]

In compiling a list of *zoharic* stories, Yissakhar Baer followed the literary precedent set by Moses Galante, whose *Mafteaḥ ha-Zohar*, printed in Venice in 1566 was the first work to have a separate section devoted to narrating "the marvelous deeds that occurred to the holy men in the land [of Israel]."[48] The major difference between the index of Galante and the one comprised by Yissakhar Baer is that while the former provides a short summary of each story in the original Aramaic of the Zohar, the latter mediates these homiletical accounts in Hebrew translation. Changing the language from Aramaic to Hebrew signals a critical shift in the reception of the Zohar as canonical and sacred text and underlines the awareness of authors that new readers require improved tools for the absorption of the original material. For Moses Galante writing in close temporal proximity to the printing of the Zohar (1558–1560), it was enough to organize the content into practical sections that reflect the study and ritual life of an early modern Jew. He therefore deconstructs the Zohar thematically into four sections: the first, a locator index collates passages from the Torah with its corresponding place in the Zohar; the second presents a locator index of topics related to Jewish ritual and halakhic life, such as prayer, tefillin, festivals, and their treatment in the Zohar; the third enumerates the stories of the Zohar; and the fourth presents a short anonymous commentary on the Torah portion, Balak. Galante could assume that his readers would be able to decipher the Aramaic of the text and therefore did not avail himself of the additional step of translating the material into Hebrew. Almost half a century later, translation becomes an important technical tool in Yissakhar Baer's authorial hands to successfully mediate between text and intended readership, who lacked the linguistic confidence to read these stories in the Aramaic original.

Apart from the primary function of the composition to serve as a dictionary and reference guide, *Imrei Binah*, from the outset boasts a number of interesting and distinctive features, which I will now explore. While this piece was printed a few weeks before *Meqor Ḥokhmah*, it was actually written and designated by Yissakhar Baer as his last work. We learn about this in the author's introduction, half of which is devoted to acquainting the reader with the titles and brief content of his other compositions. In the absence of book catalogs and dust jackets, author's introductions constituted effective tools to advertise and entice the audience to read and purchase their other publications. Entrepreneurial considerations that time and again informed the intellectual commitments of secondary elites are clearly evident in Yissakhar Baer's publishing program. In writing *Imrei Binah*, he wished to present readers "who are far removed from the words of the Zohar, because they are shut and sealed," with a practical key to unlock those mysteries. However, the conservative stance he took against citing laws in *Yesh Sakhar* that contradicted normative practice, is expressed here in his own admission that none of his compositions touch on the more recondite texts of *zoharic* literature, which he identifies as the *Sifra di-Zniuta* (*Book of Concealment*), the *Idra Rabbah*, and the *Idra Zuta* (*Large and Small Assembly*).[49] His admission discloses an ostensible awareness of not merely the esoteric stratification of the Zohar but also of his own reticence as author to probe and expose the concealed hermeneutic strata of the text, which like "Noah's Ark," are closed to most but a few exceptional individuals.[50]

One of the most striking literary features of *Imrei Binah* is the insertion of a lengthy kabbalistic poem arranged in the acrostic of the author's name.[51] The poem serves as a literary point of departure for Yissakhar Baer to compose an elaborate kabbalistic commentary, which over a few pages sets down the foundational principles for understanding the main concepts of Kabbalah.[52] That even a relatively technical genre such as a dictionary to the Zohar begins with an outline of the correct beliefs concerning Jewish mysticism demonstrates that any discussion of Kabbalah is inextricably bound up with authority, control, and deflecting any inclination toward antinomian thought.[53] In this he focuses primarily on enumerating the ten *Sefirot* and elucidating their basic characteristics and internal dynamics. The principal source that informs the writing of this commentary is the author's first composition, *Pithei Yah*, which he further digests to provide the reader with a primer to the basics of Kabbalah. Pedagogically, the poem with its brief stanzas, rhymed prose, and acrostic structure, serves to enhance memorization while the longer commentary elucidates the meaning in a concise and lucid manner. The integrated presentation of poetry and narrative commentary demonstrates Yissakhar Baer's awareness of the communicative value and pedagogical potential inherent in diverse literary genres. Adjusting the form of presentation to the function he assigns to it lends his work innovative dimensions. *Imrei Binah* is addressed to readers of diverse backgrounds satisfying a variety of educational needs in the area of Kabbalah.

Another remarkable feature of *Imrei Binah* is the appearance of a poem in praise of Rabbi Shimeon bar Yohai (*Rashbi*), which originated in the land of Israel. The poem's stanzas consist of several lines and begin with the name of one of the ten *Sefirot*, which are emphasized in larger and bolded font type. The *Sefirot* are presented in ascending order, with *Malkuth* (Kingdom) appearing at the top and *Keter* (Crown) at the bottom of the page. Rashbi's name, "Bar Yohai," functions as a form of poetic refrain, opening and closing stanzas, and connecting one *Sefirah* conceptually to another. This song, written originally by R. Shimeon ibn Lavi in North Africa, became quickly diffused and enjoyed enormous popularity in the Land of Israel at the end of the sixteenth century.[54] However, in Ashkenazi lands it is Yissakhar Baer's *Imrei Binah* that records it for the first time; previously it was printed in *Heikhal Ha-Shem* by Yehiel Luria Ashkenazi.[55] It can be tentatively suggested that this song was mediated to Yissakhar Baer via his connection with Shlomiel Dresnitz or the cultural agency of Ashkenazi's book, which may have been available to him or the printers.

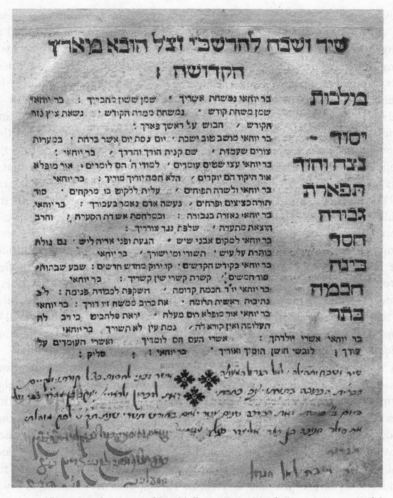

Figure 5.3. "Song and Praise of Rashbi" in *Imrei Binah* (Prague, 1610), fol. 4b, from the Scholem Collection, National Library of Israel.

The transmission and circulation of ideas in the early modern period followed well-established transregional networks that shuttled individuals, books, and traditions between Eastern Europe, Italy, and the land of Israel.

Kabbalistic poems were intended to mediate between the written text and the oral transmission of mystical secrets. Like the visual aspect of Kabbalah and the construction of Lurianic tree diagrams or *Ilanot*,

they are linked to the performative dimensions of religious life. Today
we are in the possession of several kabbalistic poems that functioned as
songs, including the welcoming of the Shabbat Bride *Lekha Dodi* widely
sung in synagogues all over the world at the onset of Shabbat. The poem
was composed by R. Solomon Alkabets, one of the Spanish exiles, who
eventually settled in Safed and became an important disseminator of
Kabbalah there in the sixteenth century.[56] The sixteenth-century rabbi and
scholar, Menaḥem de Lonzano, also penned a poem for Shabbat titled
Shivḥa de-Matrunita (The Praise of the Lady) in Aramaic adopting the
language of the Zohar. In a short preface to the poem he explains that it
was to be recited for the welcoming of the Shabbat and "thus Menaḥem
de Lonzano will sing this song to God reciting His name and with it I
shall build 32 houses corresponding to the thirty-two pathways, thirty-two
words of the King, the thirty-two letters, in addition to *yud* or ten corresponding to the words of the Queen, which are the ten *Sefirot*.[57] Besides
the first one, De Lonzano wrote another poem, intended for recitation
three times on Shabbat, evening, morning, and afternoon. This poem,
alluding to the symbolic significance of twenty-six, the numerical value
of the Tetragrammaton, was supposed to be chanted before the recital of
Eshet Ḥayyil (Prov. 31:10–31) in the liturgical sequence of the blessings
(*kiddush*) at the Shabbat table Friday evening.[58]

In the main section of *Imrei Binah*, Yissakhar Baer employs four
pedagogical strategies to ease the reader's understanding of the foreign
terms that appear frequently in the Zohar: (1) translation; (2) explication
based on rabbinic texts; (3) reference to other kabbalistic compositions;
and (4) relating word to *sefirotic*/kabbalistic symbolism. It must be stressed
that given Yissakhar Baer's fourfold pedagogic strategy, *Imrei Binah* does
not function as a conventional dictionary, which would provide the
reader with direct Aramaic to Hebrew correspondence. Rather as I will
demonstrate below, lexical difficulties emerging from the *zoharic* text,
provided an educational opportunity for the author to augment the simple
translation of words from Aramaic into Hebrew with deepr explication of
how these terms relate to specific kabbalistic symbols and processes. He
guides the reader at multiple levels interfacing traditional sources, such
as the Talmud, with prominent works of Kabbalah, such as Cordovero's
Pardes Rimonim, Yehudah Ḥayyat's *Minḥat Yehudah*, along with *Sefer
Yeẓirah* and the *Bahir*.

Translation of *zoharic* words and passages from Aramaic to Hebrew
constituted one of the earliest and most effective technical tools to facilitate

the exoterization and popularization of the Zohar. Yissakhar Baer's repeated use of this technique in *Imrei Binah* ensures a crisp, to the point, and easy-to-follow rendition of difficult Aramaic expressions. In explaining the word, *tanra takifa* (טנרא תקיפא), for instance, which appears in the Biblical chapter, *Terumah*, in the Zohar, the Hebrew equivalent is promptly provided for the reader without any additional explanation, "a solid rock" and the corresponding page number in the *zoharic* base text is supplied in brackets.[59]

The second strategy is devoted to explaining words by reference to their source in rabbinic literature. To clarify the word *me-susita de-ḥoshekh* (מסוסיתא דחשך), Tractate *Sota* in the Talmud Bavli is cited and the meaning of the Aramaic is given in Hebrew to denote the "hewing of the dark."[60] Reference to additional compositions, the third strategy pursued by Yissakhar Baer, expands the kabbalistic library and broadens the sources that can be studied and consulted by the reader. In employing this particular tool, he not only mentions the title of these works but, at the same time, meticulously outlines the exact location of the word under consideration. For instance, to elucidate the term, *itparshin dargin*, he says, "see its explanation in *Minḥat Yehudah*, fol. 9, and [also] in *Derekh Emunah*, fol. 15, where you will find a slightly different description; nonetheless they all allude to the same thing."[61] Clearly, Yissakhar Baer is mindful of the diversity of approaches available to explicate kabbalistic terminology and he considers it important to alert his readers to these theoretical alternatives.

The fourth method affords the highest degree of authorial creativity and freedom, where the writer can define and nuance the depth of kabbalistic explanation he is ready to deploy. Using the *Bi'ur Milim ha-Zarot* as a point of departure, Yissakhar Baer interprets the enigmatic word, *tiqla* טיקלא, that appears in *Parashat Beshalaḥ* in the Zohar, as "a potter's wheel, which he rotates with his feet."[62] The image of a wheel, which a potter rotates in order to fashion clay vessels, serves to delineate the literal, or *pshat*, layer of exegesis that Yissakhar Baer promptly complements with the more kabbalistic rendition of the word; "it is also an allusion, *remez*, to the whirling or spinning of the soul at the time of one's death in this world as the heavenly voice, the *bat kol*, proclaims to this wheel, 'this soul has just flown out.' "[63] The contextualization of the *zoharic* expression within an alternative mythical-symbolic nomenclature opens up multiple hermeneutic pathways for interpreting the linguistic strata of the Zohar. Conceived in this way, words as linguistic units dispersed within the narrative conceal concentric circles of multivalent associations each one amplifying and deepening the ostensible meaning.

Thus, as Yehudah Liebes and Ruth Kara-Ivanov Kaniel have demonstrated, a survey of the use of the word *tiqla* in the Zohar yields a hierarchy of parallel meanings, ascending from the mundane signifier of a potter's wheel, that moves about to define the size, shape, and measurement of earthenware to corollary epistemes of a balance, weighted scales, a plomb or surveyor's rod, and a water clock, the latter functions in the narrative as a particularly useful invention for the villagers of Kfar Tarsha, who wished to wake up and study Torah by night (*Parshat Lekh Lekha*).[64] At the same time, when projected unto the realm of divine structures and processes, the word *tiqla* assumes a number of semantic inflections in its various permutations in the mythical-symbolic nomenclature of the Zohar. In several places *tiqla* is identified with the activities of the *Sefirah* of *Malkuth*, the house of lower judgment that can, like a wheel, rotate toward the left or the right, toward judgment or mercy, depending on the deeds of the lower beings.[65] This interpretation is further supported by two other kabbalists, the thirteenth-century mystic, Rabbi Joseph ben Avraham Gikatilla who in *Sha'arei Orah* relates *Malkuth* to the lower court of justice, while the sixteenth-century Safedian kabbalist, Rabbi Moses Cordovero, in his multivolume commentary on the Zohar, *Or Yakar*, explicitly identifies the word *tiqla* with the *Sefirah* of *Malkuth*.[66]

Other scholars have pointed to the close association between *tiqla* and the zoharic expression, *mathkala* (sharing the same verb root but changing the letter *tet* to a *tav* מתקלא).[67] In explicating the term, "*ma'arei mathkala*," Yissakhar Baer notes that these are the masters of weights, who incline neither to the left nor to the right but focus on the middle line, identified with compassion (*rahamim*).[68] In more mythical layers of the Zohar the *mathkala* denotes the *Sefirah* of *Yesod*, which is arrayed in a middle position in the Sefirotic diagram responsible for conveying the divine flow from the higher *Sefirot* to *Malkuth*.[69] Furthermore, in his commentary on *Sefer Yeẓirah*, the medieval Kabbalist, Rabbi Yizhak Sagi Nahor, explains that metaphorically the divine scales or *mathkala* play an instrumental role in the creation of new worlds, and in this sense, is related to the Zohar's treatment of the death of the Edomite Kings, who symbolize worlds that aborted due to a lack of proper measure, balance, and complementarity in the world of the *Sefirot*. In its association with *Yesod*, the *mathkala* then encompasses the dialectical motion of upward and downward movement of divine energy and the cosmic measurement of balance.[70]

In compiling a *zoharic* lexicon, Yissakhar Baer's exegetical approach resonates with the inner hermeneutic stance of the Zohar, moving between multivalent semantic associations of zoharic terms that are critical in the mythological and symbolic construction of the narrative as the analysis above has demonstrated. As a pedagogue, however, he resists the temptation to delve deeper into the theosophical complexities of *zoharic* terms and merely hints at variant readings and additional kabbalistic associations, inviting his readers to continue their learning and engagement with the text. In this sense, *Imrei Binah*, goes beyond the framework of a straightforward dictionary in order to guide the reader through the multifaceted images and rich symbols of the original composition. It is instructive to note that by comparison, a rival lexicon, *Yesha Yah*, published in Venice in 1637, constitutes a much more compressed work that leaves out reference to other compositions—rabbinic or kabbalistic—as well commenting on the mythical and symbolic aspects of words found in the Zohar.[71]

To be sure, *Imrei Binah* adopts a very different organizational structure than *Yesha Yah*, thus signaling a departure from the formal layout of the *Bi'ur*.[72] Accordingly, while the former orders the foreign and difficult words into the sequence of Biblical chapters (*parashiyot*) reflecting the original literary structure of the Zohar, *Yesha Yah* faithfully reproduces the *Bi'ur*'s alphabetical organizational template. The tension between the alphabetical and the thematic approaches of ordering *zoharic* words finds expression in the ways in which manuscript witnesses treat *Imrei Binah*. In at least two manuscripts (RSL 676 and Montefiore 479), the alphabetical chapter-by-chapter indexes are presented together implying that perhaps these approaches are more complementary than contradictory and that the preferred mode of consultation of one dictionary, or the other, is conditioned by the intellectual endeavor the reader is engaged in. Furthermore, textual fluidity that is endemic to textual practices associated with manuscript culture, is poignantly illustrated in one manuscript (RSL 302), where the copyist writing in Modena takes the liberty to compress and reorganize *Imrei Binah* into an alphabetized index (fols. 60a–72b).

The fact that *Imrei Binah* was reproduced in several printed editions of the Zohar may also confirm that those printers that included it in their books, regarded it as a more valuable learning tool to accompany the reading of the Zohar than some of its competitors.[73] It should be underlined that in fact *Imrei Binah* is the only printed lexicon to the Zohar arranged not alphabetically but in the order of Biblical chapters. One might posit that a word index that follows the order of Biblical chapters was more expedient to the traditional manner in which the Zohar was studied, where the elucidation of difficult or foreign words unfolded in a more organic fashion embedded in the context of the original narrative exposition. The alphabetical exposition style, by contrast, is more valuable in a scholastic context as a tool for quick and easy referencing. In this sense, *Imre Binah* was addressed primarily to beginners embarking on the reading and study of the Zohar, which is supported by the fact that it was the dictionary of choice for the Sulzbach editors of the Zohar (1684), printed as a running reference on each page.[74] The Sulzbach Zohar was the cultural product of collaborative efforts between Jewish and Christian Kabbalists and printers and responded to the needs of an emerging Christian readership drawn from various denominations centered at the court of Prince Christian August in the late seventeenth century.[75]

Conclusion

This chapter has shown that Kabbalah, language, and meaning have an imbricated relationship in the intellectual history of early modernity. In early modern Prague, Yissakhar Baer rose to the intellectual challenge of composing a *zoharic* dictionary, *Imrei Binah*, that would reformulate and expand the sources he inherited from earlier authors. His ambition was to offer readers a pragmatic reference tool that functioned on multiple levels: as a direct translation from Aramaic into Hebrew; as a commentary that embellished the plane meaning of a *zoharic* term with additional kabbalistic interpretation; and as a place locator to improve usability by enabling the reader to locate the word in the original source. His organizational principles were informed by didactic considerations to complement the daily reading of Torah chapters (*parashiyot*) with the explicatory tool of a lexicon aimed at translating and illuminating difficult words in the chapter under consideration. *Imrei Binah* continues in the tradition of earlier lexicographic attempts, such as the anonymous *Bi'ur*, while at the same time charts a new trajectory. It aims to remythologize the Jewish textual and literary heritage—the Torah, Tanakh, and their rabbinic commentaries—using the symbolic language of Kabbalah that his lexicon renders more accessible. At the same time, Yissakhar Baer's lexical study guide to the Zohar points beyond knowledge organization to bring into sharp relief the relationship between language and identity. Gershom Scholem and later Yehudah Liebes have emphatically underlined the potential of the language of Kabbalah to generate new opportunities for meaning construction in our postmodern society as a multifaceted and rich source for the revival of the Hebrew language in the Land of Israel.[76] As Liebes highlights, many words adopted into Modern Hebrew have derived from kabbalistic works, yet Even Shoshan's comprehensive dictionary to modern Hebrew, which provides the reader with the etymological roots of each word, has failed to account for the philological sources of phrases that stem from the Zohar. A number of entries, such as *rahimu*, *'itkasia*, and *'itgalia*, are merely identified as Aramaic in Even Shoshan without a clear mention of the Zohar as their source.[77] This ostensible marginalization of Kabbalah in its semantic and lexicographic dimensions invited the writer S. Y. Agnon to wryly remark: "The scholarship in which Scholem is engaged invigorates his language. I can already visualize the ridicule with which future students of language will scoff at our dictionaries, which claim to contain all the words of the Hebrew language but which fail to recognize the language of the Kabbalah."[78] The cultural and intellectual significance of *zoharic* dictionaries developed in the medieval and the early modern periods continue to play an important role in connecting the present with the past and reinvigorating not only the Hebrew language, but also Jewish identity in an era of Jewish history that opens up hitherto unexplored avenues for the scholarly and popular appreciation of Kabbalah.

Chapter 6

The Plain Meaning of the Zohar

An Anthological Approach

What does it matter who is speaking?

—Samuel Beckett

The postmodern notion of assigning cultural merit to compilatory literary genres, which seek to assemble discrete selections from earlier literary sources, has recently received renewed scholarly appreciation.[1] Refining earlier scholarly conceptions that marginalized anthological and compilatory genres based on an ostensible lack of originality in authorship, the postmodern position rehabilitates the compiler and sees the process of textual selecting as carrying significant hermeneutic and cultural value.[2] Far from being marginal, anthological compositions have constituted a long-standing genre within the Jewish textual corpus from the ancient, through the medieval, to the modern period. It was a preferred form for transmitting Scriptural interpretations, poetry, stories, and more recently, for remembering and cultural retrieval as expressed in early Zionist and Yiddish sources.[3] While a major impetus for the anthological task was preservation, compilatory works differ significantly from one another depending on the ideological orientation and didactic focus of the compiler. The mode of reframing an original text, the depth, structure, and sequence of presentation all disclose the larger conceptual and ideological programs that informed the work of the editor.[4] Thus, no two anthologies of an original work are the same, each applies methods it deems most suitable to address a particular reading audience.

An attractive feature of anthologies is the elasticity of the genre that encourages multifarious reading of an original work or works while resisting monolithic representation. As such, rabbinic collections such as the Mishnah can function on multiple levels: as a notebook, a legal code, textbook, or even as a philosophical text.[5] Not only does an anthology accommodate easily the hybridity of literary genres, it also allows an author to insert himself into the flow and transmission of earlier Jewish traditions and thus align his work with authoritative traditions of the past.[6] An important fifteenth-century anthological compilation of the Talmud, the *En Yaaqov*, was written by Rabbi ibn Ḥabib in order to emphasize the *aggadic* portions of the Talmud, leaving out the legal discussions in an effort to present the Talmud as a "theological document" that could be a source of spiritual sustenance to Jewish communities following the vicissitudes of the expulsion.[7] Released from the burden of creative brilliance and original thought, the compiler's voice became intertwined with and incorporated into the voices he was transmitting. This was certainly true in the case of mystical anthologies, where the personal imprint of the receiver of divine revelation was secondary to the authority of the tradition he was meant to transmit. In fact the pseudepigraphic compilations of the Middle Ages can be regarded as arising from the compilatory or anthological impulse since the main purpose of authorial activity is not the authoring of new ideas but the transmission of existing teachings.[8] Thus, the literary form of pseudepigraphy, that the medieval kabbalistic classics such as the Zohar and the *Bahir* adopt, serves to reconnect traditions and teachings with a time, figure, and place that had been associated with and represented an authentic source of divine revelation.[9] Therefore, the literary genre adopted for certain medieval mystical collections reflects not necessarily an attempt to plagiarize the works of others, but a consciously cultivated theological stance that privileges reception over originality, mediation over creative production.

Kabbalistic anthologies begin to appear already in the Middle Ages and assemble earlier authoritative teachings, which they repackage in more accessible formats, often abridging the original composition or reformulating it with clearer explanation and commentary. These works constituted important yet largely underappreciated literary genres for the exposition of kabbalistic ideas since the Middle Ages and as texts disclose important information regarding the compiler's purpose and cultural-theological reference reflected in the selection of material included in a particular work.[10] In contrast to compositions lauded for their original insights, innovative symbolic or mythic elements, kabbalistic anthologies preferred tradition to innovation[11] and seemed content with transmitting earlier material albeit in newly recombined narrative frames. The individual voice of these compilers is firmly embedded in and muted by the authority of tradition from which they speak, while the methods that inform their re-presentation of older mystical writings reveal important information regarding their unique scholarly interests and intellectual stance.

Two basic approaches can be distinguished with regard to an author's anthological objective: the expansive-syncretistic and the reductionist-simplifying. The first allows a compiler to take excerpted sections as the base text and assemble around it additional primary sources or explanatory material in an effort to synthesize diverse schools of thought and variant homiletic material that readers may have encountered in other mystical or rabbinic works. Menaḥem Recanati's *Commentary on the Torah* is a fine example of this tendency, as he engages copious kabbalistic and midrashic sources, each of which presents an alternate mystical or mythic reading of the original text, to create a multifaceted and an elaborately textured exegetical composition. This model was also pursued by elite kabbalists of Safed, who tended to embellish and enlarge the *zoharic* corpus by providing comprehensive, expansive and multilayered kabbalistic commentaries to it. Moses Cordovero's *Or Yaqar* constitutes the most prominent example of this tendency, the sheer length of which and the associated financial commitment delayed its publication until the twentieth century.[12] It took thirty-three years between 1962 and 1995, and twenty-six volumes to finally print a complete version of Cordovero's exegetical masterpiece on the Zohar.

The second strategy, *reductive* in focus, was adopted not exclusively but frequently by secondary elites, who saw the Zohar as an already difficult and complex text not only from the linguistic but also from the theosophical point of view, and therefore sought strategies to simplify, digest, and reorganize its content. Yissakhar Baer's *Meqor Ḥokhmah* fits into this model. His aim is to zoom in and extract a zoharic unit that offers a concise, uncomplicated, often ethically motivated reading of Scripture. Thus, the methods that informed each author's independent style of re-presenting the Zohar were reflective of the readership they wished to target yet still working within the general intellectual framework of legitimating and promoting the study of Kabbalah.[13]

Concurrently with promoting the study of Kabbalah, anthologizers also engaged in one of the main functions of this genre that is to legitimate and canonize certain traditions, while at the same time marginalize and exclude others.[14] In penning their kabbalistic commentaries on the Torah, both Menaḥem Recanati in the thirteenth and Menaḥem Ziyyon in the fourteenth centuries adopt the anthological format for the purpose of authorizing, in other words, for defining which sources constituted legitimate textual representatives of Jewish mystical knowledge.[15] Recanati and Ziyyon were among the first anthologizers to incorporate large portions of *zoharic* fragments, which are presented together with other kabbalistic compositions contributing both to its circulation and ascribed sanctity. While Ziyyon cites Recanati's Zohar segments frequently without an explicit acknowledgment, he deploys images associated with the building of the Solomonic Temple to authorize twelve earlier mystical tractates that constitute the textual sources of his anthology, which are enumerated by him in descending order of prominence beginning with Nachmanides, the "stream" (*afik*), followed by Shem Tov Ibn Gaon's *Keter Shem Tov*, "the structural beam of the ceiling of the gallery," and the triad of "hewn stones"—the *Bahir*, the Zohar, and the *Sefer Yeẓirah*.[16] While the textual repository that Recanati draws on differs slightly from Ziyyon's, as we shall soon see, these last three pseudepigraphic and anonymous compositions appear as common sources in both compilations that play a central role as authoritative mediators in the textual repertoire of medieval and early modern authors of Kabbalah.

Carefully navigating the theological tension between the divine word and its human inscription, kabbalistic anthologies retained a sense of fluidity through collecting and assembling diverse textual sources into one unified volume that promoted authority while it obfuscated human creativity. Presenting Onkelos's interpretation of Deuteronomy 5:19, Meir ibn Gabbai describes the voice of God as an ever-flowing fountain that flows from the beginning, without interruption, to the end of time. Therefore any expression of human wisdom is conceived by ibn Gabbai as a mere resounding of the original voice and cannot be singled out and exulted for its originality.

'A great voice that did not cease speaking.' That great voice sounds forth without interruption; it calls with the eternal duration that is its nature; whatever the prophets and scholars of all generations have taught, proclaimed, and produced, they have received precisely out of that voice which never ceases, in which all regulations, determinations and decisions are implicitly contained as well as everything new that may ever be said in any future . . . Everyone received that which is his from Sinai, from that continuous voice, and certainly not according to his human understanding and reckoning.[17]

As a literary genre, anthologies that affirm continuity with the voices of the past and efface the value of innovation keenly epitomize the theological outlook of kabbalists, who in contrast to philosophers, ascribed these teachings not to the brilliant efforts of the human intellect but to the conferral of the divine effluence of prophecy on select individuals going back to Moses and the revelation at Sinai.[18] Mystical anthologies, consequently, refrain from inserting a strong authorial voice into the narrative continuity of a sacred text and assert individuality only surreptitiously within the framework of received kabbalistic traditions. In contrast to our modern insistence on clearly delineating authorship and vigorously protecting its rights, kabbalistic anthologies compel us to modify how we define the relationship between textual traditions and authorship within the field of Kabbalah, where transmission, whether through the medium of orality or writing, aims to destabilize the fixed nature of the spoken and the written word and reintroduce the receiver into the fluidity of the lived spiritual experience.[19]

Another emerging literary practice for anthologizing the Zohar in the early modern period was the composition of indexes that involved some topical reorganization of the Zohar's often rambling, associative, and disjunctive narrative. *Zoharic* indexes varied in their thematic sorting and editorial decision to include only a list of verse locators or commentary as well; nevertheless authors strove to ease retrieval and offer a device of ordering and making the Zohar searchable. While a number of important indexes were printed in the sixteenth century, such as Galante's *Mafteah ha-Zohar* (Venice, 1566), this genre became particularly widespread in the first half of the seventeenth century. Indexes therefore provide important information to cultural historians regarding the material practices and pedagogic expectations that informed the work of compilers in transmitting the Zohar. I will discuss the cultural significance of indexes in greater detail below, however, suffice to emphasize here that Yissakhar Baer's *Meqor Ḥokhmah* was influenced by Galante's conceptual layout and incorporated principles of indexing into his anthology.

One of the earliest attempts to produce an anthology to the Zohar is undoubtedly Menaḥem Recanati's *Commentary on the Torah*, written not long after the appearance of the Zohar, toward the end of the thirteenth century. Recanati's important initiative to excerpt the Zohar and present parts of the original with a substantial commentary served two mediating functions: first, to provide a translation of the Zohar from Aramaic to Hebrew and, second, to elucidate its unique symbolism by supplementing it with additional mystical texts, teachings, and doctrinal expositions devoted especially to the ten *Sefirot*. The *Commentary* was the first kabbalistic work to appear in print in 1523 at one of the most prestigious ateliers, the Daniel Bomberg press in Venice. An interesting feature of the book is the inclusion of other primary kabbalistic and midrashic sources such as the *Bahir, Bereshit Rabbah, Midrash Ruth, Midrash to Lamentations, Midrash Telim, Sefer Maʾayan ha-Hokhmah*, and *Sefer ha-Heikhalot*.[20] Thus, *zoharic* passages are explained by intertextual references and affinity to other midrashic and kabbalistic compilations. The point of departure for Recanati's exegetical strategy is to zero in on a specific word chosen from the Torah section under discussion, which functions as a kind of topical header or point of departure for elucidating its mystical and symbolic valences. He does this by reference to the corresponding narrative sections in the Zohar as well as by citing pre-*zoharic* kabbalistic authors, such as Ezra and Azriel of Gerona, and Nachmanides, communicated through Shem Tov Ibn Gaon's *Keter Shem Tov*.[21] Thus, as a hermeneut Recanati presents a variety of sources and ideas in order to disclose the secrets of the Torah. That his hermeneutic approach was met with popularity is confirmed by a large number of extant manuscripts as well as by its early appearance in print as the first published book on Kabbalah.[22]

Recanati's *Commentary on the Torah* became an influential source for interpreting the Zohar among several early modern writers of Kabbalah working in the Italian cultural milieu, including R. Reuven Zarfati, R. Moshe ben Yoav, and R. Yehudah Ḥayyat,[23] in addition to authors active in Ashkenaz such as the Polish rabbi, Mordekhai Yaffe, who penned a commentary to it titled, *Levush Even ha-Yekarah*. It may have been the mediating agency of the *Levush* published in 1595 that provided the literary impetus for Yissakhar Baer to present his last book, *Meqor Ḥohmah*, based on the organizational style of Recanati's *Commentary*, without an explicit acknowledgment. Accordingly, the typographical display of Recanati's exegesis highlights a word, selected from the Torah passage under consideration, which is presented in square Hebrew typeface, bolded, and using a larger font. This highlighted expression in turn serves as the hermeneutic pivot around which Recanti arranges the various textual sources he deploys, the titles of which receive the same visual emphasis as the highlighted word, and finally weaves them together with his own interpretation of these kabbalistic fragments producing a work that presents a rich and complex exegetical tapestry for the reader. *Meqor Hokhmah* adopts the model of Recanati's *Commentary* in both its page layout as well as in its general organization of content. As such, words under consideration from the Torah are set in larger and bolded Hebrew, however unlike Recanati's work, which interfaces square and cursive Hebrew fonts using the former only to present passages from the Torah, Yissakhar Baer's entire text is printed in square font arguably to facilitate faster absorption on the part of the reader, who did not have to switch back and forth between the styles. Another notable difference in *Meqor Hokhmah* is the lack of systematic presentation of additional kabbalistic sources beyond the base text of the Zohar, which is never presented in its original Aramaic as Recanati arranges it, but is rather excerpted in Hebrew translation only keeping in line with Yissakhar Baer's pedagogic intention to simplify and clarify the Zohar.

It is of significance that Recanati represented a kabbalist who acquired mystical teachings, mainly from books indirectly and not directly from an authoritative master. His predilection for a mosaic presentation of diverse kabbalistic schools and sources, therefore, serves to underline the authority of these textual witnesses while at the same time creating a sophisticated and variegated hermeneutic presentation of the mystical meaning of the Torah. Each textual source adds a new kabbalistic exposition to the Biblical word under consideration, inviting the interpreter to step in and fuse the various mystical systems into a unified theological framework.[24] Not closely aligned with a particular kabbalistic center, Recanati prefigures the rise of a new cadre of writers in the age of print, such as Yissakhar Baer, who pursued a more flexible attitude toward diffusing kabbalistic knowledge to a broader readership. The twofold deployment of the anthological genre underlines its diverse function apposite to the hermeneut's intellectual objective: in the case of Recanati, it served as a tool in the exegete's repertoire to forge a unified theological message while Yissakhar Baer adopted it as a convenient instrument for mediating the original in a simplified, translated, abridged, and generally more accessible literary presentation.

In the case of both Recanati and Yissakhar Baer, standing outside the institutional framework of a particular kabbalistic school accorded them as

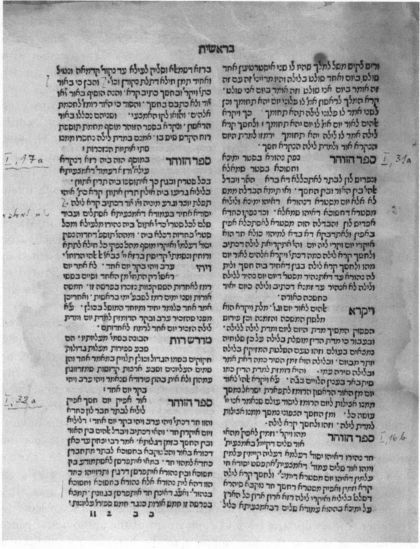

Figure 6.1. Recanati, *Commentary* (Venice, 1523), from the Scholem Collection, National Library of Israel.

hermeneuts and editors greater opportunity for innovation and independence in the exposition of earlier kabbalistic systems. A major difference between their distinct anthological approaches is that Recanati works at a scholastic and highly erudite level, citing sources in their original without

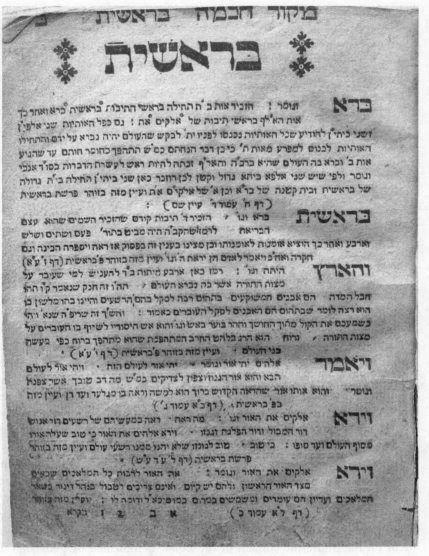

Figure 6.2. Page Layout in *Meqor Ḥokhmah* (Prague, 1610), fol. 2a, from the Scholem Collection, National Library of Israel.

a parallel translation and explaining only the *sefirotic* and kabbalistic but not the linguistic implications of these texts, Yissakhar Baer's hermeneutic focus in *Meqor Ḥokhmah* is directed less toward resolving theological ideas and difficulties and more toward exposing and explaining the *peshat* or literal layer of the Zohar. As an anthologizer, Recanati's approach is expansive-syncretistic, as he aims to expose with great intellectual subtlety and scholastic erudition the hidden facets of Torah and to capture its manifold mystical valence using earlier kabbalistic sources, which in this process of editing become legitimized and synthesized into a new product that bears his unique interpretative stamp and theological authority.[25]

By contrast, Yissakhar Baer introduces his work by drawing the reader's attention to the main binary textual divisions in the Zohar: the literal, which is likened by Yissakhar Baer to a ladder, which leads a person to the worlds above, Beit El; while the second, the mystical aspect of the text, is "'the knowledge of the upper beings and those above them by way of concealed mystery . . . beyond the human intellect."[26] In this hermeneutic bifurcation of the *zoharic* layers, the literal (*peshat*) mode of exposition is seen as a vehicle that provides the reader with the necessary instrument with which to begin the ascent toward the more sublime summits of the divine world. The author's formulation expresses an inherent didactic warning against readers who think they can jump immediately into the more recondite layers of the Zohar. That esoteric knowledge is to a certain degree bestowed and cannot be attained by the mere application of the human intellect is underlined by Yissakhar Baer in his explanation that the second path of penetrating the hidden registers of the *zoharic* text is not accessible for every individual and generation. He laments the ostensible inability of his generation to gain access to the Zohar's deeper registers, which necessitates his task of composing *Meqor Ḥokhmah* in the hope that the elucidation of the plain meaning of the Zohar using concise and lucid language will prime readers and refine them for receiving the more concealed textual strata.[27]

A brief comparison of parallel sections in Recanati and Yaffe, on the one hand, with *Meqor Ḥokhmah*, on the other, accentuates Yissakhar Baer's exegetical stance to move the interpretation of the Zohar away from the dense *sefirotic* imagery and closer to the genre of midrash, more familiar to his intended readership. The author's consideration to focus on the midrashic content of the Zohar is informed by pedagogical considerations to offer a more gradual introduction to the Zohar's layered literary and symbolic universe, the basic elements of which are rooted in classical midrash.[28] In contrast to Recanati and Yaffe, who from the outset establish and highlight the *sefirotic* correlation between a particular word of the Torah and the *sefirotic* analogue signified by that word, Yissakhar Baer refrains completely from engaging the language and symbolism of the divine emanations. The difference in literary strategies adopted for the elucidation of the Zohar signifies diverse readership addressed by Recanati and Yaffe, both of whom decidedly address an audience already familiar with the *sefirotic* nomenclature, in contrast to the intended audience of Yissakhar Baer, who were not.

In explaining the first word of the Torah, "at the beginning [*bereshit*]," Recanati promptly establishes a correspondence between the signifying word and the signified *Sefirah*, *Ḥokhmah*, the second divine emanation counting from the top.

> 'In the beginning, He created the heavens and the earth' [Genesis 1:1]. According to the opinion of the sages and also from what we can glean from their allusions in *Sefer ha-Zohar* the word *reshit* alludes to supernal wisdom (*ḥokhmah elyonah*), which is also called 'the wisdom of God (*Elohim*)' and in the Zohar it is referred to as 'a hidden point above.' This is the second *Sefirah* which is emanated from the first one and is called beginning (*reshit*) for reasons that we will explain by the decree of God as the sages have already explained in *Sefer ha-Bahir*, 'there is no other beginning except *Ḥokhmah*.'[29]

It becomes evident from the above excerpt that Recanati's main goal in explicating the Zohar was to expose the symbolic layers and establish a proper alignment between words of Torah and their corresponding *sefirotic* signifiers. This approach assumes some familiarity on the reader's part with the concept and language of the *Sefirot* and uses the Zohar as a base text for presenting a comprehensive theology of the *Sefirot* using a variety of textual sources, such as *Sefer ha-Bahir*, to support and nuance his argument.

In contrast, when commenting on the word *bereshit*, Yissakhar Baer opts to draw on the midrashic text of the *Alfa Beita de-Rabbi Aqiva*, which appears in *Haqdamat Sefer ha-Zohar* in the Mantua edition[30] and in the first chapter of the Cremona version, to present a brief synopsis of the significance of the Hebrew alphabet. The authors of the Zohar quote and rework this midrash extensively, inserting a mystical layer into the narrative. According to the midrash, God resolves the competition between the two initial letters of the Hebrew alphabet, the *aleph* and *bet*, each vying for primacy among the other letters by appointing a unique status to each of them: the *aleph* becomes the first letter of the alphabet and the Ten

Commandments, while the *beit* is appointed to be the first letter of the Torah, through which the entire world is created, and the first letter of the word blessing (*berakhah*).[31] In reshaping this midrash, the Zohar invokes the concept of unification as a defining function of the letter *aleph*, which is designated to unite the various powers of God, including the *Sefirot*: "Only through you do I become one."[32] Furthermore, the simultaneous emanation of two parallel alphabets—one consisting of high and large, and another made up of low and small letters, orthographically encoded in the initial letters of the first four words of the Torah ("*bereshit bara elohim et*")—also receives a mystical interpretation in the Zohar. Accordingly, using *sefirotic* symbolism, the large letters derive from *Binah*, designating the higher world, while the small letters emanate from *Shekhinah*, denoting the lower, material world.[33] In presenting the literal reading of the Zohar, Yissakhar Baer relates the mystical idea of the two alphabets, but stops short of assigning any *sefirotic* signifier to it. By extracting this portion from the various interpretations the Zohar offers on the word *bereshit*, he keeps the exegetical focus away from the abstruse theological categories of the *sefirot* and more directed toward establishing the theological principle of creation by speech and the primordial existence of the Torah.[34]

Ethical objectives often informed the selection criteria of anthologizers, as is evident in the following example from *Meqor Ḥokhmah* commenting on the initial verses of Genesis: "and the earth was unformed (*tohu*) and void (*va-vohu*) and darkness (*ḥoshekh*) was upon the face of the great deep, and the spirit (*ruaḥ*) of God hovered upon the face of the waters" (1:2). In this excerpt Yissakhar Baer selects a passage from among the various homiletic interpretations the Zohar offers on this verse, one that transposes these words hyperliterally unto the level of human conduct where abstract Biblical words, *tohu*, *bohu*, *ḥoshekh*, and *ruaḥ*, come to designate concrete forms of divine punishment for those who transgress the commandments.

> This alludes to four types of death, to punish the person who transgresses the commandments of the Torah, by which the world was created. '*Tohu*,' refers to strangulation, as it is said, 'the line of *tohu* is a measured rope' and [designates also] the stones that are sunk within the great deep, [used] for stoning the wicked; *bohu*, from the expression 'he is in it (*bo hu*)' implying that the stones are in the great deep for stoning, as has been explained. *Ḥoshekh* this is fire, as it is said, 'and as

you heard the voice from amidst the darkness (*hoshekh*), and the mountain was burning with fire.'[35] This is elemental fire, to burn those who transgress the commandments of the Torah. And *ruah*, this is beheading by a rotating sword, which moves about in the wind as the deeds of the world [revolve]. And see more on this in [the Zohar] *Parashat Bereshit*. (fol. 10a)[36]

The selection of this particular *zoharic* reading exposes the anthologizer as pedagogue, who shows concern for concrete moral conduct and uses Kabbalah as an instrument to bolster this message rather than engage in transmitting complicated theories of divine processes and conjunctions, the primary reoccupation of Recanati's compilatory enterprise.

At the same time, by comparing *Meqor Ḥokhmah* to *Me'ulefet*, an anthology very similar in scope, size, and intended audience, we can get a better idea of how pedagogical and theological considerations informed another author's selection of excerpted passages and how they chose to organize the content and layout of their books in an effort to popularize Kabbalah. *Me'ulefet* was written by Shlomo Algazi and was printed by Avraham Gabbai in Constantinople in 1660. The printer explains that he found "this delight, a precious pearl hidden away, a book filled with delightful words small in size but great in quality hidden in the house of the anthologizer. The distinguished Sage abandoned it for lack of means necessary to bring it to print . . . together with his other excellent compositions . . . but I realized its great benefit for all of Israel—especially for the zealous ones who return to God with all their hearts . . . and decided to print it."[37] The majority of the book is printed in cursive script while new sections are denoted by recurring headers "it is written" (*katav*) or "and it is written" (*ve-katav*), printed in square script and slight distance from the rest of the text. The format of the volume is pocket size, facilitating easy handling for a person carrying it from home to a place of study and back. *Zoharic* excerpts are referenced according to Biblical books (Genesis, Exodus, etc.) and their page locators are provided without either the author or the printer specifying the edition of the Zohar being used. In contrast to *Meqor Ḥokhmah*, where the anthologizer organizes the *zoharic* citations following their original order as a running commentary on the books and chapters of the Torah, in *Me'ulefet Sapirim* the anthological activity is topically organized based on three major headers: Torah, a theoretical introduction to the world of Judaism; service of God (*avodah*), consisting of topics related to religious observance and ritual; and acts of loving kindness (*gmilut ḥasadim*). This tripartite division is informed by a similar conceptualization of the foundational pillars of Judaism delineated in the ancient rabbinic tractate, *Pirkei Avot*.[38] Moreover, all religious subjects are apportioned into a thirty-day cycle and are divided into thirty units, enabling daily study.[39]

This anthological arrangement was particularly valuable to preachers and other readers who lacked access to the *zoharic* volumes or had limited time to spend on reading, deciphering, and grasping the original. A preacher who wished to devote a sermon to ethical dilemmas concerning sin and how to understand and overcome the evil inclination, could pick up *Me'ulefet Sapirim*, find the appropriate header for the topic, "Issues of the Evil Inclination and the Angel of Death,"[40] and read the Zohar's mythic rendering on this issue in Algazi's Hebrew paraphrase of excerpted passages from the original. *Meqor Ḥokhmah* as a running commentary on the Torah was less useful for topical consultation but enhanced more regular study of the Torah study following the weekly portion. Whether used as a topical reference or a supplement, in a more traditional commentary style, in spite of the increased availability of kabbalistic books after printing new authors, like Algazi and Yissakhar Baer, looked to the genre of anthological compilations to reorganize kabbalistic knowledge into more manageable intellectual frameworks while at the same time controlling the mediated content and keeping it at the level of simple rendition of the original work.

The format of Yissakhar Baer's *Meqor Ḥokhmah*, with its concise and straightforward commentary, concerned only with the literal (*pshat*) layer of the Zohar, which he presents in clear Hebrew, and the use of scriptural words as the starting point of the author's exegetical activity, places the work between a commentary and an index. That indexing was of paramount importance for Yissakhar Baer is underscored in his introduction: "concerning each verse I indicated the place of its source in the Zohar and I neither intended to add nor to confound, only to establish the true meaning of each topic."[41] The typographical setting of the printed page that displays a Biblical word as the starting point of his commentary is addressed to readers whose learning was primarily oriented toward Torah study, and only secondarily toward assimilating the Zohar's mystical exegesis, which Yissakhar Baer defines as too complex and multivalent for most people to understand. Therefore, the aim of his composition is to offer select passages from the Zohar as an authoritative and valuable source that would be "an aid and guide to all"[42] in expanding a person's traditional mode of learning Torah. As a pedagogue he explains that his two works, *Imrei Binah* and *Meqor Ḥokhmah*, were meant to constitute complementary compositions to aid the absorption and popularization of the Zohar with a clear messianic undertone that the study and knowledge of Kabbalah filtered through the teachings of the Zohar will contribute to hastening redemption: "an open gate and an introduction to all aspects of the Zohar, and through this may we merit the coming of the Messiah."[43]

As in his other compositions, Yissakhar Baer is conscious of both format and content and therefore explicitly justifies his editorial decision to include page references to the original source material and adopt clear language for the educational benefit of his readers. Although the modern reader is accustomed to locating sources with ease by reference to citation indexes included in most books, in the sixteenth and early seventeenth centuries, citation indexes to the Zohar represented a major innovation for reorganizing the content into more manageable units. Making the Zohar searchable as a text enabled readers to relate its content to other textual sources in the classical rabbinic canon such as the Tanakh, the Talmuds, and the midrashim. The compilation of *zoharic* indexes that displayed Biblical verses cited in the Zohar with its corresponding location in the Torah and other Biblical books promoted the homiletical application of the text for preachers, assisted commentators and rabbinic scholars with expanding their exegetical scope, and contributed to solidifying the canonical status of the work as a mystical commentary on Scripture. It is therefore not accidental that within a decade after the Italian publications of the Zohar in Cremona and Mantua, one of the first explicatory reference works to appear was an index to the Zohar, *Mafteaḥ ha-Zohar*, written by Moses Galante and printed in Venice in 1566.

Galante's index, the first printed attempt to present an index to the Zohar,[44] is significant in its organizational layout for several reasons. His editorial strategy to provide easier access to the Zohar was based on creating four main sections: a citation index covering Biblical verses that the Zohar employs and its corresponding source in Tanakh; a thematic index divided into twelve topical sections related to Jewish ritual life, learning, and various theological issues;[45] a catalog of *zoharic* tales, presented in the order of Biblical chapters, which was particularly expedient for preachers, who could incorporate some of these stories into their sermons imparting greater cultural prestige to their rhetoric;[46] and finally, a short commentary on the Zohar's interpretation of the Biblical chapter, Balak. By repackaging a lengthy and conceptually abstruse kabbalistic composition into more user-friendly shorter sections convenient and simple for consultation, Moses Galante, succeeded in presenting the reader with cognitive shortcuts that aided the assimilation of the original work.

The printed version of Galante's index, however, is but one of many additional manuscript versions of this text to the extent that there are more versions of the *Mafteah* in manuscript than what is available in print.[47] The large number of manuscript witnesses to *zoharic* indexes underlines the cultural prestige and theological importance of the work as well as attests to its frequent deployment among various study groups where each editor compiled an index according to his own style and learning objectives. Editorial considerations and goals were stated by writers in their introductions, and even though the editorial methods lacked a standardized approach they were nonetheless united by one purpose to make the content of the Zohar more accessible by devising search tools that effectively managed the dense symbolism and narrative of the text.[48] We gain a better perspective on the cultural and religious significance of the reasons and the methods that informed the production of these indexes from the account of R. Mordehai Dato, a sixteenth-century rabbi and kabbalist. As discussed earlier, Dato left Italy in the middle of the sixteenth century to study Kabbalah in Safed with R. Moses Cordovero and authored an abridgement to his master's work, *Pardes Rimonim*.[49] We are fortunate to have his autiobiographical comments recorded in the introduction to his Zohar index, only extant in manuscript,[50] as it reveals important information about the reasons that informed an author's decision to produce *zoharic* indexes and the pedagogic considerations they deployed to justify their organizational strategies.

Dato does not shy away from admitting that a major impetus for his endeavor to compile an index was his own intellectual limitation to retain information from one day to the next and in order to abet his memory he decided to make a list of key words from his readings on a daily basis, especially in regard to issues in the Zohar. By a curious coincidence, shortly after his decision, a man arrived from Safed who visited him and showed him a notebook that contained both a Biblical citation and a thematic index to the Zohar. With great excitement Dato borrowed the manuscript but could only complete a partial copy of it before the traveler was compelled to continue his journey and Dato reluctantly returned the notebook to him. The twelve thematic subsections incorporated in Galante's published *Index* are clearly reflected in Dato's description, however, with some significant variances both in the order of the topics presented as well as in their content. In addition, while Dato expresses his appreciation of Galante's efforts he nonetheless does not shy away from unstintingly exposing its shortcomings in order to correct them by composing an alternative version of what he regards paradigmatic in a *zoharic* index. More specifically, he identifies two sections that such an index must include: first, a primer or general introduction to Kabbalah that everyone who embarks on its study needs to complete and, second, a more focused treatment of the major theological principles of Kabbalah, such as the *Sefirot*.[51]

The methodological and pedagogical diversity that we witness here in the selective adaptation of strategies by which authors made the Zohar more comprehensible seemed to have stimulated intellectual competition among writers to present a more superior reference tool to the Zohar than the ones already available on the market. In fact, one may argue that the diffusion of a large number of zoharic indexes extant in manuscript may reflect the authors' need to structure these learning aids based on their unique educational objectives and theological focus in presenting the Zohar.[52] In *Mar'eh Kohen*, R. Yissakhar Baer ben Naftali Katz adopts a significantly different approach to indexing and organizing the content of the Zohar than Galante. Printed by the Prostitz press in Crakow in 1589, *Mar'eh Kohen*, represents an early attempt by an Ashkenazi author to not merely accept an Italian index already in circulation, but offer an alternative version more in conformity with the needs of an Ashkenazi reader. He justifies his task by reference to the different editions of the Zohar in circulation and use in Ashkenaz (Cremona), in contrast to Italy (Mantua). He divides the index into seventeen parts corresponding to the numerical value of the Hebrew word, *tov* (good), which are topically closely aligned with Galante's index. He adds, however, a separate section devoted to the subject of death and dying as well as collectanea devoted to various topics that he could not fit into the other categories. He concludes the index with a list of the stories in the Zohar (*ma'asiyot*).

A highly sophisticated and comprehensive thematic index to the Zohar is presented in *Maftehot ha-Zohar*, the first part of which is divided into more than eighty topical categories that are listed alphabetically in a handy reference table at the end of the work.[53] Originally written by a Rabbi Shmuel, whose last name was not recoded, it was arranged for print by the editor R. Israel Berakhiah Fontanella and published in Venice in 1744. Compared to Galante's index, the *Maftehot* organizes the Zohar's content not only into more comprehensive topics but also in some places provides a brief commentary on the literal meaning (*peshat*) of the topic under consideration. In this regard, the *Maftehot* represents an intermediary stage between a straightforward thematic index and the commentary genre such as Yissakhar Baer's *Meqor Hokhmah*, which stays close to plain, literal meaning of select *zoharic* passages. It is important to emphasize that the *Maftehot* constitutes a highly edited version of the original work, which was considerably reworked by Fontanella, who discloses with slight unease that he had decided to substantially abridge the original work.

> The author explains that he intented and and endeavored to collect, arrange, and present along with the indexes also the [corresponding] passages each in its proper place as I mentioned in the introduction. However, I the printer, young in age, included the indexes only in an abridged form in the holy tongue; and this is for the better so as not to slow down the printing process . . . and in order to gladden the hearts and souls of those who walk in the truth and to illumine their eyes when they are able to locate the subjects in their proper place . . . on the precise folio and page indicated [in this book lying] before them.[54]

The second part of the work offers a cross-reference between a particular verse of the Torah and its locator in the Zohar. The index is presented in three columns with the verses printed in larger typeset to facilitate the reader's search and follows the canonical order of biblical chapters beginning with Genesis.

A common sentiment expressed in the introduction of several learning aids printed in the early modern period was that certain layers and parts of kabbalistic knowledge could be, and should be, studied by nonspecialists. These authors argued that even an uninformed encounter with the mysteries of the Torah could potentially enhance Jewish commitment to religious life, the *mizvot*, and thus benefit learners of all types. For instance, in creating a digest for Elijah de Vidas's *Reshit Hokhmah* (Venice, 1579),

R. Yehiel Mili was motivated to produce a more affordable product than the original and one that addressed the needs of ordinary readers, "even those among us, who are empty [of kabbalistic wisdom] and who grasp only the plain meaning of the subject matter, from it [this book] they will perceive and thus learn the knowledge and fear of God and will be filled with the commandments."[55] Another abridger of *Reshit Hokhmah* widens the intended circle of readers to include even children maintaining that even their curriculum should include his kabbalistic précis. In other words, far from restricting this knowledge to Sages and elites, the author wrote his digest in the hope of marketing it not only among the adult reading population but presenting it also as a useful educational tool for teachers in instructing schoolchildren: "and moreover, I go forth in my work, a holy undertaking, with a double potion of goodness, for [even] the teachers of small children will be able to teach this book to their students [. . .] which is not the case with the original composition."[56]

One way of coping with the Zohar's literary and semantic complexities was to underscore the hermeneutically layered style of the narrative and direct the interpretive focus on the plain meaning (*peshat*) while bypassing the more complex symbolic, and often *sefirotic*, layers of the work. Correlating the revelation of the mysteries of the Torah with the merit of the generation, authors of kabbalistic study guides were quick to emphasize that as each generation of Jews decreased in merit and good deeds, the ability to understand the esoteric mysteries diminished as well. R. David ben Abraham Shemaryah argues, for instance, that in his generation the kabbalistic secrets of the Zohar can only be grasped in their totality by a select few; therefore, for the benefit of the many "these hidden mountains should be skipped" in favor of short explanations of a literal reading of the *zoharic* texts. It is revealing that this author admits to committing errors and omissions due to his own inability to properly decipher and comprehend all the inherent mysteries of the original work.[57] He thus demonstrates that while incomplete comprehension and reception of a text poses certain limitations on its transmission, by demarcating between the exoteric and more esoteric strata, learning aids represent powerful new instruments in reshaping Jewish knowledge and identity.[59] At the same time, the selective communication of esoteric content in kabbalistic works, like the Zohar, afforded authors a degree of self-censorship as they engaged in controlled revelation of divine mysteries.[59]

Conclusion

In summary, Yissakhar Baer's last two works exemplify a central concern that preoccupied kabbalistic secondary elites in the early modern period: to bring the Zohar, the magisterial work of Jewish mysticism, to a new readership that lacked the intellectual tools to access its linguistic and semantic layers. These two works constitute a clearly formulated educational program to present mystical knowledge to a new readership with the help of systematic learning tools: a dictionary of foreign words, a catalog of *aggadic* homilies, and a concise anthology of the *zoharic* midrash.

It was not a coincidence that the Zohar was singled out from within the kabbalistic corpora as a medium for the transmission of esoteric ideas to wider circle of readers spawning scores of anthologies, commentaries, and learning aids. The Zohar's reception as sacred, canonical, and holy text,[60] demanding serious study and exegesis, was predicated to an extent, on its midrashic compositional format.[61] This sentiment was contrary to mystical-magical treatises, the *Heikhalot* literature, *Sefer Yeẓirah*, *Shimmush Torah*, and *Shimmush Tehillim*, that viewed the Torah as identical with God. Thus these treatises regarded exegetical activity as tantamount to a magical operation that directly affected the Divine and therefore demanded serious expertise and circumspection.[62]

While these mystico-magical works presupposed extensive training in, and deep familiarity with, the theosophical systems and mystical techniques of Kabbalah, the hermeneutic approach invoked in the Zohar appeared more fluid and associative facilitating and easing the transmission of esoteric ideas.[63] An early modern Jew without any previous training in kabbalistic discourse could pick up the Zohar in print and connect with the midrashic elements of the narrative discourse. Thus, ostensibly, the narrative style of the Zohar enabled the successful mediation of Jewish mysticism to a broad segment of specialist and lay readers, who might have lacked the requisite expertise to acquire its deeper and abstract substrata, but who, nevertheless, were able to encounter it as a new iteration of a midrashic commentary on the Pentateuch already familiar to readers from the Jewish religious curriculum. Anthologies and indexes such as Yissakhar Baer's *Meqor Ḥokhmah*, constituted important but often underappreciated genres for the transmission of Jewish mystical knowledge. The reconfiguration of the original source material in new literary frames allows us to gain an insight into the pedagogical imperatives that informed the works of various authors and the intended reading audience they sought to address.

Chapter 7

The Influence of Kabbalistic Study Guides and Concluding Remarks

The literary production of R. Yissakhar Baer tells a story of a stratum of Jewish society, the secondary elites, whose daily lives revolved around education and whose primary task was to provide the pedagogical foundation and ensure continuing learning for members of the Jewish community. With the dissemination of kabbalistic knowledge in printed books, these individuals became important cultural agents who had the technical means to offer effective pedagogical tools to communicate complicated esoteric ideas in more accessible literary frameworks to facilitate popular consumption. They understood the theological importance of popularizing kabbalistic ideas and texts, for they viewed such a process as ultimately leading to the moral and spiritual perfection at the level of both Jewish individuals as well as communities. At the same time, the diffusion of kabbalistic literature, even at a basic or literal level, was believed to generate profound religious consequences in refining the Jewish soul, which in turn will hasten the Messianic redemption.

At the economic level, these new authors recognized the inherent benefit to be gained from publishing study manuals for Kabbalah, which due to their smaller size and lower production cost, provided a more reliable investment for printers than larger books. In this context, it is instructive that while Yissakhar Baer's four short works were printed in quick succession over a two-year period, his longer manuscript, an elaborate and detailed commentary on the Zohar, was met with less enthusiasm by the printers, and it seems that he was forced to either self-publish it, or at least contribute to its printing, for which he lacked the appropriate funds.[1] Therefore one may presume that whereas the short compositions constituted economically profitable outlets for the printers, Yissakhar Baer's extensive and detailed commentary on the Zohar, *Yod'ei Binah*, did not. Their decision to refrain from financially supporting the publishing of *Yod'ei Binah* may have been motivated either by its literary genre, a Zohar commentary, which was represented by several excellent volumes on the market, or by the sheer length of the material product that required greater financial commitment from the printers than what they were willing to invest. Be that as it may, the fact that *Yod'ei Binah* remained in manuscript, no longer extant today, while his other three works were printed within a brief span of two years, highlights the complex interplay between author, editor, market conditions, and the literary and material dimensions of texts.

The shift from manuscript production to printing redefined both the parameters of and access to knowledge and provided secondary elites with an important cultural platform for expressing an independent voice in mediating and reformulating traditional tenets and ideas. These books addressed both other secondary elites, such as preachers, who benefited from reference works that facilitated expedient consultation, as well as lower echelons of Jewish society, for whom Kabbalah presented a highly coveted religious language poised to enrich their traditional beliefs and expand their newly established libraries. At the same time, printing did not displace manuscript production in an absolute sense and authors continued to copy and create personal notebooks for individual study.[2] A case in point is the circulation of Luranic *Ilanot* diagrams and instructions, many of which survived into the twenty-first century as precious and hidden commodities of their owners.[3]

The reception history of Yissakhar Baer's works demonstrates that "reading takes no measures against the erosion of time,"[4] and that new readers rediscover and reappropriate in creative ways the written compositions of earlier generations.[5] Following their initial printing, Baer's works enjoyed several reprints in subsequent centuries. In Berlin, Meshullam Zalman ben Wolf Fischof printed *Pithei Yah* and *Meqor Hokhmah* in a single volume set in 1710–1711. He also released *Meqor Hokhmah* in 1711, which was reprinted in Warsaw in 1889, bearing the mark of the Kiev censors from 1882. Nathan Schriftgiesser published *Yesh Sakhar* in 1882 in Warsaw. For its part, the relatively recent reprinting of this work in 1993 by the Jerusalem printing press Torat Moshe reflects a new interest in what Boaz Huss calls the "recanonization of the Zohar," an emerging cultural phenomenon in the modern period.[6]

An important mediator of Yissakhar Baer in the twentieth century was Rabbi Yudel Rosenberg (1859–1935), an Orthodox rabbi who immigrated from Poland to North America and finally settled in Montreal (Canada) in 1919. A prolific writer in both Hebrew and Yiddish, Rabbi Rosenberg embarked on a major literary undertaking to translate and reedit the Zohar, which would occupy him for nearly twenty years. He shared Rabbi Yissakhar Baer's vision to popularize the Zohar with the aim of refocusing Judaism on its spiritual dimensions and away from the tide of secularism, while at the same time, hastening the final redemption and the coming of the Messiah.[7] By his own admission, his efforts to re-present the Zohar anew to the masses in his generation were greatly indebted to the pioneering works of Yissakhar Baer that anticipated his own by three centuries.

> And when I began to occupy myself with [the translation of the Zohar into Hebrew] I saw that I was not the first with this idea . . . Thus, there arose one great man [*gadol*] in the days of the *Shelah* and the *Levush* . . . Our teacher Rabbi Yissakhar Baer, author of the commentary, *Imrei Binah*, on the Zohar. He translated the passages of the Zohar, that are easily understood, to the Holy Language and arranged them according to the order of the chapters (*parshiyot*) in the Torah and called his book *Meqor Ḥokhmah*. The Holy Rabbi author of the *Shelah* [Rabbi Isaiah Horowitz] . . . and the excellent [gaon] Rabbi Mordecai Yaffe, author of the *Levush*, and other great ones of the generation approved the printing of his book. In his introduction, he [Yissakhar Baer] wrote that his work would be of use so that all the words of the Zohar will be open and explained for the eyes of all those who read it. And this is what he said in his introduction . . . [followed by an extensive quote from Yissakhar Baer's introduction].[8]

At the same time, Yissakhar Baer's didactic efforts to teach Kabbalah and disseminate its tenets widely reached beyond a Jewish audience and became influential among Christian intellectuals as well. His role as effective cultural mediator of kabbalistic ideas and language from one religious and geographical context to another is underscored by the fact that out of the eleven kabbalistic books enumerated in the library of the celebrated Hebraist, Johannes Buxtorf, four are Baer's compositions.[9] Buxtorf's acquisition and ownership of these works illustrates the cultural and intellectual entanglement of Jews and Christians in the early modern period and emphasizes the unique status Kabbalah enjoyed in this interchange. Stephanus Rittan-

Figure 7.1. Zohar (Sulzbach, 1684) with *Imrei Binah* printed at the bottom of the page, from the Scholem Collection, National Library of Israel.

gelius (1606–1652), a theologian and professor of Hebrew language at the University of Konigsberg, incorporated passages from *Imrei Binah* into his own commentary on *Sefer Yeẓirah* and translated these sections into Latin.[10] In addition, the inclusion of *Imrei Binah* in the bottom margins of the Sulzbach edition of Zohar (see Figure 7.1 above) printed in 1684, a collaborative effort between Jews and Christian Hebraists at the court of Christian August, affirms its didactic value as a reference tool.[11]

The juxtaposition of reading and writing, the original intent of the writer and the renewed encounters of a text by future readers, who probe the old text with the tools of new intellectual and cultural paradigms, is illustrated by the 1897 publication of a small book, titled *Yissakhar Baer's Commentary on the Song of Songs*.[12] This short fifty-four-page composition is a French translation of the section of *Meqor Ḥokhmah* devoted to explaining the Zohar on the Song of Songs. The work, printed in Paris by the Chamuel press, appeared as the second publication in the Rosicrucian Library series (Bibliothèque Rosicrucienne). The editors provide the reader with a brief conceptual introduction, aimed at establishing the Song of Songs as the holiest book of the Hebrew Bible ('*Kodesh ha-Kodashim*') and R. Yissakhar Baer and his father Rabbi Moshe Petaḥyah as authoritative interpreters of its mystical associations. That the French editors of the Rosicrucian Library series decided to excerpt a short section of *Meqor Ḥokhmah* and present it as a book that complements their other esoteric offerings in the series confirms the unexpected ways in which new readers recontextualize the written word for their specific needs and times.

The technological possibilities engendered by the spread of print technology were tempered in the early modern period by the growth of institutional control that shaped the boundaries of religion, literature, and culture in European society. At the same time, new intellectual directions, the promotion of humanism, and a concomitant return to ancient sources created shared intellectual spaces where encounters between Jewish and Christian scholars opened possibilities to harmonize rather than localize diverse religious and ideational systems. Exposure, however, did not guarantee comprehension. Thus, within a few decades after the Zohar's appearance in print, demand for abridgments, study aids, and anthologies provoked creative literary responses that aimed to ease both the linguistic and the conceptual limitations of these texts. Cultural agents, such as Yissakhar Baer, embodied an alternative voice in relation to elite hegemony, which came under attack in the dissemination of printed matter. Their literary strategies promoted the diffusion of Jewish esoteric ideas downward to the level of the nonspecialist reader. At the same time, the authorial impetus to reorganize Kabbalah into innovative literary frameworks clearly attests to an autonomous voice that comes " 'from below" and shapes new cultural values and ideals.[13]

That the intellectual impulse to produce study guides to the Zohar did not cease in the seventeenth century and continued well into the modern and postmodern eras is attested to by the scholarly efforts of Professor Isaiah Tishby, whose most celebrated work, the *Mishnat ha-Zohar*, was printed several times in the lifetime of the author and appeared in Littman Library series of Oxford University Press in the English translation of David Goldstein in 1989. The original Hebrew work appeared in two volumes printed with a considerable time gap, in 1949 and 1961, respectively, which was justified in the preface by the author that he hoped to correct the lack of "unexplained things" that appeared in the first volume.[14] Tishby's organizational framework was designed to accomplish three educational goals: (1) to organize the Zohar's content into larger topical categories such as, the "Doctrine of Man," "Sacred Worship," "Practical Life," and so on, and to subsequently create subcategories within these larger themes; (2) to deploy the tool of translation from Aramaic to Hebrew in order to render the selected passages more comprehensible for a reading audience that was comfortable with Hebrew but had difficulty deciphering the Aramaic original; and (3) to add introductions that provided not only an overview to the topics within the field of Kabbalah but, especially in the second volume, aimed to frame them in the broader intellectual context of traditional rabbinic texts and the literature of Jewish speculative thought, "aggadic literature . . . philosophy, and in pre-Zoharic Kabbalah" and to trace their development within the field of the history of ideas.[15]

The expansive strategy that Tishby adopts, which goes beyond the mere anthological presentation of the Zohar and seeks to define its place in relation to other major ideational and textual traditions, no longer addresses itself to the uninitiated reader and departs sharply from the efforts of Yissakhar Baer and other early modern authors who produced *zoharic* study tools discussed in this book. In contrast to his sixteenth- and seventeenth-century predecessors, I contend, Tishby aspires to reach out to a largely academic readership and open the Zohar's rich repository of literary, linguistic, and theologic-symbolic elements to an audience who would gain access to a primary resource that intersects and dialogues not only with other kabbalistic texts but also with rabbinic literature, medieval philosophy, history, religion, linguistics, and society. That this purpose crystallized later on in the creative process after he and the literary scholar Fishel Lachower had already completed the first volume, is affirmed by Tishby's admission that he felt the individual anthological sections required more extensive introductions with expanded explanations, notes, and a general comparative discussion in contextualizing the ideas and passages. Tishby's work gained additional momentum in 1989 when the work appeared for the first time in Goldstein's English translation, further spurring its dissemination among circles of popular readers.

The Pritzker project launched in 2004 confirmed that wide-scale popularization of the Zohar in the postmodern period demanded a superior translation of the original into a sophisticated English rendition that reflects the literary ambiguities and nuances of the original Aramaic text. The intended audience for this new edition of the Zohar was a readership interested in supplementing their learning of Torah with commentary that went beyond the traditional rabbinic canon comprised of midrashic literature and medieval commentary and introduced a fundamentally different language and symbolic universe in disclosing the hidden facets of the Pentateuch.[16] The readers of the new edition therefore were both specialists and nonspecialists, who devoted time to Jewish learning with a keen interest to encounter Jewish mysticism through the gateway of the Zohar but ultimately to remain in the linguistic sphere of the English language. In contrast to Tishby's anthology of textual selections, Daniel Matt decided to compile the Pritzker edition based on Reuven Margoliot's edition of Sefer ha-Zohar, which drew first on the Vilna and originally on the Mantua printing of the work. An important feature in Daniel Matt's contribution as translator and commentator was not only to enlist the expertise of a team of scholars who are specialists of zoharic literature but also to consult a variety of extant manuscript witnesses[17] as well as commentaries to the Zohar, such as Cordovero's Or Yaqar, in order to determine the best recension of individual passages.

If we adopt Daniel Abrams's contention that the Zohar as a book has never existed and its printing in the sixteenth century produced merely one edition of the Zohar rather than offering some kind of urtext,[18] then we might posit that in fact an intrinsic and deeply embedded characteristic of this text is that it invites innovation and re-presentation from new generations of readers. Just as the protagonists of the zoharic narrative extol the virtue of producing hermeneutic novelty (ḥiddushim),[19] the work itself survives and becomes received anew by the mediating efforts of new generations of scholars and interpreters. Therefore, we may conclude that the mission of Yissakhar Baer and other secondary elites like him, to make the Zohar more accessible to future readers, will be taken up in the future by new authors who will bring their own unique paradigms, perspectives, and priorities to the project. In the crucible of Matt's scholarly laboratory, the Zohar was refined again to sparkle for many generations to come and provide the foundation and starting point for new explorations, affirming Moses Cordovero's statement that "this composition is not a work that will vanish, rather it will be composed, and (re)written and (re)arranged."[20]

Notes

Introduction

1. See Agata Paluch, "Intentionality and Kabbalistic Practices in Early Modern East-Central Europe," *Aries* 19 (2019): 84.

2. See Jeremy Stolow's insightful investigation of the impact of ArtScroll books in reshaping Jewish religious sensibilities, attitudes and praxes in *Orthodox by Design*, 4.

3. Carpenter and McLuhan (eds.), *Explorations in Communications*, IX.

4. Carpenter and McLuhan, *Explorations in Communications*, IX.

5. Benedict Anderson, *Imagined Communities*.

6. Stock (1983, 90–91, 522; and 1990, 23, 150). See Huss, *Like Radiance of the Sky*, 152.

7. See Marshall McLuhan, *The Gutenberg Galaxy*, 206.

8. A similar device was employed by printers who used embedded citation indexes in printing the Talmud. The work *'En Mishpat*, printed in 1546, for instance, provides a reference to the discussion of Talmudic laws in subsequent legal codes such as Maimonides. In published editions of the Talmud this index is printed in the margins of a Talmudic page enhancing and easing cross-referencing. See Bella Hass Weinberg, "The Earliest Hebrew Citation Indexes," 318–19. Weinberg's article provides a useful overview of citation indexes and how they functioned in the early centuries of the circulation of the printed book.

9. See the discussion of hypertext and its relevance to philosophical thought in George P. Landow, "Critical Theory in the Age of Hypertext" and David Kolb, "Socrates in the Labyrinth."

10. On the concept of multivocality see Mikhail Bakhtin, *Problems of Dostoevsky's Poetics*.

11. Julia Kristeva defines intertextuality as "a mosaic of quotations; any text is the absorption and transformation of another. The notion of *intertextuality* replaces that of intersubjectivity, and poetic language is read as at least *double*" in "Word, Dialogue and Novel," 85.

12. George P. Landow, "Critical Theory in the Age of Hypertext," 1.

13. Christina Hass, *Writing Technology*, X.

14. Christina Hass, *Writing Technology*, XIII.

15. Walter Ong, *Orality and Literacy*, 124–25.

16. Alberto Cevolini, "Storing Expansions: Openness and Closure in Secondary Memories," 171.

17. A comprehensive treatment of this subject is presented in Moshe Halbertal, *People and the Book: Canon, Meaning, and Authority* (1997). See especially the chapter, "Esotericism and Censorship" in section 3.

18. Stern, *The Anthology in Jewish Literature*, 4–5.

19. Alsted is only one of a number of Christian theologians and thinkers active in the seventeenth century who aimed to devise various methods and systems for coping with the explosion of information and knowledge in print. For a more detailed discussion of other Alsted and other authors, see Ann Moss, *Printed Common-Place Books and the Structuring of Renaissance Thought*, 228–54.

20. J. H. Chajes, "Kabbalah and the Diagrammatic Phase of the Scientific Revolution," 111–12. Chajes and his team are further involved in an unprecedented undertaking supported by the Israel Science Foundation to catalog, digitize, and analyze the extant Lurianic *Ilanot*. For more on the development of this project consult the following website: http://ilanot.haifa.ac.il/site/. Other works that engage the questions of visual aspects of Kabbalah are Giulio Busi, *Qabbalah Visiva* (Torino: Einaudi, 2005) (Italian); Marla Segol, *Word and Image in Medieval Kabbalah*; recent articles by J. H. Chajes, "Durchlässige Grenzen," and Eliezer Baumgarten, "Drashot 'al ha-Ilan ha-Kabbali le-Yosef ibn-Ẓur." *Kabbalah* 37 (2017): 101–57.

21. http://ilanot.haifa.ac.il/site/.

22. See Scholem's discussion of Shabbatai Zvi and his approach to messianism in *Sabbatai Ṣevi: The Mystical Messiah, 1626–1676*.

23. Drawing on Hegel's dialectical understanding of history, Scholem maintained that Jewish history had a mainstream normative tendency that was always counterbalanced by a subterranean current, which he identified as the mystical element in Judaism. For Scholem, Kabbalah was not a marginal, but an essential element in Jewish history, which over time contributed to the renewal of Judaism and ensured its continuity and spiritual vitality. The spiritual crisis engendered by the expulsion of the Jews from the Iberian Peninsula intensified and activated the irrational impulses inherent in Judaism, culminating in the Safedean "mystical revolution," which further contributed to the broader popularization of Kabbalah in nonelite circles in the seventeenth century. See Biale, *Gershom Scholem: Kabbalah and Counter-History*, 8; Scholem, *Major Trends in Jewish Mysticism*, 244.

24. See also Garb, "The Cult of the Saints in Lurianic Kabbalah," 203–05 and Idel, "On Mobility, Individuals, and Groups."

25. The Italian rabbi, physician, and writer, Abraham Yagel, a slightly older contemporary of Yissakhar Baer, sought to collate Kabbalah, scientific discourse, and traditional rabbinic literature in his autobiographic work, *Gei Hizzayon*.

For an extensive and erudite treatment of this important early-modern figure, see David Ruderman, *Kabbalah, Magic and Science* (Cambridge, MA: Harvard University Press, 1988).

26. The largest one at the time was Rome. For a comprehensive study on communal memory in the Prague Jewish community, see Rachel Greenblatt, *To Tell Their Children: Jewish Communal Memory in Early Modern Prague.*

27. Jonathan Israel, *European Jewry in the Age of Mercantilism*, 32.

28. R. J. W. Evans, *Rudolf II and His World: A Study in Intellectual History 1576–1612*, 240.

29. Jonathan Israel *European Jewry in the Age of Mercantilism*, 33; Sharon Flatto, *The Kabbalistic Culture of Eighteenth-Century Prague*, 5.

30. Marvin Heller, *The Sixteenth Century Hebrew Book*, 779.

31. Andre Neher, *The Jewish Thought and the Scientific Revolution of the Sixteenth Century: David Gans (1541–1613) and His Times*, 23–24.

32. Neher, *The Jewish Thought and the Scientific Revolution of the Sixteenth Century*, 20.

33. Joseph Davies, *Yom Tov Lipmann Heller: Portrait of a Seventeenth-Century Rabbi*, 27.

34. R. J. W. Evans, *Rudolf II and His World: A Study in Intellectual History 1576–1612*, 237.

35. R. J. W. Evans, *Rudolf II and His World*, p. 238.

36. Joseph Davies, *Yom Tov Lipmann Heller: Portrait of a Seventeenth-Century Rabbi*, 59–60.

37. It should be noted nonetheless that the Maharal seldom cited kabbalistic sources such as the *Zohar* in his writings.

38. Joseph Davies, *Yom Tov Lipmann Heller: Portrait of a Seventeenth-Century Rabbi*, 8.

39. Gershom Scholem, *Sabbatai Sevi: The Mystical Messiah*, 86.

40. Joseph Davis, *Yom Tov Lipmann Heller: Portrait of a Seventeenth-Century Rabbi*, 33.

41. Joseph Davis, *Yom Tov Lipmann Heller: Portrait of a Seventeenth-Century Rabbi*, 33.

42. Davis, *Yom Tov Lipmann Heller*, 42.

43. Davis, *Yom Tov Lipmann Heller*, 47.

44. Andre Neher, *The Jewish Thought and the Scientific Revolution of the Sixteenth Century: David Gans (1541–1613) and His Times*, 34–35.

45. On the matter of secrecy and disclosure of esoteric secrets in Jewish medieval mystical and philosophical discourse, see Moshe Halbertal, *Concealment and Revelation*. See also Elliot R. Wolfson, *Abraham Abulafia—Kabbalists and Prophet: Hermeneutics, Theosophy, and Theurgy.*

46. There are several accounts that highlight the frequency with which rabbis who wished to study Kabbalah with an authoritative master undertook arduous

trips, leaving their families and homes to spend time "at the feet" of a renowned kabbalist. See, for example, Solomon Shlomel Dresnitz, who left Moravia in his early twenties in order to study Lurianic Kabbalah in Safed; see his letters to Yissakhar Baer in Meir Benayahu, *Toldot ha-Ari*, 39–60. See also Joseph Delmedigo, *Taʿalumot Ḥokhmah*, fol. 41b–49b. Rabbi Menaḥem Azariah da Fano recounts that a Polish rabbi left not only his native land but also his family in order to study with him for a period of time: "My friend, the polish Sage R. Yizḥak ben R. Mordechai, adjured me. He is a venerated disciple who seeks good for his people, a warrior in the war of Torah [. . .] and now he decreed upon himself complete exile and has become ruthless to his wife and children for the love of this wisdom Kabbalah and came from the ends of the Earth, the remote parts of the North to hear the word of God," see *Pelah ha-Rimmon*, fol. 3.

47. Rosman, "Innovative Tradition," 532.

48. Rosman, "Innovative Tradition," 532.

49. See Elbaum, *Openness and Insularity*, 185. Elbaum notes that authors in the lands of Poland and Ashkenaz, in the early modern period, chose to synthesize and integrate the knowledge of the past, rather than embark on the composition of conceptually original treatises in the field of Kabbalah.

50. Reiner, "A Biography of an Agent of Culture," 229–30. See also Ruderman, *Early Modern Jewry*, 99–103.

51. My work on secondary elites builds on Elhanan Reiner's argument that attributes the transformation of traditional Jewish learning, discourse, and curriculum to the presence of fundamental cleavages in early modern Ashkenazi society. Reiner further posits that the central line of division was not based on wealth or economic status that pitted rich against the poor, but rather on a more nuanced understanding of four social strata: the traditional rabbinic aristocracy; the emerging secondary elite; the nouveaux riches; and the poor. Reiner concludes that the most important line of division was drawn between the first two groups: members of the established primary and the rising central secondary elites. It was the competition between these two groups in Ashkenazi society that would define the main contours of theological change and any subsequent religious development. See Reiner, "Transformations in the Polish and Ashkenazi Yeshivot."

52. Ruderman, *Early Modern Jewry*, 103.

53. This aspect of messianic thought has been largely overlooked in previous studies and it deserves a more focused treatment that I hope to undertake in the near future. See Scholem, *The Messianic Idea in Jewish Mysticism*; Idel, *Messianic Mystics*; Liebes, *Studies in Jewish Myth and Messianism*, "The Messiah of the Zohar"; Saperstein (ed.), *Essential Papers on Messianic Movements and Personalities in Jewish History*; Sharot, *Messianism, Mysticism, and Magic*; and *The Messianic Idea in Jewish Thought: A Study Conference in Honour of the Eightieth Birthday of Gershom Scholem*. A more recent volume on the messianic idea in Judaism is *Rethinking the Messianic Idea in Judaism*, edited by Michael L. Morgan and Steven Weitzman.

54. See Baer, *Imrei Binah*, Author's Introduction, fol. 1b.

55. This book was recently translated into English and published by Littman Library; see Huss, *The Zohar: Reception and Impact*.

56. Boaz Huss, *Like the Radiance of the Sky*, vii.

57. Elbaum, *Opening and Insularity*.

58. Ruderman, *Early Modern Jewry*, 14–15.

59. J. Davis, *Yom Tov Lipmann Heller*, 59–60; J. Israel, *European Jewry*, 78–81; A. Coudert, *The Impact of Kabbalah*, 342–45.

60. Rosman, "Rethinking European Jewish History," 25–27.

61. Elbaum, *Openness and Insularity*, 191. Elbaum specifically highlights the gap in the academic study of works produced by kabbalists, such as Rabbi Yissakhar Baer and R. Shabbtai Sheftel Horowitz.

62. Barzilay, *Yoseph Shlomo Delmedigo*, 106; Meir Benayahu, *Toldot ha-Ari*, 39–60. See also the primary source, Joseph Delmedigo, *Ta'alumot Hokhmah*, Folios 41b–49b. On the transmission of the Cordoverean system versus Lurianic Kabbalah, see Idel, "One from a Town, Two from a Clan," Gries, *The Book in the Jewish World*; Weinstein, *Breaking of the Vessels*; Tishby, *Studies in Kabbalah and Its Branches*, 177–254.

63. R. Solomon Shlomiel explains that upon his arrival to Safed he was excluded from the circles that taught and disseminated Lurianic Kabbalah. His entry into this rarified lore was through marriage to the daughter of Israel Sarug, a defining proponent of Lurianic Kabbalah at the end of sixteenth and early seventeenth centuries, who made both his knowledge and library accessible to him. See Benayahu *Toldot ha-Ari*, 58. On Sarug, see Scholem, "Israel Sarug—Disciple of Luria?" For a more recent reevaluation of Scholem's conclusions regarding Sarug, see Meroz, "Contrasting Opinions" and "The Saruq School of Thought."

64. Idel, "One from a Town," 83 and Tishby, "Confrontation," 8–20.

65. Michel de Certeau, *The Practice of Everyday Life*, 174.

66. Guglielmo Cavallo and Roger Chartier, eds., *History of Reading in the West*, 1–2.

Chapter 1

1. Printing using woodblocks began in China already during the Tang dynasty in the seventh century, and the movable type appeared in the eleventh century. See Carter, *The Invention of Printing in China*, and Blair, *Too Much to Know*, 28–29.

2. See Richardson, *Manuscript Culture in Renaissance Italy*; Beit-Arie, "Publication and Reproduction of Literary Texts," and Febvre and Martin, *The Coming of the Book*, 15–28.

3. Cavallo and Chartier, *A History of Reading in the West*, 22.

4. See for instance Febvre and Martin, *The Coming of the Book*, 87.

5. Cavallo and Chartier, *A History of Reading in the West*, 22–23.

6. It took 10–12 animal skins to print a book of 150 pages on parchment, which made production considerably more expensive than printing the same text on cheap paper, Baruchson-Arbib, "The Prices of Hebrew Printed Books in Cinquecento Italy," 151.

7. Baruchson-Arbib, "The Prices of Hebrew Printed Books in Cinquecento Italy," 22.

8. Eisenstein, *The Printing Press as an Agent of Change*, 45–46 and Blair, *Too Much to Know*, 13. Ann Blair notes, based on the estimates of an Englishman in 1630, that what took four men to print in one day took ten men a full year to copy; a poignant example that illustrates the technological potential of the printing press in contrast to manuscript production. See *Too Much to Know*, 47.

9. Eisenstein, "Some Conjectures about the Impact of Printing," 7.

10. See the library of the Italian miller, Domenico Scandella, who in the sixteenth century possessed several religious books, including the vernacular translation of the Bible and even an Italian translation of what may have been the Qur'an. Clearly, Scandella, or as he was popularly called Menocchio, did not belong to the educated elite, nonetheless he acquired either by purchasing or by borrowing several books that shaped his own idea of the world in general and the Christian religion in particular. For more on Menocchio, see Ginzburg, *The Cheese and the Worms*.

See also Eisenstein, "Some Conjectures about the Impact of Printing on Western Society and Thought: A Preliminary Report," 7n16.

11. Grafton, "The Humanist as Reader," 196.

12. Grafton provides the example of Hieronymus Muenzer, a scholar in Nurnberg, to illustrate the process by which a text, printed or in manuscript form, became personalized by its owner. Muenzer carefully recorded in his books how he acquired them noting for instance that one of his medical books was imported from Venice in 1478, while another one purchased on a trip to Italy during his student years in Pavia in 1477. In addition, he relates the joy of finally meeting the writer of a manuscript he acquired. Muenzer, like his contemporaries, felt a need to transform the book from a commercial, into a highly personalized, object, see "The Humanist as Reader," 195–96.

13. Blair, *Too Much to Know*, 47.

14. Blair, *Too Much to Know*, 53.

15. Blair, *Too Much to Know*, 52. Blair notes that some of the cities featured in the book, offered financial assistance in the printing, which represents an early example of economic networks that emerged among political entities (the cities), cultural agents (the printers) and the public (the readers). On how printing affected political consciousness see Benedict Anderson, *Imagined Communities: Reflections on the Origin and Spread of Nationalism*, especially 37–46.

16. Blair, *Too Much to Know*, 53.

17. Blair, *Too Much to Know*, 13.

18. Eisenstein, "Some Conjectures about the Impact of printing on Western Society and Thought: A Preliminary Report," 4.

19. Febvre and Martin, *The Coming of the Book*, 249. Febvre and Martin note that 45 percent of all books printed before 1500 were religious texts; classical, medieval, and contemporary literature comprised 30 percent, and legal and scientific texts, made up 10 percent and 11 percent, respectively.

20. Febvre and Martin, *The Coming of the Book*, 250. See also Brian Richardson, *Printing, Writers and Readers in Renaissance Italy*, 150–51. Richardson described the controversy that accompanied the vernacular printing of the Bible. In the late sixteenth century, at the Council of Trent, a certain discomfort was registered concerning the access that even "uneducated women" enjoyed to the Biblical text.

21. Febvre and Martin, 350n345.

22. In the fifteenth century, the distribution of vernacular versus the Latin Bible were the following: 77 percent in Latin; 7 percent in Italian; 4–6 percent in German; 4–5 percent in French, and over 1 percent in Flemish; see Febvre and Martin, *The Coming of the Book*, 249.

23. Stolow, *Orthodox by Design*, 20.

24. Ginzburg, *The Cheese and the Worms*, 4.

25. Ginzburg, 5.

26. Febvre and Martin, *The Coming of the Book*, 244–45.

27. An Italian translation was printed in Venice in 1547.

28. For a complete list of Menocchio's textual sources, see Ginzburg, *The Cheese and the Worms*, 28–32.

29. Ginzburg, *The Cheese and the Worms*, 45.

30. See Gilmont, "Protestant Reformations and Reading;" Eisenstein, *The Printing Revolution*, 164–208, and Eisenstein, *The Printing Press as an Agent of Change*, 303–450.

31. Eisenstein, *The Printing Press as an Agent of Change*, 378.

32. Eisenstein, *The Printing Press as an Agent of Change*, 424.

33. Eisenstein, *The Printing Press as an Agent of Change*, 425.

34. Wright, *Middle Class Culture*, 239–41, cited in Eisenstein, *The Printing Press as an Agent of Change*, 425.

35. Gilmont, "Protestant Reformations and Reading," 218.

36. Gilmont, "Protestant Reformations and Reading," 219.

37. Gilmont, "Protestant Reformations and Reading," 218.

38. Eisenstein, "Some Conjectures," 37.

39. Heller, *The Seventeenth Century Hebrew Book*, xiii; and also Heller, *The Sixteenth Century Hebrew Book*, xiii.

40. Posner and Ta-Shema, *The Hebrew Book*, 85.

41. Heller, *The Sixteenth Century Hebrew Book*, xv.

42. Heller, "Early Hebrew Printing from Lublin to Safed," 106 and *The Sixteenth Century Hebrew Book*, xiv. At the same time, Jews on occasion undertook printing as a secondary economic activity such as the press that was operated by three silk manufacturers in Bologna, with a relatively modest output of nine books over five years; see Baruchson, "Money and Culture," 36.

43. Baruchson, "Money and Culture," 27.

44. Heller, *The Sixteenth Century Hebrew Book*, xviii, and Baruchson, "Money and Culture," 27. The humanist, Conrad Gesner, included one extant Bomberg catalog in his *Bibliotheca Universalis*, which according to Heller included seventy-five titles with prices.

45. Heller, *The Sixteenth Century Hebrew Book: An Abridged Thesaurus*, xvii.

46. Baruchson, "Money and Culture," 26. Baruchson's article provides a good overview of the four major Venetian presses. For more information regarding these presses, see also Heller, *The Sixteenth Century Hebrew Book*. On printing in the Ottoman Empire in the same period, see Hacker, "Authors, Readers and Printers."

47. Heller, *Studies in the Making of the Early Hebrew Book*, 278–83.

48. Hacker, *The Alphabet of Ben Sira*, p. 29, cited in Heller, *The Sixteenth Century Hebrew Book*, xlviii.

49. Benayahu, *Yosef Behiri*, 192.

50. Dweck, *The Scandal of Kabbalah*, 34–35.

51. Baruchson-Arbib, "The Prices of Hebrew Printed Books in Cinquecento Italy," 154.

52. Baruchson bases herself here on three income categories collected and tabulated by the historian, Fernand Braudel. Accordingly, the lowest income level up to 20 ducats covered only basic necessities; the second, with 20–40 ducats was still substantially low; the third, with 40–150 ducats, was considered reasonable. Those with income levels above 150–200 ducats were considered wealthy. See Baruchson-Arbib, "The Prices of Hebrew Printed Books in Cinquecento Italy," pp. 157–58.

53. Baruchson, "Jewish Libraries," 23.

54. Bonfil, *Jewish Life in Renaissance Italy*, 126. Rabbi David Ibn Yahia, rabbi in the city of Naples, when asking the community to raise his salary to 100 scudi explained that anything less would require him to beg for charity and would hinder him in fulfilling his communal functions; see Baruchson-Arbib, "The Prices of Hebrew Printed Books in Cinquecento Italy," 160.

55. Baruchson-Arbib, "The Prices of Hebrew Printed Books in Cinquecento Italy," 160.

56. Baruchson, "Jewish Libraries in Italy," 26.

57. Baruchson, "Jewish Libraries in Italy," 20–21.

58. By contrast, one of the outstanding Jewish intellects of his generation, the scholar and physician, Yoseph Shlomo Delmedigo (Yashar), boasted a library that contained 7,000 books! Having acquired a comprehensive education in all

fields of Jewish learning as well as years of secular-scientific studies at the University of Padua, he exemplifies one of the most ardent bibliophiles of his time. See Barzilay, *Yoseph Shlomo Delmedigo*, 48.

59. Baruchson, "Jewish Libraries in Italy," 23.

60. Baruchson, "Jewish Libraries in Italy," 23–24. Baruchson notes the lack of any reference to the complete Talmud, or even individual tractates, which must be attributed to the strict ecclesiastical ban on this work. Ownership of the Talmud or its tractates would have had to be done in a clandestine manner, hidden away from the Inquisition.

61. Italian titles included classics, such as the Homer's *Iliad* and the Boccaccio's *Decameron*, along with the popular epic, *Orlando Furioso* by Ludovico Ariosto. See Baruchson, "Jewish Libraries in Italy," 25 and Baruchson, *Book and Readers*, 108–19 and 176–90.

62. Baruchson, "Jewish Libraries in Italy," 25.

63. Price, *Johannes Reuchlin*, 13.

64. Yates, *Giordano Bruno and the Hermetic Tradition*, 12–13.

65. According to Ficino, Hermes was called Trismegistus "because he was the greatest philosopher and the greatest priest and the greatest king." See Copenhaver, *Hermetica*, xlviii.

66. Ruderman, *Kabbalah, Magic, and Science*, 140–41.

67. Pico della Mirandola evokes the idea of "poetic theology," according to which ancient pagan authors concealed the esoteric meaning of their compositions by way of hiding the truth behind a veil of legends and stories. See Ruderman, *Kabbalah, Magic, and Science*, 141.

68. For a comprehensive study on Pico in the context of Jewish mysticism, see Wirszubski, *Pico della Mirandola's Encounter with Jewish Mysticism*.

69. Giovanni Pico della Mirandola, *Oratio*, cited in Ruderman, *Kabbalah, Magic, and Science*, 142.

70. Ruderman, *Kabbalah, Magic, and Science*, 142.

71. Fabrizio Lelli, "Jews, Humanists," 50.

72. Fabrizio Lelli, "Intellectual Relationships," 153–54.

73. The Latin inscriptions are quoted in Yates, *Giordano Bruno and the Hermetic Tradition*, 42. The translation from Latin into English is mine.

74. For a different interpretation of the inscriptions, see Yates, *Giordano Bruno and the Hermetic Tradition*, 43.

75. Ruderman, *Early Modern Jewry*, 120–22. On Abraham Yagel see the penetrating study of Ruderman, *Kabbalah, Magic, and Science*. On other important Jewish humanists, see Idel, *Kabbalah in Italy, 1280–1510: A Survey*. On Yohanan Alemanno, see Idel, "The Study Program of R. Yohanan Alemanno," and *Kabbalah in Italy*, 177–91 and 340–43.

76. Ruderman, *Jewish Thought and Scientific Discovery*, 106.

77. Barzilay, *Yoseph Shlomo Delmedigo*, 48.

78. Ruderman, *Early Modern Jewry*, 122.

79. Freudenthal, *Science in Medieval Jewish Cultures*, 406.

80. It was published multiple times in major printing centers: 1513 (Constantinople); 1534 (Salonika); 1535–1539 (Venice); 1548 (Basel); 1548 (Paris); 1568 (Wittenberg), see Heller, *The Sixteenth Century Hebrew Book*, 197.

81. Freudenthal, *Science in Medieval Jewish Cultures*, 407.

82. Reprints: 1508 (Pesaro); 1519 (Ortona); 1519 (Hagenau); 1520 (Augsburg); 1531, 1536 (Basel); 1545 (Rome); 1546, 1552 (Venice); 1563, 1578 (Mantua).

83. On the engagement of Christian thinkers with Kabbalah in the Renaissance, see Brian Ogren, *Renaissance and Rebirth: Reincarnation in Early Modern Kabbalah*.

84. Price, *Johannes Reuchlin*, 66.

85. Price, *Johannes Reuchlin*, 66–67.

86. Price, *Johannes Reuchlin*, 67. It is instructive, that Reuchlin's studies with Jewish scholars, such as Obadiah Sforno, positively impacted his attitude toward Judaism and prompted him to defend the Jewish faith in his scholarly compositions. In his *Art of the Kabbalah*, Judaism is represented as a religion that is defended and not denounced or marginalized. One of the protagonists, Simon, the Jew, is portrayed as the humanist ideal, integrating thorough knowledge of Judaism with moral uprightness and humanist expertise. Jews and Christians are depicted not as rivals but as allies in search of divine wisdom. The conversionary subtext that informs the works of other Christian Hebraists of the time, is absent in Reuchlin's writings as he aspires to portray a Judaism to his Christian readers, that constitutes a model of piety, a powerful theological voice, and a religion unrelenting in its pursuit of God. See Price, *Johannes Reuchlin*, 91–92.

87. Price, *Johannes Reuchlin*, 86. Also in Morlok, *Rabbi Joseph Gikatilla's Hermeneutics*, 311. Ricius's translation, titled, *Portae Lucis*, was printed in Augsburg in 1515.

88. Price, *Johannes Reuchlin*, 87, where Price cites Idel's observation that Reuchlin must have used the JTS manuscript or something very similar to it, see Idel, "Introduction to *On the Art of Kabbalah* by Johann Reuchlin," xvi–xix. He also highlights that Saverio Campanini convincingly demonstrated the close correspondence between MS Halberstam 444 and Reuchlin's kabbalistic excerpts, see Price, *Johannes Reuchlin and the Campaign to Destroy Jewish Books*, 257n155.

89. It is worth quoting his praise of Gikatilla's *Ginat Egoz*: "But in my opinion no one up to this time has ever written about that art more scientifically, more distinctly, and more lucidly than has Rabbi Joseph ben Abraham of Castile, a citizen of Salem. He studiously built up three volumes on this discipline, in which he clarified the entire teachings of the Kabbalists—the first volume is on words, the second on letters, and the third is on points [i.e., diacritics and punctuation]." Cited in Price, *Johannes Reuchlin*, 87.

90. Coudert, *The Impact of the Kabbalah in the Seventeenth Century*, 84–86. According to Reuchlin's formulation, Hebrew constitutes a natural and not a

conventional language: "the Cabala is nothing else but . . .symbolic theology in which . . . letters and names are the signs of things" (88).

91. Coudert, *The Impact of the Kabbalah in the Seventeenth Century*, 88.

92. Ruderman, *Preachers of the Italian Ghetto*, 6.

93. On the esoteric potential of the Hebrew language, see Chapter 1 in Brian Ogren, *The Beginning of the World in Renaissance Jewish Thought*.

94. Pico studied with the noted kabbalist, Joseph Alemanno and the physician and philosopher, Elijah del Medigo. Pico's conclusions were in large part based on Recanati's *Commentary on the Torah*, which incorporated substantial portions of *zoharic* literature, see Blau, *The Christian Interpretation of the Cabala in the Renaissance*, 28. On Pico see also important studies by Chaim Wirszubszki, *Pico della Mirandola's Encounter with Jewish Mysticism*; Giulio Busi, "Who does not wonder at this Chameleon? The Kabbalistic Library of Giovanni Pico della Mirandola"; and Giulio Busi's introduction in Severio Campanini's work, *The Book Bahir. Flavius Mithridates' Latin Translation, The Hebrew Text and the English Version*.

On Alemanno, see a number of important studies by Idel, "The Magical and Neoplatonic Interpretations," "The Study Program of R. Yohanan Alemanno," and *Kabbalah in Italy 1280–1510*.

When Pico died in 1494 his private library collection contained some 1,100 books and competed with the most rarified inventories of his contemporaries. On Pico, his reading interests, and library, see Grafton, "Giovanni Pico della Mirandola." On the inventory of his library, see Cesis, *Giovanni Pico della Mirandola* and Kibre, *The Library of Pico della Mirandola*.

95. Lelli, "Intellectual Relationships," 161.

96. Cooperman, "*Amicitia* and Hermeticism," 98.

97. Christian debates whether to burn the Talmud in its entirety or merely expurgate blasphemous content from it were informed by a sentiment shared by prominent Christian theologians that rabbinic literature, including the Talmud, could prove useful in the conversion of Jews, see Stow, "The Burning of the Talmud in 1553," 436–37.

98. Blau, *The Christian Interpretation of the Cabala*, 20–21. Bernard McGinn argues that Pico delineated three strata in Jewish thought: (1) talmudic Judaism, which he discounted as heretical; (2) philosophical Judaism, which he deemed as late and therefore irrelevant; and (3) kabbalistic Judaism, the oldest and "true more than any other because established opinion is that it was made known to Moses by the best and greatest God"; see in McGinn, "Cabalists and Christians," 11.

See also Idel's assessment of Pico's tripartite response to Kabbalah: (1) where Kabbalah can be used to support Christianity, Pico advocates for its exploitation for missionary purposes; (2) if Kabbalah disagrees with Christianity, Pico attacks it; and (3) when an esoteric tenet is found in Kabbalah but not in Christianity, Pico calls for its usurpation and transfer to Christianity. See Idel, "Jewish Thinkers versus Christian Kabbalah," 52.

99. Pico della Mirandola, *Opera Omnia*, "Kabblistic Conclusion 7," cited in Coudert, *The Impact of the Kabbalah in the Seventeenth Century*, 85.

100. Kaufmann, "Elia Menachem Chalfan," 501–2.

101. R. Ḥalfan depicts the persistence with which Christians pursued Jews who were learned in Kabbalah: "Especially after the rise of the sect of Luther, many of the nobles and scholars of the land [namely the Christians] sought to have a thorough knowledge of this glorious science. They have exhausted themselves in this search, because among our people there are but a small number of men expert in this wisdom, for after the great number of troubles and expulsions but a few remain. So seven learned men grasp a Jewish man by the hem of his garment and say: 'Be our master in this science.'" Idel, *Absorbing Perfection: Kabbalah and Interpretation*, 462.

102. Leon da Modena thus laments the diffusion of Kabbalah among non-Jews:

> But even several members of the uncircumcised nations [studied Kabbalah], as is well known about Giov[anni] Pico, Count of Miran-dola. Among the nine hundred theses he established and proposed at Rome, there were one hundred and sixteen that derived from this Kabbalah: forty-five from other authors and seventy-one of his own invention as I shall discuss later in chapter [thirty] of the third section, with the help of God. This very year I saw in the possession of a French gentile twelve manuscript books of Kabbalah in Hebrew, of the choiciest and most prominent by the aforementioned Count.

Cited in Dweck, *The Scandal of Kabbalah*, 158.

103. See Bonfil, *Cultural Change among the Jews of Early Modern Italy*, 13.

104. Stow, "The Burning of the Talmud in 1553," 457. For a general study on Christian Kabbalah, see Dan, *The Christian Kabbalah*.

105. For a comprehensive treatment on the textual traditions and reception associated with the Zohar, see Abrams, *Kabbalistic Manuscripts and Textual Theory*.

106. Yehudah Ḥayyat, Introduction to *Maʾarekhet ha-Elohut*, fol. 2a, cited in Huss, "*Sefer ha-Zohar* as a Canonical, Sacred, and Holy Text," 283.

107. Abrams, *Kabbalistic Manuscripts and Textual Theory*, 246.

108. Abrams, *Kabbalistic Manuscripts and Textual Theory*, 247. Abrams carefully traces Cordovero's own theories regarding how the various strata of the Zohar were created highlighting Cordovero's attempts to account for the striking inconsistencies that abound in the text. Abrams repeatedly underlines Cordovero's role as an editor, and not merely a commentator, by citing several examples from *Or Yakar* where Cordovero is shown to critically evaluate textual variants and makes decisions based on inference drawn from the manuscript evidence before him: "I went over all the manuscript witnesses and found agreement between

them." *Or Yakar*, vol. 21, cited in Abrams, *Kabbalistic Manuscripts and Textual Theory*, 254n60.

109. Boaz Huss enumerates four main scholarly positions in delineating the date or historical event associated with the canonization of the Zohar: (1) Gershom Scholem and Isaiah Tishby emphasized the Spanish Expulsion and its immediate aftermath as the turning point; (2) Roland Goetschel, who argued that the kabbalists of Safed played a decisive role in the canonization process in the sixteenth century; (3) Moshe Idel highlights the early fourteenth century as pivotal, just a few decades after the Zohar began to circulate in manuscript form; and (4) Zeev Gries, who argued for a significantly later date, the eighteenth century, when according to him the Zohar's unique status was unequivocally confirmed. See Huss, "*Sefer ha-Zohar* as a Canonical, Sacred, and Holy Text," 268–69.

110. Huss, "*Sefer ha-Zohar* as a Canonical, Sacred, and Holy Text," 259.

111. On the marginal penetration of the Zohar into the study programs and speculative universe of the Italian kabbalists in contrast to their Spanish counterparts, see Idel, *Kabbalah in Italy, 1280–1510*, 224–26. Furthermore, an important representative of the Italian Kabbalah, Yohanan Alemanno, omits any mention of the Zohar in his suggested book list, which he compiled around 1470, with the explicit aim of establishing a proper hierarchy among discrete disciplines of knowledge, including Torah, Talmud, philosophy, the sciences, Kabbalah, and magic. It is worth emphasizing that Alemanno reserved the highest level of intellectual attainment not for Kabbalah but for mastering the art of magical operations. See Idel, *Kabbalah in Italy, 1280–1510*, 343 and Idel, "The Study Program of Rabbi Yohanan Alemanno," 303–31.

112. Menaḥem Recanati was one of the first kabbalists to incorporate large sections of the Zohar into his kabbalistic compositions. His *Commentary on the Torah*, printed twice in the sixteenth century (Venice, 1523 and 1545), cited extensive passages from the Zohar. For more on Recanati, see Idel, *Rabbi Menahem Recanati: The Kabbalist*.

The sixteenth century produced two seminal examples of comprehensive commentaries on the Zohar: Shimeon ibn Lavi's, *Sefer Ketem Paz*, and Moses Cordovero's *Or Yakar*. On Ibn Lavi, see Huss, *Ketem Paz: The Kabbalistic Doctrine of Rabbi Shimeon Lavi in His Commentary of the Zohar* and Huss, *Sockets of Fine Gold: The Kabbalah of R. Shimon Ibn Lavi*. In addition the great legal Ashkenazi codifier, R. Moses Isserles also wrote a commentary to the *Zohar* extant in manuscript form, see Giller, *Reading the Zohar*, 28n194 and B. Richler, "From the Collections of the Institute of Microfilmed Hebrew Manuscripts," 196–197.

113. See Cooperman, "Political Discourse in a Kabbalistic Register," 47–68. See also his oral comments to Boaz Huss: http://condor.wesleyan.edu/openmedia/emw/video/2004/huss_2004.mov.

On the inclusion of *zoharic* and other kabbalistic ideas in sermons, see Bonfil, "Preaching as Mediation between Elite and Popular Cultures"; Horowitz,

"Speaking of the Dead"; Idel, "Judah Moscato"; and Saperstein, "Italian Jewish Preaching: An Overview."

114. Gueta, "The Hebrew Imprints of 'Shin' Years," 141.

115. I will engage the literature on Kabbalah and halakhah in greater depth in chapter 4, but certainly the works of Jacob Katz are pioneering in this field, see his, *Halakhah and Kabbalah*; "Halakhic Statements in the Zohar;" and "Post-Zoharic Relations between Halakhah and Kabbalah." Two other comprehensive sources are Hallamish, *The Kabbalah in Liturgy, Law, and Custom* and Ta-Shma, *The Revelaed within the Concealed*.

116. Cited in Hallamish, *The Kabbalah in Liturgy, Law, and Custom*, 167 using my translation.

117. Hallamish, *The Kabbalah in Liturgy, Law, and Custom*, 106 and 168.

118. The *Arba'ah Turim* was composed by R. Jacob ben Asher based on the legal positions of his father, R. Asher ben Yehiel, who fled from Ashkenazi lands and settled in Spain in the thirteenth century. The structure of the *Tur* became paradigmatic for the organization of other legal codes and influenced Joseph Qaro's own categorization and presentation of Jewish law in the *Shulhan Arukh*.

119. In Ibn Gabbai, *Tola'at Ya'akov*, fol. 16b, cited in Huss, "Sefer ha-Zohar as a Canonical, Sacred, and Holy Text," 280.

120. Elijah de Vidas, *Reshit Ḥokhmah*, "Sha'ar ha-Kedusha," chapter 16. Cited in Hallamish, *The Kabbalah in Liturgy, Law, and Custom*, 51, my translation.

121. Huss, "*Sefer ha-Zohar* as a Canonical, Sacred, and Holy Text," 277 and Elbogen, *Jewish Liturgy: A Comprehensive History*, 159–60.

122. Cooperman, "Organizing Knowledge for the Jewish Market: An Editor/ Printer in Sixteenth-Century Rome," 90.

123. An allusion to Habbakuk 2:14. This verse appears as a recurrent refrain in introductions to kabbalistic works that are written and printed in the sixteenth and seventeenth centuries. See Yissakhar Baer, *Yesh Sakhar*, Author's Introduction; Also, Cooperman, "Isaac de Lattes's 'Imprimatur' to the Mantua edition of the Zohar," as well as the online resource of the Early Modern Workshop: http://condor. wesleyan.edu/openmedia/emw/video/2009/cooperman_2009.mov.

124. Leviticus, 25:10. The context concerns the Jubilee year (*Yovel*) and the concept of freedom associated with it. For a general introduction on the kabbalistic significance of the Jubilee year, and the doctrine of cosmic cycles, see Gershom Scholem, *Kabbalah*, 116–21. Ḥayyat is citing from *Tikkunei Zohar*, fol. 23a–24b.

125. See Moshe Idel, *Kabbalah in Italy*, 215.

126. Slightly modified version of Boaz Huss's translation: http://www.wesleyan. edu/socsci/Develop/emw/workshops/summer04/huss/hayat/english2.html.

127. *Shemita* (sabbatical year) alludes to the seven-year agricultural cycle in the land of Israel, when Israel was commended by God to leave the land fallow and refrain from planting, pruning, and harvesting; see Leviticus 25:1–24.

128. *Pirkei Avot* 1:14.

129. Cooperman, "The 'Imprimatur' by Isaac de Lattes" in "*Early Modern Workshop: Jewish Resources*, vol. 6, 'Reading across Cultures,'" 23.

130. According to this theory, like the land that a Jew works for six years but leaves fallow in the seventh, the world also is sustained and nourished by God for a fixed period of 6,000 years and in the seventh it is destroyed. It is before this apocalyptic destruction of the world every seventh cycle that Messianic redemption becomes manifest. The highly esoteric notion of cosmic cycles are rarely discussed in writing by the kabbalists; one such exception is the *Sefer ha-Temunah,* see Gershom Scholem, *Kabbalah,* 120–22.

131. As a doctoral student participant, I am indebted to the presentation of Professor Bernard Dov Cooperman at the Radcliffe institute of Harvard University titled, "Technology, Preservation, and Freedom of Expression: Isaac de Lattes as Printer in Sixteenth-Century Italy." See the online resource of the Early Modern Workshop: http://condor.wesleyan.edu/openmedia/emw/video/2009/cooperman_2009.mov.

132. Stow, "The Burning of the Talmud in 1553," 440. On the censorship of Jewish books, see Baruchson-Arbib and Prebor, "Sefer ha-Ziquq" and the comprehensive treatment of Raz-Krakotzkin, *The Censor, the Editor, and the Text;* "The Censor as a Mediator," and "From Safed to Venice: The *Shulhan 'Arukh* and the Censor."

133. Raz-Krakotzkin, *The Censor, the Editor, and the Text,* 189–91.

134. Raz-Krakotzkin, *The Censor, the Editor, and the Text,* 190.

135. Raz-Krakotzkin, *The Censor, the Editor, and the Text,* "Major Trends in Italian Kabbalah between 1560–1660," 248–69.

136. The debate over the printing of the Zohar in Italy has been extensively discussed. See Isaiah Tishby's elaborate treatment in "The Debate over the Zohar in the Sixteenth Century in Italy"; see also Hacker, "A New Letter Regarding the Debate over the Printing of the Zohar in Italy"; Kupfer, "New Documents on the Controversy over the Printing of the *Zohar*"; and Assaf, "On the Controversy over the Printing of Kabbalistic Books." On the social consequences of the printing Kabbalah in Italy, see Bonfil, *Cultural Change,* 12–14.

137. R. Moshe Basola argued for instance that the elevation of the study of Kabbalah over Mishnah, Talmud, and Torah, would lead to the marginalization of rabbinic teachings, the abandonment of halakhic adherence, and the eventual loss of Jewish particularity, Raz-Krakotzkin, *The Censor, the Editor, and the Text,* 191.

138. Assaf, "On the Controversy over the Printing of Kabbalistic Books," 4.

139. *Sha'arei Orah* (Mantua, 1561) was written by R. Joseph Gikatilla in the thirteenth century and constitutes an important introduction to understanding the *sefirotic* system, see Scholem, *Kabbalah,* 59.

140. Cited in Dweck, *The Scandal of Kabbalah,* 73–74.

141. *Hilkhot Talmud Torah* 1:11–12.

142. It should be noted that even the kabbalist, R. Moses Cordovero, underlined the need for the student to gain proficiency in the traditional Jewish curriculum (Scripture, Mishnah, and Talmud) before embarking on the study of the Kabbalah, See Robinson, *Moses Cordovero's Introduction to Kabbalah*, 55–56.

143. In another place, Moses Cordovero also takes issue with the unregulated study of kabbalistic texts: "Some in our generation, study this wisdom [Kabbalah], without any preparatory study of Scripture, Mishnah and Gemarah, and undoubtedly they commit a grave error for several reasons." Cited in Elbaum, *Openness and Insularity*, 182.

144. Benayahu, *Yosef ha-Behiri*, 191–92 and 214–15. Benayahu cites Elijah de Vidas in his Introduction to *Reshit Hokhmah*, where he explains that he finally gained permission to print his work in 1579 four years after he had completed it.

145. Idel, *Absorbing Perfection*, 463. Idel explains that "foxes in the vineyard" is a literary trope that refers to heretics, who inflict damage either on Israel or on the Torah.

146. "Such a person should not aggrandize himself with false knowledge, saying 'the wisdom of Kabbalah is intended to benefit the masses,' for Kabbalah for him is only a way to make money for his own pocket." See Tishby, *Studies in Kabbalah and Its Branches*, 87.

147. Isaiah 35:6.

148. *Tikkunei ha-Zohar*, Mantua, 1557, fol. 1b.

149. Abrams, "When was the 'Introduction' to the Zohar Written"; Bendowska and Doktor, "*Sefer ha-Zohar*: The Battle for *Editio Princeps*," 143.

150. Raz-Krakotzkin, *The Censor, the Editor, and the Text*, 117–18. Raz-Krakotzkin emphasizes that this edict represents the first internal attempt by the Italian Jewish community to regulate individual copyright and exercise control over textual content.

151. Raz-Krakotzkin, *The Censor, the Editor, and the Text*, 118, where he cites the edict of R. Meir Katzenellenbogen, the Maharam of Padua, to enforce greater rabbinic control in suppressing the wide circulation and dissemination of esoteric ideas.

152. Bendowska and Doktor, "*Sefer ha-Zohar*: The Battle for *Editio Princeps*," 147.

153. Abrams carefully traces the ostensible typographic and semantic differences between the extant *editio princeps* printed in Mantua and Cremona. On the basis of these variances he concludes that there were two variant editions printed in Cremona and Mantua, respectively, giving us on total four slightly different editions, see "When was the 'Introduction' to the Zohar Written." See also Bendowska and Doktor, "*Sefer ha-Zohar*: The Battle for *Editio Princeps*," 146.

154. Bendowska and Doktor, "*Sefer ha-Zohar*: The Battle for *Editio Princeps*," 147.

155. The traditional expression for printing in Hebrew is *le-hosi la'or*, to bring to light.

156. Jacob Elbaum, *Openness and Insularity*, 184.

157. Elbaum, *Openness and Insularity*, 184. Elbaum cites a remarkable example that evinces the degree of prestige associated with citing the Zohar. The case in point is Abraham Rapoport, a famous Talmudist living in Poland at the end of the sixteenth through the middle of the seventeenth century, who concluded his bar mitzvah speech titled, *Neqi Khapayim*, by citing a passage from the Zohar. Rapoport's example confirms that those educated in elite *yeshivah* settings were expected to demonstrate familiarity with the Zohar, even at a fairly young age.

158. Anat Gueta, "The Hebrew Imprints of 'Shin' Years as a Resource for the Research of Jewish Society's Spiritual Life," 118, table 3.

Chapter 2

1. Cited in Rosman, "Innovative Tradition," 537.

2. Gueta, *The Hebrew Imprints of the Shin Years*, 183. The notably high number of Talmud/Mishnah tractates printed in Poland in comparison to Bohemia, may reflect the abundance of *yeshivot* in Polish lands, the educational curriculum of which became standardized, so that if a student moved and had to change his *yeshivah*, he was able to continue his studies exactly at the place where he left it off. See Shulvass, *Jewish Culture in Eastern Europe*, 83.

3. See Shulvass, *Jewish Culture in Eastern Europe*, 87. Shulvass notes that *yeshivah* heads preferred the to use the title *resh metivta*, the Aramaic designation, in their written correspondence, while the title *av bet din* was used to refer to the post of a communal rabbi. He further states that while in small towns these two positions were usually filled by one individual, in larger cities, these professions were kept separate. On the use of these titles see also, Katz, *Tradition and Crisis*, 142–43, 167–68, and 198–99.

4. Shulvass, *Jewish Culture in Eastern Europe*, 88.

5. Shulvass, *Jewish Culture in Eastern Europe*, 80.

6. Rabbi Jacob Polack and his student, Rabbi Shalom Shakhna, both *yeshiva* heads and legendary personalities in the history of Polish Jewry, refrained from writing down their teachings into books. Yet it is instructive that R. Shakhna's student, Hayyim ben Beṣalel (the Maharal of Prague) did not refrain from recording some of his teachings in his notebook: "I found written down in explaining Asheri (R. Asher ben Yehiel), which I wrote down as I studied Asheri with my teacher, Rabbi Shakhna." See Reiner, "The Ashkenazi Elite," 89 and Rosman, "Traditional Eastern European Jewish Book" (Prepared for Ninth Manfred R. Lehmann Workshop), 13.

7. Reiner, "A Biography of an Agent of Culture," 238.

8. Reiner, "A Biography of an Agent of Culture," 237–38.

9. Moses Shulvass, *Jewish Culture in Eastern Europe*, 95.

10. Rosman, "Innovative Tradition," 541.

11. Shulvass, *Jewish Culture in Eastern Europe*, 91 and Rosman, "Innovative Tradition," 532–33.

12. Shulvass, *Jewish Culture in Eastern Europe*, 91.

13. Rosman, "Innovative Tradition," 536–37.

14. Rosman, "Innovative Tradition," 537.

15. Rosman, "Innovative Tradition," 537.

16. Rosman, "Innovative Tradition," 538–39 and Shulvass, *Jewish Culture in Eastern Europe*, 92.

17. Rosman, "Innovative Tradition," 541.

18. Jacob Elbaum notes the lack of a thorough examination of certain types of kabbalistic works written by authors such as Yissakhar Baer, see *Openness and Insularity*, 191.

19. Scholem, "The Sabbatean Movement in Poland," 36. Jacob Elbaum observes wryly that in spite of Scholem's strong words regarding Kabbalah in Poland, he failed to consider and discuss the nature and types of compositions produced in Poland and Bohemia in this period; see Elbaum, *Openness and Insularity*, 191.

20. For a recent work on this Bracha Sack, *Keeper of the Orchard: The Kabbalist Shabbetai Sheftel Horovitz from Prague* (Jerusalem: Bialik, 2002) (Hebrew).

21. Two of his works were printed in the last decades of the sixteenth century: *Matenot Khehunah, Priestly Endowments* (Krakow, 1587/1588), is an explication of the Midrash Rabbah, using simple words and short passages to make it accessible for the less learned. His other work, *Mar'eh Kohen* (Krakow, 1589) is comprised of an index and recommendations for ethical conduct (*hanhagot*) collected from the Zohar. It is noteworthy that like David Darshan, he also studied at the famous *yeshivah* of Rabbi Moses Isserles, where he acquired knowledge of midrash, halakhah, and Kabbalah. See Gries, *Conduct Literature*, 71.

22. Elbaum, "Ethical Literature in Poland," 148.

23. Reiner, "A Biography of an Agent of Culture," 244.

24. Reiner, "A Biography of an Agent of Culture," 244.

25. Yissakhar Baer, *Meqor Ḥokhmah*, fol. 48a.

26. Yissakhar Baer, *Meqor Ḥokhmah*, fol. 48a.

27. Jacob Elbaum notes that both Fano and Gedalyah Cordovero, praise Yissakhar's Baer's ability to faithfully represent Moses Cordovero's Kabbalah, and yet *Meqor Ḥokhmah* to which these *haskamot* are appended does not discuss Cordovero's Kabbalah directly; see *Openness and Insularity*, 188. In my opinion, the printers may have acquired approbations for various works at different times, and decided to print them together at the end of *Meqor Ḥokhmah*.

28. Kahanah, *The Literature of Israeli Literature*, 220.

29. He is also called the *Levush* (garment), reflecting the title of his main composition.

30. Yissakhar Baer, *Meqor Ḥokhmah*, fol. 48a.

31. Baer, *Meqor Ḥokhmah*, fol. 48a.

32. The author of the popular commentary on the Torah, *Shnei Luḥot ha-Berit*, which incorporates different kabbalistic systems into its exegesis, including both Cordoverean and Lurianic Kabbalah. The work was printed in Amsterdam in 1649, by the author's son, R. Sheftel Horowitz. On R. Isaiah Horowitz see S. A. Horodetzky, *Ha-Mistorin be-Yisrael*, 54–113.

33. Yissakhar Baer, *Meqor Ḥokhmah*, fol. 48a.

34. Elbaum, *Openness and Insularity*, 188n24.

35. *Ẓafnat Pa'aneakh*, a name given to Joseph in Genesis 40:45.

36. Song of Songs 5:15.

37. Proverbs 24:26.

38. Allusion to Psalms 57:2.

39. Issakhar Baer, *Meqor Ḥokhmah*, fol. 48b.

40. Jacob Elbaum, *Openness and Insularity*, 189n27.

41. Gershom Scholem notes that evidence suggests that Sarug spent time in Poland and he must have played an instrumental role in spreading the Lurianic lore in Ashkenazi lands. See "The Sabbatean Movement in Poland," 37.

42. He was sometimes called Joseph ha-Ma'aravi, a reference to his North African extraction, probably from Dr'aa Morocco. Ibn Tabul belonged to the premier circle of Isaac Luria's students according to R. Hayyim Vital's hierarchical classification, see Fine, *Physician of the Soul, Healer of the Cosmos*, 83. See also, David, *To Come to the Land*, 159.

43. The expression used in Hebrew: *yo'sim ve-lo yo'se*. Issakhar Baer, *Meqor Ḥokhmah*, fol. 48b.

44. Garb, "The Kabbalists of Prague," 349. Garb lists the following works as reflective of each academic's position on this questions: Tishby, "Debate between the Kabbalah of the Ari and the Kabbalah of the Ramak" in *Studies in Kabbalah and Its Branches*, 177–254; Elliot R. Wolfson, "The Influence of the Ari on the Shelah;" Idel, "One from a Town, Two from a Clan;" Gries, *Conduct Literature*, 76. See also Bracha Sack, "The Influence of Cordovero on Seventeenth-Century Jewish Thought."

45. Menaḥem Azariah da Fano, *Pelaḥ ha-Rimon*, fol. 4a.

46. These are two of the most recondite compositions within *zoharic* literature. Daniel Matt observes that there is an interpretive reciprocity between these texts, so that the *Sifra di-Sniuta* (*Book of Concealment*) functions as a Mishnah, which the *Idra* (*Threshing Floor*) interprets and expands. Daniel Matt, *Zohar* (Pritzker Edition), vol. 5, 535. See also Huss, "Anthologies of Zohar Commentaries."

47. Menaḥem Azariah da Fano, *Pelaḥ ha-Rimon*, Venice 1600, fol. 4a. A short excerpt of this passage is cited by Dweck, *The Scandal of Kabbalah*, 138.

48. According to Boaz Huss, Hayyim Vital was the first to associate Cordovero's method of studying Kabbalah with *peshat* in his *Sefer ha-Ḥezyonot*. In this book, Vital describes a dream in which he inquires from Cordovero whether his or Luria's system is the one promulgated in the heavenly academy. Cordovero's reply reflects Fano's own formulation: "Both methods are true: my method is

according to the plain way (*peshat*), appropriate for the beginners in this wisdom. The way of your master [i.e., Isaac Luria], on the other hand, is the inner and principal one. Now that I am in the supernal realm, I also study only according to the method of your master"; see Huss, "Anthologies of Zohar Commentaries," 10–11. Since, however, Vital's book was not printed until the twentieth century, Fano's dichotomy between the two kabbalistic schools represents one of the earliest explicit and printed formulations on this question.

49. For a recent article devoted to the impact of R. Solomon Shlomiel of Dresnitz's hagiographic accounts of Safed in the late sixteenth century, see Koch, "Of Stinging Nettles and Stones."

50. Delmedigo, *Ta'alumot Hokhmah*, fol. 42a.

51. Delmedigo, *Ta'alumot Hokhmah*, fol. 42a.

52. Delmedigo, *Ta'alumot Hokhmah*, fol. 42a. On Israel Sarug's activities to spread Lurianic teachings to the kabbalists of Italy in the last decade of the sixteenth century, see Scholem, "Israel Sarug—Disciple of Luria?"; Barzilay, *Yoseph Shlomo Delmedigo*, 226n5; and Ronit Meroz, "Contrasting Opinions."

53. Ruderman, *Early Modern Jewry*, 26.

54. Delmedigo, *Ta'alumot Hokhmah*, fol. 42b. R. Solomon Shlomiel explicitly alludes to this ban in his letter to Yissakhar Baer.

55. R. Abraham Azulay, the author of zoharic anthologies, *Or ha-Hamah* and *Or ha-Ganuz*, written in the first two decades of the seventeenth century, states that he immersed himself in the study of Zohar in his hometown Fez, but wanted to learn more than what his teachers in North Africa could provide. After reading the *Pardes Rimonim*, he decided to travel to the land of Israel in search of Cordovero's commentary on the Zohar, *Or Yakar*. Once there he became acquainted with Lurianic Kabbalah and accepted its supremacy over Cordovero's method. See Huss, "Anthologies of Zohar Commentaries," 5 and 11.

56. Scholem, "The Sabbatean Movement in Poland," 37. On Israel Sarug's visit to Poland to disseminate Lurianic teachings among the rabbis there, especially regarding transmigration and soul roots, see Scholem, *Sabbatai Sevi*, 79n117. One of the first few exponents of Lurianic Kabbalah in Poland was Nathan Neta Shapira in his *Megalleh 'Amuqot* printed in 1637. On this kabbalist, see the article of Agata Paluch, "The Ashkenazi Profile of Kabbalah," and her more recent book, *Megalleh 'Amuqot*. More discussion on Shapira can be found in Scholem, *Sabbatai Sevi: The Mystical Messiah*, 80–81.

57. Benayahu, *Toldot ha-Ari*, 42–43.

58. Regarding these rabbis see David, *To Come to the Land*, 131. For Dresnitz's letter see Delmedigo, *Ta'alumot Hokhmah*, fol. 42a and Benayahu, *Toldot ha-Ari*, 43.

59. Which corresponds to Exodus 27:20–30:10.

60. Zeilig explains in his introduction that he copied these excerpts from a manuscript, which suggests that some parts of *Yod'ei Binah* circulated in such a form even after the author's death. See Aharon Zeilig, *'Amudei Sheva* (Krakow

1635), fol. 2b. See also Jacob Elbaum, *Openness and Insularity*, 193n39 and Boaz Huss, *Like the Radiance of the Sky*, 185n24.

61. Benayahu notes that it is unclear why it was not printed, whether perhaps due to its large size, as even Yissakhar Baer refers to it in his introduction to *Pith ei Yah*, as "my large composition, my commentary on *Sefer ha-Zohar*," *Pithei Yah*, Prague 1609, fol. 1b. Another possibility, suggests Benayahu, is that perhaps some of the Ari's writings may have reached him later on and he wanted to change parts of his original composition. See Benayahu, *Toldot ha-Ari*, 44.

I do not think that the Luria's writings would have reached Yissakhar Baer at this time. They were still promulgated mostly in manuscript form, with a limited circulation and constituted expensive investments. In addition, R. Solomon Shlomiel himself refrains from revealing too much about Lurianic ideas in the letter. Instead, he urges Yissakhar Baer to muster strength and journey to the Land of Israel in order to learn the Ari's Kabbalah first hand. See Joseph Delmedigo, *Ta'alumot Hokhmah*, fol. 47b.

62. *Those Who Know Understanding*, this expression comes from 1 Chronicles 12:33 and the word *binah* is used in this context to refer to those who can properly interpret the signs of the times to determine what the right action is for the Jewish people.

63. Proverbs 24:32.

64. Allusion to Psalms 60:13. For this excerpt see Yissakhar Baer, *Yesh Sakhar*, Prague 1609, fol. 1b.

65. Delmedigo, *Ta'alumot Hokhmah*, fol. 43a.

66. Joseph Delmedigo, *Ta'alumot Hokhmah*, fol. 47b. The *urim* and *thummim* were precious stones set in the breast plate of the High Priest, which were used to inquire from God in times of need, see Exodus 28:30.

67. Joseph Delmedigo, *Ta'alumot Hokhmah*, fol. 47b and Meir Benayahu, *Toldot ha-Ari*, 44. It should be noted that at the time of this correspondence Vital had already moved and resided in Damascus moving there in 1597 (Moshe Feierstein ed. *Sefer Hezyonot: Book of Visions* (Jerusalem: Makhon ben Zvi, 2006), 22. This discrepancy raises a number of possibilities: first, that even though Vital was residing in Damascus, the proper place to receive his teaching was in Safed where his students were presumably active at this time; second, that Vital may have traveled back to Safed on occasion to transmit his knowledge directly as the distance between Damascus and Safed is less than 100 kilometers.

68. His name does not appear in *Sefer ha-Kremenets*, which records the rabbinic personalities in the Jewish community of Kremenets.

69. Jacob Elbaum, *Openness and Insularity*, 193n39. In another kabalistic work, *Emeq ha-Melekh* printed in 1648, fol. 13a, he is listed among the dead.

70. See *Family Tree of the Rivlin Family*, compiled by Eliezer ben ha-Rav Benjamin Rivlin (Jerusalem: 1935), under the number 2 in the second generation of the family; Yissakhar Baer is mentioned under 3 as part of the third generation.

71. Alexandr Putik, "Review of Abraham David, ed., *Anonymous Hebrew Chronicle from Early Modern Prague,*" *Judaica Bohemiae* 48, 2 (2013): 136. See also Koppelman Lieben, *Gal Ed: Grabsteininschriften des prager ihr. alten Friedhofs* (Prague: Landau, 1856), 62–63 and Simon Hock, *Die Familien Prags: Nach den Epitaphien des alten Jüdischen Friedhofs in Prag* (Pressburg: Alkalay, 1892), 233, col. B, no. 2482.

72. David Lidda, *Sod ha-Shem*, Amsterdam, 1680 or 1694, 2 and 4. See Benayahu, *Toldot ha-Ari*, 43.

73. The description of this work is based on Heller, *The Seventeenth Century Hebrew Book*, 231.

74. Heller, *The Seventeenth Century Hebrew Book*, 231. I modified the translation slightly.

75. Heller, *The Seventeenth Century Hebrew Book*, 255.

76. Cited in Heller, *The Seventeenth Century Hebrew Book*, 255.

77. This section is borrowed from Heller, *The Seventeenth Century Book*, 239.

78. Reiner, "A Biography of an Agent of Culture," 233–34.

79. Reiner, "A Biography of an Agent of Culture," 234–36.

80. See Olga Sixtova, "Jewish Printers and Printing Presses in Prague 1512–1670 (1672)," 48–49. Heller, *The Seventeenth Century Book*, liv–lv and 479. See also Moritz Steinschneider, *Catalogus Librorum Hebraeorum in Bibliotheca Bodleiana* (Berlin: Friedlander, 1852–1860), col. 2970 and Zunz, "The Gersonids," *Scientific Journal of Jewish Theology* 5 (1844): 35–44.

81. Heller, *The Seventeenth Century Book*, 257.

82. Heller, *The Seventeenth Century Book*, 259.

83. This section is based on Heller, *The Seventeenth Century Book*, 265. *Keli Yakar* was the author's homiletic commentary on the Torah.

Chapter 3

1. Lombard, *Libri Sententiarum*, Preface, cited in Hamesse, "The Scholastic Model of Reading," 109.

2. *Florilegium* comprised a literary genre consisting of excerpted passages from authoritative writings culled together by Christian scholars and writers. The term comes from the Latin *flores*, flowers and *legere*, to collect. See Ann Blair, *Too Much to Know*, 34–35.

3. Jacqueline Hamesse explains that the establishment of the first universities in Europe in the twelfth century led to an unprecedented explosion in the availability of books, which in turn transformed in a fundamental way the organization of knowledge in scholastic circles. Scholars and students who sought to cope with the information overload required specific working tools to access and cognitively assimilate the new material, see "The Scholastic Model of Reading," 108–9.

4. Jacqueline Hamesse, "The Scholastic Model of Reading," 113. Original works stored in libraries as large manuscripts, were very difficult to consult and

replicate. Parchment was very expensive and copying was expensive and labor intensive. Easy and quick consultation of short summaries made knowledge accumulation more effective.

5. Aristotelian florilegia, for instance, served an important function to facilitate comprehension of a required but highly abstract and difficult body of knowledge that comprised a compulsory subject matter within the university curriculum. Hamesse, "The Scholastic Model of Reading," 113.

6. Jacqueline Hamesse, "The Scholastic Model of Reading," 111.

7. Hamesse, "The Scholastic Model of Reading," 115.

8. Hamesse, "The Scholastic Model of Reading," 112.

9. Jacqueline Hamesse, "The Scholastic Model of Reading," 116. Philosophic works were especially fertile grounds for the cultivation of heretical thoughts and therefore Jordan of Saxony decreed that Dominican friars were barred from reading such works without the guidance and interpretation of a senior Dominican cleric.

10. Ann Blair, *Too Much to Know*, 35.

11. Blair, *Too Much to Know*, 236.

12. Blair, *Too Much to Know*, 237. Ann Blair cites and interesting example of acquiring reference tools for the explicit use of correctors, who worked in print shops. In 1563, the humanist printer, Plantin, bought volumes of reference works in Antwerp: four thesauruses, seven dictionaries, two Biblical concordances, a Latin Bible, and a Greek New Testament.

13. Ann Blair, *Too Much to Know*, 254. See also Elizabeth L. Eisenstein, *The Printing Press as an Agent of Change*, 398, on the decline of ecclesiastical influence on the activities of Italian printing presses.

14. Cited in Ann Blair, *Too Much to Know*, 254.

15. Cited in Cooperman, "Organizing Knowledge for the Jewish Market," 95. I thank Prof. Cooperman for sharing his unpublished work with me.

16. Galinsky, "On Popular Halakhic Literature," 320–21. On the abridgments of the medieval halakhic code, the *Mordechai*, see Zeev Gries, *Conduct Literature*, 55. Zeev Gries differentiates between two types of halakhic abridgments: those used for individual study and another, which encompassed instruction on legal jurisprudence.

17. Ta-Shma, "Rabbi Joseph Caro and His *Beit Yosef*: Between Spain and Germany," 192–97.

18. Proverbs 7:4.

19. Qaro here plays on the double meaning of wisdom: on the one hand, his digest will help Jews become more confident in their knowledge of legal matters; at the same time, increased halakhic wisdom and knowledge will make them cognizant of the minutiae of the Biblical precepts, such as the laws concerning incest.

20. Song of Songs 4:4.

21. Qaro, *Shulḥan Arukh*, Introduction.

22. The first edition was printed in Venice in 1565.

23. Cited in Dweck, *The Scandal of Kabbalah*, 55.

24. Gries, *Conduct Literature*, 55.

25. Fine, *Safed Spirituality*, 87.

26. For a comprehensive treatment of digests to de Vidas's *Reshit Ḥokhmah* see Pachter, "The Book *Reshit Ḥokhmah*."

27. A case in point is Menaḥem Azariah da Fano, who explains in his introduction to *Pelaḥ ha-Rimon*, that the leaders of the Jewish community in Venice pleaded with him to teach them a section of the *Pardes* every day. See Dweck, *The Scandal of Kabbalah*, 147.

28. The National Library of Israel has a holding of close to fifty manuscripts of the *Pardes Rimonim* that display a striking variance within each copy.

29. Stern, *The Anthology in Jewish Literature*, 4–5.

30. G. Thomas Tanselle, *A Rationale of Textual Criticism* (Philadelphia: University of Pennsylvania Press), 1992).

31. On his works see Avivi, "The Writings of R. Menahem Azariah da Fano on Kabbalah"; Altmann, "Notes on the Development of Rabbi Menahem Azariah Fano's Kabbalistic Doctrine." *Jerusalem Studies in Jewish Thought* 3 (1983/4).

32. On Mordeḥai Dato, his life and works, see Jakobson, *Along the Path of Exile and Redemption*.

33. Job 11:9.

34. Literally, "who poured water," a reference to discipleship.

35. Genesis 19:11. Contextually, the Sodomites in this passage are blinded by God for their evil intention to harm Lot's two guests.

36. Literally, "there can be no sour grapes worse than them," invoking Jeremiah 31:2.

37. I Samuel 18:3, an allusion to the type of love that characterized the relationship of King David and Jonathan, the son of King Saul.

38. Literally "wallowing in the blood of confusion," the entire sentence is evocative of Ezekiel 16:6.

39. *Assis Rimonim*, Mantua 1623, fol. 1a–b.

40. Oxford 359 (17278) folios 91–175 which is a highly corrupt copy barely visible in places and another Oxford 1806 (18098), an incomplete manuscript on folios 1–76. Benayahu notes that they were both copied in Italy. See Meir Benayahu, *Yosef ha-Behiri*, 216. I would like to thank Dr. Yoed Kadary for bringing these manuscripts to my attention.

41. According to his admission he finished the work in 1605 on the seventh day of Shevet, *ha-Netzo ha-Rimonim*, Oxford 359, fol. 175a. Cited in Benayahu, *Yosef ha-Behiri*, 118.

42. *Ha-Netzo ha-Rimonim*, Oxford 359, fol. 91a.

43. Benayahu, *Yosef ha-Behiri*, 221.

44. Benayahu, *Yosef ha-Behiri*, 219.

45. Benayahu, *Yosef ha-Behiri*, 219.

46. Benayahu, *Yosef ha-Behiri*, 221.

47. Menaḥem Azaria da Fano, *Pelaḥ ha-Rimon*, Venice, 1601, Introduction, fol. 4b.

48. Daniel 12:3.

49. A variant of Daniel 12:3 and 12:10.

50. *Pithei Yah*, Prague 1609, Folio 1a.

51. Numbers 8:1.

52. *Pithei Yah*, Prague 1609, fol. 1a. The expression, "one from a town and two from a clan," comes from Jeremiah 3:14, and it is a recurrent expression in Jewish literature invoked to describe the exceptional and infrequent nature of an event or deed. For more on the use of this expression especially in seventeenth-century kabbalistic texts and correspondence, see Idel, "One from a Town, Two from a Clan," especially 85–91. For identification of this passage, see Idel, "One from a Town, Two from a Clan," 100n30.

53. *Pithei Yah*, Prague 1609, fol. 1a.

54. See Babylonian Talmud, Tractate *Hagigah* 14b.

55. Robinson, "Moses Cordovero and Kabbalistic Education in the Sixteenth Century," 157.

56. Elbaum, "The Influence of Spanish-Jewish Culture," 187. See also Elbaum, *Openness and Insularity*, 186.

57. It seems from this passage that he was able to secure some approbations from the kabbalists in the land Israel in spite of the negative reaction to his work as revealed by R. Solomon Shlomiel of Dresnitz in his reply to Yissakhar Baer. His words indicate here that at this point he was ready and prepared to publish his major commentary on the Zohar, *Yod'ei Binah*. In his introduction to *Yesh Sakhar*, however, he informs the reader that it was too expensive for him to print this work and had to put it off until such time that he would become financially more established.

58. *Pithei Yah*, Prague 1609, Folio 1a.

59. The human potential to unlock divine mysteries with the use of the rational intellect was regarded as limited at best, and therefore proper instruction in Kabbalah could only derive from an authoritative master who himself received esoteric wisdom from a reliable transmitter, see Eitan P. Fishbane, *As Light Before Dawn*, 54.

60. See Robinson, "Moses Cordovero and Kabbalistic Education," 157. See also, Bracha Sack, "Galut Yisrael ve-Galut ha-Shekhinah be *Or Yakar* le-Rabbi Moshe Cordovero," and Scholem, *Major Trends in Jewish Mysticism*, 408n13.

61. Allusion to BT *Shabbat* 104a: "Resh Lakish said, 'If one comes to defile himself, he is provided an opening; if one comes to purify himself, he is assisted.'" (For this translation I used Daniel Matt, *The Zohar: Pritzker Edition*, vol. 2, 1.)

62. For a similar expression see 2 Samuel 22:37 and Psalms 18:37.

63. The wording here follows Isaiah 9:6.

64. Genesis 1:15.

65. Malachi 3:23.

66. Isaiah 11:9. This verse from Isaiah is a recurrent phrase found usually as part of an author's preface in a number of kabbalistic guides and manuals that I examined in this period. This observation is quite significant because it highlights the self-perception of the kabbalists in this period, who perceived their importance in the period as unique in that kabbalists had a major role to play and to some extent were obliged to educate the populous and raise their awareness of the esoteric overtones in traditional Jewish texts, liturgy, and ritual.

67. *Sefer Yezirah,* Mishnah 3.

68. Cordovero also engaged this topic later in the *Pardes,* in Gate 1, chapter 8, but his discussion is more focused on the relationship between the *Sefirot* and the Divine, examining more specifically if the *Sefirot* could reflect changes in God or not. In other words, he poses the question of whether the ubiquitous multiplicity in the number of the *sefirot,* ten in total, denotes a multiplicity in the Godhead as well.

69. See *Ma'arekhet ha-Elohut,* chapter 1 and chapter 2, respectively.

70. See Maimonides, *Guide of the Perplexed,* fol. 50a–56b, especially fol. 51b and 52a, where he discusses Biblical references to God's limbs and sensory organs, such as "the hand of the Lord," "the mouth of the Lord," and so on and wrestles with integrating them into a rationalistic framework.

71. *Pithei Yah,* Prague 1609, fol. 1b.

72. Moses Isserles was a major proponent of harmonizing Kabbalah and philosophy and regarded these essentially distinct fields as forming an integral part of the Rabbinic tradition. Isserles repeats this notion several times in *Torat ha-Olah*: "For the science of Kabbalah is [identical with] the science of philosophy except that they speak in two [different] languages." (*Torat ha-Olah,* part 3, chapter 4). Cited in Lawrence Kaplan, "Rationalism and Rabbinic Culture," 79 and 90.

73. On this Kabbalist see Horodetzky, *Ha-Mistorin ba-Yisrael,* 7–13.

74. Again it is helpful to recall that Cordovero uses 32, Gallico 32, and Fano 22 gates to present kabbalistic content, and thus Yissakhar Baer's structure displays no affinity with either the original work or its Venice abridgements.

75. Kaplan, "Rationalism and Rabbinic Culture," 76.

76. Kaplan, "Rationalism and Rabbinic Culture," 76.

77. Kaplan, "Rationalism and Rabbinic Culture," 78.

78. *Pithei Yah,* Prague 1609, fol. 7a.

79. Kaplan, "Rationalism and Rabbinic Culture," fol. 5a.

80. I note here that Cordovero's original work, the *Pardes* uses the methods of rationalistic philosophical discourse to organize and present the subject matter, which includes the occasional reference to Maimonides and his works.

81. See Cordovero, *Pardes Rimonim,* Gate 1, chapter 8.

82. *Pithei Yah,* Prague 1609, fol. 1b.

83. *Pithei Yah,* Prague 1609, fol. 2a.

84. These sources are incorporated into different chapters of Gate 1 in the *Pardes*. Rav Ḥai Gaon's responsum, the *Baraʾita* of Shimon the Righteous, and *The Bahir*, are all discussed in Gate 1, chapter 7, see *Pardes Rimonim*, Krakow 1592, fol. 9a–b.

85. *Pitḥei Yah*, Prague, 1609, fol. 10b.

Chapter 4

1. An earlier version of this section was published as a chapter in Maoz and Gondos (eds.), *From Antiquity to the Postmodern World: Contemporary Jewish Studies in Canada*, permission was granted for using it here.

2. The ethical will of R. Shabbtai Sheftel Horowitz, cited in Rosman, "Innovative Traditions," 549.

3. See especially Katz, "Halakhic Statements in the Zohar," 9–30; "Post-Zoharic Relations between Halakha and Kabbalah," 31–55; and "Halakhah and Kabbalah as Competing Disciplines of Study," 56–87.

4. While from the rabbinic period on, halakhah enjoyed greater weight and prestige than aggadah in defining Jewish ritual life, Marc Saperstein incisively notes that these two disciplines cannot be regarded as entirely distinct. For one, the Talmud adopts a literary format in which these rabbinic genres appear intertwined and complementary, therefore, questioning the authority of the aggadic material would consequently undermine the validity of the halakhic exegesis. He further argues, that in the Talmud a *Tanna* or *Amora* often pronounces both legal and homiletic statements and if one were to question any aspect of their aggadic sayings it would surely cast doubt on their legal ruling as well. See *Decoding the Rabbis: A Thirteenth-Century Commentary on the Aggadah*, 10–11.

5. Katz, *Divine Law in Human Hands: Case Studies in Halakhic Flexibility*, 57.

6. Katz, *Divine Law in Human Hands*, 57.

7. Such as Alfasi's *Sefer ha-Halakhot* (eleventh century), Maimonides's *Mishneh Torah* (twelfth century), Mordechai ben Hillel's *Sefer Mordehai* (thirteenth century), Isaac ben Moses' *Or Zarua* (thirteenth century), Asher ben Yehiel's *Pisqei ha-Rosh* (thirteenth century), and Jacob ben Asher's *Arbaʾah Turim* (fourteenth century), to include some of the most outstanding examples of the codificatory activity of this time.

8. Katz, *Divine Law in Human Hands*, 32.

9. Meir Sendor observes that medieval legists relied on a principle, formulated in the Geonic period that defined the relationship between the Talmud and other extra-Talmudic literature commonly known as *baraʾitot*. According to Amram Gaon in the ninth century: "Any *baraʾita* that is not contradicted by the Talmud of our Rabbis the Amoraim, the accepted law is according to it . . . Any *barʾaita* that is contradicted by the Talmud, the accepted law is not according to

it . . . Therefore there is no absolute status to the *Tosefta, Sifra,* and *Sifrei,*" Sendor, "The Rule of Admissibility of Kabbalah in Halakhah," 274. This precedent continued to be applied in the Middle Ages by halakhists such as R. Joseph Qaro and R. Abraham Zacuto, as a model to define the admissibility of kabbalistic legal positions into normative halakhah. See Sendor, "The Rule of Admissibility of Kabbalah in Halakhah," 269 and 274.

On the limitations of a theological compromise between the Talmud and rationalism, see I. Epstein, who maintained that Maimonides' Code excluded certain Talmudic formularies and imperatives that were irreconcilable with his rationalistic proclivity. Cited in Katz, *Divine Law in Human Hands: Case Studies in Halakhic Flexibility,* 33n2.

10. For a survey of the relationship between philosophy and Kabbalah in the late-sixteenth to early-seventeenth-century Ashkenaz, see Joseph Davis, *M. Yom Tov Lipmann Heller,* 5–7 and 39–65. Robert Bonfil provides a broad analysis of this question with a larger geographical and temporal scope, including Spain and Italy; see *Rabbis and Jewish Communities in Renaissance Italy,* 280–98. See also Twersky, "Talmudists, Philosophers, Kabbalists: The Quest for Spirituality in the Sixteenth Century"; Ira Robinson, "Halakhah, Kabbalah, and Philosophy in the Thought of Joseph Jabez;" and Lawrence Kaplan, "Rabbi Mordekhai Jaffe and the Evolution of Jewish Culture in Poland in the Sixteenth Century."

11. Katz, *Divine Law in Human Hands,* 59–60. See also Bonfil, *Rabbis and Jewish Communities in Renaissance Italy,* 280–98.

12. On the general cultural and intellectual effects of printing see Eisenstein, *The Printing Revolution in Early Modern Europe.* See also Ruderman's concise summary on the aftermath of Jewish book printing, *Early Modern Jewry,* 103–11. On the consequences of Medieval Jewish scribal practices see Beit-Arie, "Publication and Reproduction," 225–47. On the circulation of ethical literature see Elbaum, *Openness and Insularity,* and Gries, *Conduct Literature.* Gries provides a comprehensive overview of the place and role of the book in Jewish culture from the early modern period to 1900 in *The Book in the Jewish World 1700–1900.* For a recent treatment of the scholarship and major approaches to the cultural, intellectual, and religious impact of the Jewish book, see the focused essays by Adam Shear, Lawrence H. Schiffman, Yaacob Dweck, and Jeffrey Shandler, in *AJS Review* 34 (2010): 353–75.

13. David Ruderman, *Early Modern Jewry,* 99–100.

14. Ta-Shma's essay, "The Law Is in Accord with the Later Authority-*Hilkhata Kebatrai,*" traces important issues concerning various principles that guided the halakhic decision-making process and authorization in the Middle Ages. He draws attention to the fact that due to a lack of centralization, Ashkenazi legal deliberations were more localized than their Sephardic counterparts, allowing greater freedom for individual jurists to flex and adjust the law to local customs and needs. By contrast, in Sephardic lands, jurists would rely on the great halakhists

of the past whose legal opinions they held as normative and binding, see 106–7. See also Ruderman, *Early Modern Jewry*, 101.

15. Davis, *Yom Tov Lipmann Heller*, 252.

16. The active role printers played in diffusing halakhic codes and expanding their authority beyond the mandates ascribed to them by their original authors in order to increase their own sales and revenue can be discerned in R. Ḥayyim ben Beẓalel's criticism regarding the applicability of Isserles' *Torat ha-Ḥatat* for German lands: "There is great need to assert the differences between the customs of the Jews of Germany [*benei Ashkenaz*] and those of the land of Poland . . . Rabbi [Isserles] himself in his introduction [to *Torat ha-Ḥatat*] did not mention the customs of Germany at all, but only those of his own land . . . One may see that he expressed uncertainty whether the book applies to German Jews [*benei Ashkenaz*] or not. So the printer added that on his own and mentioned Germany as well on the title page, so that he would increase his sales in all those lands, because buyers always look at the beginning of the book." See Davis, "The Reception of the *Shulhan 'Arukh*," 264.

17. Ruderman, *Early Modern Jewry*, 101–2. In addition, Elchanan Reiner reflects on the complexities between oral and written texts in sixteenth-century Ashkenaz and asserts that authority was ascribed to oral and not written transmission based on the unique educational paradigms regnant in the Ashkenazi *yeshivot* (academies) of the time; see "The Ashkenazi Elite at the Beginning of the Modern Era: Manuscript versus Printed Book." As such, especially in halakhic matters, the written text served more as a notebook, designed to aid the memorization and learning of the student rather than constituting an authoritative source for halakhic deliberations.

18. Rachel Elior discusses the attempts by sixteenth century kabbalists such as Hayyim Vital to realign the relationship between Kabbalah and halakhah. Based on a *zoharic* dichotomy, Vital suggested that Kabbalah represented *Etz ha-Hayyim* (Tree of Life) or the spiritual-eternal aspect of Torah, while halakhah constituted *Etz ha-Da'at* (Tree of Knowledge), or the literal-legal aspect of the Torah. Vital affirmed the superiority of the former, with the attendant program to seek out and reveal the esoteric, concealed facet latent not only in the Torah, but more specifically, in Jewish law; see "Messianic Expectations," 40–41.

On the diffusion of rules and conduct literature in the sixteenth and seventeenth centuries, which were deeply infused with mystical-kabbalistic ideology, see Pachter, "Kabbalistic Ethical Literature in Sixteenth-Century Safed."

19. Werblowsky, *Joseph Karo—Lawyer and Mystic* and Werblowsky, "R. Joseph Caro, Solomon Molcho and Don Joseph Nasi."

20. Printed in 1551, Qaro began working on it in 1522, see Ta-Shma, "Rabbi Joseph Caro and His *Beit Yosef*," 194–95.

21. Ta-Shma, "Rabbi Joseph Caro and His *Beit Yosef*," 197.

22. Ta-Shma, "Rabbi Joseph Caro and His *Beit Yosef*," 194.

23. Ta-Shma, "Rabbi Joseph Caro and His *Beit Yosef,*" 200. Loops and the clasps refer to the construction of the Tabernacle, where these diverse implements are joined together in order to yield a unified structure.

24. An important study on the universal cosmic dimensions of Yosef Qaro's thought is Maoz Kahana, "Cosmos and Nomos: Rabbi Joseph Karo and Shabtai Zvi as Portable Heavenly Temples." *El Prezente: Journal for Sephardic Studies* 10 (2016): 143–53.

25. On the admissibility of halakhic conduct communicated via dreams, visions, and angelic intermediaries into normative law see Werblowsky, *Joseph Karo: Lawyer and Mystic*, 39–47 and 183–84. Furthermore, Werblowsky points to several instances where Qaro repeatedly rejects the *maggid*'s exhortations in matters of halakhah, see *Joseph Karo: Lawyer and Mystic*, 169–88. See also, Hallamish, *Kabbalah: In Liturgy, Halakah and Customs*, 127–35.

26. Werblowsky points to several instances where Qaro repeatedly rejects the *maggid*'s exhortations in matters of halakhah, see *Joseph Karo: Lawyer and Mystic*, 169–88. Also see Hallamish, *Kabbalah: In Liturgy, Halakah and Customs*, 127–35.

27. See Twersky, "The *Shulhan 'Aruk*: Enduring Code of Jewish Law," 153. Twersky also draws attention to the fact that the *Shulhan Arukh* departed completely from the legal convention of his predecessors in the following ways: (1) omission of conflicting, multivocal and diverse halakhic opinions that are so characteristic of the Talmudic rhetoric and other medieval halakhic compendia; (2) lack of interpretive comments and discussions; and (3) a pervasive absence of "ideology, theology and teleology," see "The *Shulhan 'Aruk*: Enduring Code of Jewish Law," 152–53.

28. Raz-Krakotzkin, "From Safed to Venice: The *Shulhan 'Arukh* and the Censor," 97.

29. Raz-Krakotzkin, "From Safed to Venice: The *Shulhan 'Arukh* and the Censor," 99.

30. The *Shulhan Arukh* was the only Hebrew publication that was reprinted multiple times during the lifetime of its author: Venice 1564–65; Venice 1567 (twice); Salonica 1567; Venice 1574. After Qaro's death but still within the sixteenth century: Venice 1577–78, 1597–98.

For translating the many Biblical phrases and allusions evoked by Yissakhar Baer in his introduction, I relied for the most part on the JPS Tanakh (Philadelphia 2003).

31. Job 29:4.

32. Genesis 16:13.

33. Isaiah 60:22.

34. Psalms 68:17.

35. Isaiah 40:26.

36. Isaiah 40:29.

37. Job 13:13

38. 2 Samuel 18:19 or 22.

39. Job 11:6.

40. Job 33:30, words in parentheses added by the author.

41. Isaiah 30:26 the word order differs here than in the original Biblical verse.

42. Ecclesiastes 11:7.

43. Daniel 12:3.

44. "Those who know how to interpret," comes from 1 Chronicles 12:33 and the word *binah* is used in this context to refer to those who can properly interpret the signs of the times to determine the right action for Israel. This work of Yissakhar Baer was never printed and is no longer extant.

45. Proverbs 24:32.

46. Allusion to Psalms 60:13.

47. Allusion to BT *Shabbat* 104a: " 'Resh Lakish said, 'If one comes to defile himself, he is provided an opening; if one comes to purify himself, he is assisted.' " (For this translation I used *The Zohar: Pritzker Edition*, vol. 2, 1.)

48. For a similar expression see 2 Samuel 22:37 and Psalms 18:37.

49. The wording here is close to Isaiah 9:6.

50. Genesis 1:15.

51. Malachi 3:23.

52. Isaiah 11:9.

53. Job 33:30, author's addition in parentheses.

54. This fact is supported by R. Mordechai Yaffe's magnum opus, *Levush Malkhut*, in which an entire section, *Even Yeqarah*, is devoted to a supercommentary on Recanati's original explication of the *Zohar*.

55. Zeev Gries highlights the unique status of *Yesh Sakhar* as an entirely novel genre, which paved the way to similar Lurianic compositions in the seventeenth century. See *Conduct Literature*, p. 78.

On another note, while the genre of a zoharic lexicon, such as Yissakhar Baer's *Imrei Binah*, has been established already by other kabbalists, such as ibn Lavi in his *Ketem Paz*, it did not enjoy broad circulation nor did these earlier examples constitute separate works, see Huss, "Dictionary of Foreign Terms in the Zohar."

56. *Mar'eh Kohen*, Krakow 1589, fol. 1b. Aharon Zeilig, also admits using the Cremona *Zohar* in the introduction to *'Amudei Sheva*, Krakow 1635.

57. Gries, *Conduct Literature*, 74–75 and also footnotes 115 and 116 on these pages.

58. See Cooperman, "Organizing Knowledge for the Jewish Market" (unpublished paper), 47. Also Galinsky, "On Popular Halakhic Literature and the Jewish Reading Audience," and Galinsky, "And This Scholar Achieved More Than Everyone for All Studied His Works."

59. *Yesh Sakhar*, Prague 1609, fol. 74b.

60. Galante, *Mafteah ha-Zohar*, fol. 23a–29b.

61. Gries, *Conduct Literature*, and "Hasidism: The Present State of Research," 179.

62. Gries, *Conduct Literature*, 77–78.

63. For the above translation I used the 1993 Jerusalem edition of *Yesh Sakhar*. This example is found on 207–8.

64. Exodus 17:7.

65. Scholem explains that the concept of the heavenly curtain is an ancient one, and refers to an ethereal fabric suspended in front of the Throne of Glory into which the past and future of each soul is suffused. Further, the curtain also constitutes the place of return for the righteous soul, and therefore if a soul is not meritorious it will be prevented from reentering its former abode and therefore will be "cut off," see *Kabbalah*, 159.

66. This Scriptural verse depicts Korah's agitation and rebellion against Moses and Aaron.

67. For a discussion on guttural letters, see Yehudah ha-Levi's *The Kuzari* 2:80.24.

68. *Yesh Sakhar* (1993), 208.

69. Translation became an important literary technique to broaden the audience and readership of particular texts. Beginning with the fourteenth century parts of the *Zohar* began to be translated into Hebrew. One of the first translations of the *Zohar* into Hebrew was prepared by R. David ben Yehuda, see Abrams, "New Study Tools From the Kabbalists of Today," 2. For more on translations of the Zohar, see Isaiah Tishby, *The Wisdom of the Zohar*.

70. A recent study on language and the demonic in the Zohar, see Nathaniel Berman, *Divine and the Demonic in the Poetic Mythology of the Zohar* (Leiden: Brill, 2018).

71. For a comprehensive thematic treatment on the question of evil in the Zohar, see Isaiah Tishby, *Wisdom of the Zohar*, vol. 2, 447–546.

72. Gershom Scholem, *Kabbalah*, 123.

73. On the "myhic" transformation of Jewish law in Kabbalah, see Hartley Lachter, *Kabbalistic Revolution*, especially chapter 4 devoted to the issues of Halakhah and theurgy.

74. Isadore Twersky, "Concerning Maimonides' Rationalization of the Commandments: An Explanation of *Hilkhot Me'ilah 8:8*," in *Studies in the History of Jewish Society in the Middle Ages and in the Modern Period* (Jerusalem: Magnes, 1980) (Hebrew). Maimonides argues in the both his *Mishneh Torah* and the *Guide* that while the commandments that fall into the category of *mishpatim* can be rationally deciphered, those that are designated in the Torah as *huqqim* cannot be understood by applying the human intellect. Their reasons are therefore concealed from human intellectual inquiry and comprehension, as noted by Isadore Twersky, *Introduction to the Code of Maimonides*, 407–14. Also, Roslyn Weiss, "Maimonides on Shilluah ha-Qen," *Jewish Quarterly Review* 79, no. 4 (1988): 345–66.

75. For a comprehensive treatment on Kabbalah and Halakhah in Hasidism, see Maoz Kahana and Ariel Mayse, "Hasidic Halakhah: reappraising the Interface of Spirit and Law." *AJS Review* 41, 2 (2017): 375–408. On the influence of the Zohar on halakhic practice in early modernity, see Maoz Kahana, "Mekorot ha-yeda' u-temurot ha-zeman: Zava'at R. Yehudah he-Hasid ba-'et ha-Hadashah," in *Spiritual Authority: Struggles over Cultural Power in Jewish Thought*, ed. Howard Kreisel, Boaz Huss, and Uri Ehrlich (Beer Sheva: Ben-Gurion University of the Negev Press, 2009), 223–62.

76. *Kelipot*, literally husks, designate the forces of evil, the "other side" in Kabbalah.

77. See Matt, "The Mystic and the Mizwot." In this article, Daniel Matt provides a comprehensive chronological survey of kabbalistic works with a distinctive focus on expounding the esoteric meaning of the commandments. In *Venturing Beyond: Law and Morality in Kabbalistic Mysticism*, Elliot Wolfson examines the meaning of halakhah and its implications for ethical conduct in Jewish mysticism. Talya Fishman's article, "A Kabbalistic Perspective on Gender-Specific Commandments," discusses the gender implications of important fourteenth century representatives of *ta'amei ha-mizvot* literature, the *Sefer ha-Kanah* and *Peliyah*.

78. For the precise categories and the classification of kabbalistic works into those three divisions, see Elliot Wolfson, "Mystical Rationalization," 219–20. On Moses de Leon's classification of the commandments shaped to some degree by the works of Maimonides, see Elliot Wolfson, *The Book of the Pomegranate*, 27–34.

79. *Yesh Sakhar*, fol. 21a.

80. Zeev Gries, *Conduct Literature*, 78–79.

81. *Yesh Sakhar*, fol. 21b.

82. Gries, *Conduct Literature*, 79. Gries notes that Yissakhar Baer essentially summarized what he must have read in the *Beit Yosef* regarding Asher ben Yehiel's explanation to Tractate Megillah in the Talmud.

83. Cited in Zeev Gries, *Conduct Literature*, 79–80. Gries notes in parenthesis that the *zoharic* prooftext cited by Qaro after this preamble is the same as the one Yissakhar Baer includes in *Yesh Sakhar*. At the same time, Yissakhar Baer does not reference the *Beit Yosef* as his source.

84. Davis demonstrates that Isaiah Horowitz unlike his colleague, Yom Tov Lipmann Heller, repudiated philosophy and elevated the study of Kabbalah, see his *Yom Tov Lipmann Heller*, 51–54. Further, while both rabbis were learned and in Kabbalah, Heller was hesitant and measured in accepting zoharic halakha as normative (60–63), while Horowitz remained more open and inclusive, 59–60.

85. *Shnei Luhot ha-Berit*, vol. I, Author's Introduction.

86. Meir Sendor, offers a lucid analysis on the complex relationship between halakha and Kabbalah and provides examples of how rabbinic legists were able

to cope with admitting and incorporating Kabbalah into the legal discourse, see "The Rule for the Admissibility of Kabbalah in Halakhah."

87. Yissakhar Baer, Author's Introduction. See also reference to an abbreviated version of this passage in Huss, *Like the Radiance*, 176 and Gries, *Conduct Literature*, 77.

88. See Elior, "Messianic Expectations," 41–43.

Chapter 5

1. Proverbs 2:1.

2. Considine, *Dictionaries in Early Modern Europe*, 9. See also Peter Burke, *Languages and Communities*, 5–6.

3. Considine, *Dictionaries in Early Modern Europe*, 44.

4. Blair, "Organizations of Knowledge," 8. OpenAccess. https://dash. harvard.edu/bitstream/handle/1/29674918/blair%202007%20organizations%20of %20knowledge%20for%20DASH.pdf?sequence=1&isAllowed=y. Last accessed May 26. 2020.

5. Erasmus, *Adagia* III i I (*Herculei Labores*), quoted in Considine, *Dictionaries in Early Modern Europe*, 22.

6. Considine, *Dictionaries in Early Modern Europe*, 23.

7. Considine, *Dictionaries in Early Modern Europe*, 27–28.

8. Daniel O'Callaghan, *The Preservation of Jewish Books in the Sixteenth Century*, 47 and Considine, *Dictionaries in Early Modern Europe*, 29.

9. Considine, *Dictionaries in Early Modern Europe*, 29.

10. Considine, *Dictionaries in Early Modern Europe*, 29.

11. Considine, *Dictionaries in Early Modern Europe*, 12.

12. Gershom Scholem, *Major Trends in Jewish Mysticism*; Isaiah Tishby, *Wisdom of the Zohar*, Introduction. Yehudah Liebes, "Sections of the Zohar Lexicon."

13. Yehudah Liebes, "Hebrew and Aramaic as Languages of the Zohar," 36.

14. Scholem: "The Aramaic of the Zohar Is a Purely Artificial Affair;" in *Major Trends in Jewish Mysticism*, 163 and Isaiah Tishby, *The Wisdom of the Zohar* (London, 1994), I, 64. These sources are quoted in Liebes, "Hebrew and Aramaic as Languages of the Zohar," 36.

15. Charles Mopsik, "Late Judeo-Aramaic: The Language of Theosophic Kabbalah"; Ada Rapoport-Albert and Theodore Kwasman, "Late Aramaic: The Literary and Linguistic Context of the *Zohar*"; and Yehudah Liebes, "Hebrew and Aramaic as Languages of the Zohar."

16. Liebes, "Zohar and Eros," *Alpayyim* 9 (1994): 67–119.

17. Considine, *Dictionaries in Early Modern Europe*, 15.

18. Bialik, *On Literature* (Tel Aviv, 1959), 47. Cited in Liebes, "Hebrew and Aramaic as Languages of the Zohar," 40; I made some minor adjustments in the text.

19. Meir ibn Gabbay, *Tola'at Yaakov* (Jerusalem 1967), 23 and Menaḥem Azariah da Fano, *Kanfei Yonah*, Part 3, #7. Cited in Liebes, "Hebrew and Aramaic as Languages of the Zohar," 47–48.

20. Boaz Huss, "Translations of the Zohar," 85 citing the research of Asi Farber-Ginat, *Joseph Gikatila's Commentary on Ezekiel's Chariot* (Los Angeles: Cherub, 1998), 29 and Elliot R. Wolfson, *The Book of the Pomegranate: Moses de Leon's Sefer Harimon*, 47–48.

21. Moshe Idel, "The Translation of R. David ben Judah Hehasid of the Zohar and His Interpretation of the Alfa Beita," *Alei Sefer* 8 (1980): 60–73; (1981): 84–98 (Hebrew); Daniel C. Matt, *The Book of Mirrors* (Chico, CA: Scholars Press, 1986), 13–15, cited in Huss, "The Translation of the Zohar," 85.

22. Abraham Gross, *Iberian Jewry from Twilight to Dawn: The World of Rabbi Abraham Saba* (Leiden: Brill, 1995), 68.

23. Huss, "The Translation of the Zohar," 85.

24. In the field of Jewish philosophy, the lexicon and dictionary comprised prevalent literary genres beginning in the Middle Ages. Maimonides' *Guide of the Perplexed*, for instance, traditionally appeared with Samuel Ibn Tibbon's *Commentary of Foreign Terms* (*Peirush Milim ha-Zarot*) appended to its printed editions. This lexicon was usually placed at the back of the standard editions to the *Guide*, with the exception of the 1553 Sabbioneta edition by Tobias Foa, where it appears in the front. Specialists, already conversant with philosophical nomenclature, used Ibn Tibbon's lexicon to clarify and affirm their understanding of the *Guide*, whereas for audiences who had little or no recourse to this field of knowledge the dictionary comprised an indispensable learning aid to navigate the complicated and associative narrative of the Maimonidean original. Working in Poland, Bohemia, and Italy in the sixteenth century, the prodigious rabbi Mordechai Yaffe could not assume that Maimonides' *Guide*, replete with philosophical and scientific terminology, would be easily accessible to the Eastern European reader. In composing *Levush Pinat Yikrat*, he set himself the task of creatively responding to this challenge by furnishing Ibn Tibbon's original dictionary of philosophical terminology with comprehensive explanations. The types of philosophical terms that Yaffe included in his commentary were "equivocal terms, derivative terms, amphibolus terms, univocal expressions, and species," giving in effect clarification and explication of difficult concepts and terminology, Kaplan, "Rationalism and Rabbinic Culture, 93.

A classic compendium to the foreign terms and lexicographic content of the Talmud, *Sefer he-Arukh*, was written by Nathan ben of Rome in the eleventh century and became a widely consulted and frequently cited reference work by medieval interpreters, including the eminent French Bible commentator Rashi. In his work, Nathan ben Yehiel relates the words found in the Talmud to their etymological roots in the Mediterranean and ancient Near East, including Latin, Greek, Arabic, Aramaic, and Persian. In addition, he embellishes the philological explication with information concerning the customs of diverse Jewish communities. Encyclopedic in its organizational style, *he-Arukh* incorporates linguistic novellae drawn from geonic sources and integrates commentaries and halakhic responsa from diverse rabbinic academies such as Kaioruan in North Africa, Provence, and Mainz in Northern Europe. Printed in Pesaro in 1517 by the Soncino press, *he-Arukh* was broadly consulted and circulated generating new works, which sought to emend or enhance it, such as the medieval *Agur*, the *Ma'arikh* by Menaḥem de Lonzano, printed as a section in his *Shtei Yadot* (Venice, 1618), and Benjamin Mussafia's *Musaf he-Arukh* (Amsterdam 1655), beside additional attempts in the nineteenth and twentieth centuries (David, A. "Nathan ben Yehiel of Rome," *Encyclopedia Judaica* 12, 1971: 859–60).

25. An indispensable reference tool for understanding the foreign phrases found in the Zohar is Yehudah Liebes's doctoral dissertation, "Sections of the Zohar Lexicon" (Jerusalem: Hebrew University, 1976), which in fact utilized and built on Scholem's card catalog that indexed linguistic and philological material for the preparation of a large and comprehensive lexicon to the Zohar. Scholem's card catalog has now been digitized and an expanded version can now be consulted on line, http://web.nli.org.il/sites/NLI/English/collections/jewish-collection/scholem/scholem-card-catalog/Pages/search.aspx.

26. The *Bi'ur* is related sometimes to the dictionary of R. David ben Yehudah he-Hasid. In one manuscript, Jerusalem 80 *4, R. David's book *Sefer ha-Gevul* that contains a dictionary of foreign and difficult words of the *Zohar* is presented together with the *Bi'ur,* and a note in the manuscript ascribes the authorship of the Biur to R. David. It is also of note that while the *Bi'ur* translates and explains the foreign terms of the *Zohar,* R. David often simply cites them without a translation. See Huss, "A Dictionary of Foreign Words in the Zohar—A Critical Edition," 167. Huss also cites several other academic sources on the question of Rabbi David as possible author to the *Bi'ur,* see Scholem, "Chapters from the History of Kabbalah," 325; Liebes, "Sections of the Zohar Lexicon," 162; Liebes, "How was the Zohar Written?," 58n250.

27. Huss, "A Dictionary of Foreign Words in the Zohar—A Critical Edition," 169–71, provides a complete list of the manuscript variants.

28. Huss, "A Dictionary of Foreign Words in the Zohar—A Critical Edition," 167. Huss notes that this text constitutes the first literary attempt written with the explicit aim to facilitate the study of the *Zohar.*

29. Huss, "A Dictionary of Foreign Words in the Zohar—A Critical Edition," 168. Ibn Lavi in *Ketem Paz* and Abraham Azulay in *Or Hamah.* Based on MS Cambridge 1244 and one of the printed editions, both of which mention Ibn Lavi's name as author, Huss argues in favor of accepting the authorship of Ibn Lavi for the *Bi'ur.*

30. On this work see also Gries, *Conduct Literature,* 75n117. See also Huss, *Like the Radiance of the Sky,* 246n104.

31. Tishby, *Wisdom of the Zohar*, vol. I, 103.

32. Huss, *Like the Radiance of the Sky*, viii.

33. Tishby, *Wisdom of the Zohar*, vol. I. 20–21. See also Huss, "Anthologies of Zohar Commentaries," 14n11.

34. It was printed by two Venetian printers, first by Bomberg in 1522–1523 and two decades later by Justinian in 1544–1545.

35. See Abrams, "Critical and Post-Critical Textual Scholarship," and Abrams, *Kabbalistic Manuscripts and Textual Theory*; Boaz Huss, "Anthologies of Zohar Commentaries," Huss, "Sefer ha-Zohar: As a Canonical, Sacred and Holy Text."

36. Yissakhar Baer ben Naftali ha-Kohen, *Sefer Mar'eh Kohen*, Krakow 1589, fol. 2a, cited by Zeev Gries, *Conduct Literature*, 72–73; Jacob Elbaum, *Openness and Insularity*, 186.

37. These are: "Light of Torah" ("*Or Torah*"), "House of Prayer" ("*Beit Tefilah*"), "Light of Charity" ("*Or Zedakah*"), "Gate of Repentance" ("*Sha'ar Teshuvah*"), "Judgment" ("*Erekh ha-Mishpat*"), "Gate of Holiness" ("*Sha'ar Qedushah*"), "Conduct at the Table" ("*Ma'aseh Shulḥan*"), "Gate of Holy Days ("*Miqra Qodesh*, including Shabbat, New Moon, and Festivals), "Way of the Righteous" ("*Oraḥ Ẓadikim*"), "Gate of Recompense" ("*Sha'ar ha-Gamul*"), "Gate of Souls" ("*Sha'ar ha-Ruḥot*"), "Gate of the Loftiness of Israel and the Land of Israel" ("*Sha'ar Ma'alat Israel ve-Ereẓ Israel*"), "The Deeds of the Ancestors" ("*Ma'aseh Avot*"), "Gate of Death" ("*Sha'ar Mavet*"), "Gate of the Temple and Its Holiness" ("*Sha'ar Mikhdash u-Qedoshav*"), "Gate of Gleaning" ("*Sha'ar ha-Leket*"), and "Stories" ("*Ma'aseh Rav*"); see Elbaum *Openness and Insularity*, 186n7.

38. Mystical technique comprised of adding up the numerical value of Hebrew letters.

39. See *Pitḥei Yah*, where the author explains, "my book constitutes a portal and a gateway ((which allows one)) to enter into the inner court, and to move from these preliminary ((chapters)) to the inner room, where the treasures are, filled with good (*tov*), and there is no goodness (*tov*) like Torah." Zeev Gries, has already raised the possibility that the two authors may have known each other, which he attributes to the fact that, first, R. Mordechai Yaffe provided approbations to the works of both authors and, second, that R. Samson ben Beẓalel, who gave a *haskhamah* to R. Yissakhar Baer from Szczebrzeszyn, also served as judge (*av bet din*) in Kremenets. Zeev Gries, *Conduct Literature*, 76–77.

40. Elbaum, *Openness and Insularity*, 187.

41. Elbaum, *Openness and Insularity*, fol. 44b.

42. Huss, "Text and Context of the 1684 Sulzbach Edition of the Zohar," 168.

43. See *Imrei Binah*, fol. 43a–44b.

44. *Imrei Binah*, Prague 1610, fol. 44a.

45. Eitan Fishbane, *The Art of Mystical Narrative*, 223. On the narrative dimensions of the Zohar, see also Wolfson, *Through a Speculum that Shines*;

Wolfson, "Suffering Eros and Textual Incarnation: A Kristevan Reading Kabbalistic Poetics"; Oded Yisraeli, *Temple Portals: Studies in Aggadah and Midrash in the Zohar*; Hellner-Eshed, *A River Flows from Eden: The Language of Mystical Experience in the Zohar*; Meroz, "The Path of Silence: An Unknown Story from a *Zohar* Manuscript"; Meroz, *The Pearl, the Matza, and the Fish—The Spiritual Biography of Rashbi*; Meroz, "Zoharic Narratives and Their Adaptations"; "And I Was Not There? The Complaints of Rabbi Shimon bar Yohai According to an Unknown Story of the Zohar"; "The Weaving of a Myth: An Analysis of Two Stories in the Zohar"; Greenstein, *Roads to Utopia: The Walking Stories of the Zohar*; Liebes, Benarroch, Hellner-Eshed, *The Zoharic Story*; Wolski, "Mystical Poetics: Narrative, Time, and Exegesis in the Zohar"; Wolski, *A Journey into the Zohar: An Introduction to the Book of Radiance*"; Gondos, " 'Go Your Forth': The Construction of Meaning in the Zohar."

46. Meroz, "The Path of Silence."

47. On the dissemination of Kabbalah by preachers, see Roee Goldshmidt. "*Arvei Nahal* of Rabbi David Shlomo Eybeschütz: Editing of the Sermons and Their Printing as a Means of Editing of Homiletical Literature from the Sixteenth Century and Its Conclusions for the Hassidic Movement from the Foundational Figure of the Besht."

48. *Mafteah ha-Zohar*, fol. 29b. For a recent scholarly treatment of the stories of the *Zohar* presented in a two-volume edition compiled by Yehuda Liebes, Jonathan Benarroch and Melila Hellner-Eshed eds., *The Zoharic Story* (2017).

49. *Imrei Binah*, fol. 1b. On the controlled transmission of mystical content through the vehicle of zoharic anthologies and reference books, see Huss, *Like the Radiance*, 208.

50. *Imrei Binah*, fol. 1b.

51. *Imrei Binah*, fol. 2a–2b.

52. *Imrei Binah*, fol. 2b–4a.

53. A similar tendency is evinced in a manual extant in manuscript only that gives detailed instruction on how to construct a Lurianic tree diagram or *Ilan*. The author of the treatise provides fourteen introductory principles to the proper understanding of Kabbalah before he launches into the technical details of *Ilan* construction. This manuscript is extant in several versions: National Library of Israel MS F 11088, F 11128, and F 15580. I thank Prof. J. H. Chajes for sharing the transcribed manuscript with me.

54. On Shimeon ibn Lavi see, Huss, *Ketem Paz*, PhD diss. Hebrew University, Jerusalem, 1992.

55. Elbaum, *Openness and Insularity*, 189.

56. Bracha Sack, "The Mystical Theology of Solomon Alkabeẓ" (PhD diss. Jerusalem: Hebrew University, 1977), 184–91.

57. MS Oxford, Bodleian Library Opp. 500, fol. 1r. Cited in Jordan S. Penkower, *Masorah and Text Criticism*, 70. This poem as well as another he wrote for Shabbat appear in his printed work *Shetei Yadot*, albeit with modification.

58. MS Oxford, Bodleian Library Opp. 500, fol. 2v. See Jordan S. Penkower, *Masorah and Text Criticism*, 71 and notes 171 and 172 on this page.

59. *Imrei Binah*, fol. 31b.

60. *Imrei Binah*, fol. 23a.

61. *Imrei Binah*, fol.10a.

62. See *Imrei Binah*, fol. 29b. For the *Bi'ur*, see Huss, "A Dictionary of Foreign Words in the *Zohar*—A Critical Edition," 178.

63. *Imrei Binah*, fol. 29b.

64. See Gondos, " 'Go Your Forth:' The Construction of Meaning in the Zohar." MA Thesis (Montreal: Concordia University, 2005); Omri Shasha, " 'Words are Revealed Only Among Us': On the Story of Kfar Tarsha and Its Adaptation," in *The Zoharic Story*, edited by Yehudah Liebes, Jonathan M. Benarroch, and Melila Hellner-Eshed, 463–514 (Jerusalem: Ben Zvi, 2017); Melila Hellner-Eshed, *A River Flows from Eden: The Language of Mystical Experience in the Zohar* (Stanford, CA: Stanford University Press, 2011), 211–26.

65. See for instance, Daniel Matt, *The Book of Mirrors* (Chico: Scholars Press, 1982), 29. For an insightful analysis of the term *tiqla* in the Zohar related particularly to notions of gender and messianism, see Ruth Kara-Ivanov Kaniel, "Lot's Daughters and the Mothers of Davidic Dynasty in the Zohar: The Enigma of the Word, 'Tiqla.' " *English Language Notes* 50.2 (2012): 113–27. For a detailed analysis of the use and appearance of the term, *tiqla*, in the Zohar see Yehudah Liebes, "Sections of the Zohar Lexicon" (PhD diss. Jerusalem: Hebrew University, 1976), 17–18 and 359–68.

66. Moses Cordovero, *Or Yakar* (Jerusalem: Aḥuzat Israel, 1970), commentary to the Zohar I. 109b. Joseph Gikatilla, *Sha'arei Orah*, in Sha'ar 2. Both sources cited in Liebes, "Sections of the Zohar Lexicon," 362.

67. Liebes, "Sections of the Zohar Lexicon," 361.

68. *Imrei Binah*, 31b. commenting on *Parashat Mishpatim* in the Zohar.

69. Liebes, "Sections of the Zohar Lexicon," 362.

70. Ruth Kara Ivanov-Kaniel, "Lot's Daughters," 123. On the *tiqla* in the Zohar as an eschatological middle pillar equipped with scales on the left and on the right, upon which the souls are judged, after which they "ascend and descend, enter and return," see Moshe Idel, *Ascensions on High in Jewish Mysticism: Pillars, Lines, Ladders* (Budapest: Central European University Press, 2005), 113–14.

71. On this work see earlier sections of this chapter.

72. Aharon Zeilig in his *'Amudei Sheva* includes some exposition of *imrei zarot* in the *Zohar*. He explains in his introduction that while he is familiar with Yissakhar Baer's *Imrei Binah*, he prefers his teacher's R. Tiktin's *zoharic* dictionary, no longer extant today. See Elbaum, *Openness and Insularity*, 193n39. For a recent

reprint of *'Amudei Sheva* with an introduction and analysis of the text, see Daniel Abrams, *Sefer Hibbur Amudei Sheva by R. Aaron Zelig Ben Moshe Cracow 1675: A Chapter in the History of Textual Criticism to the Editio Princeps of the Book of the Zohar Cremona 1558* (Los Angeles: Cherub, 2017).

73. Huss, "A Dictionary of Foreign Words in the Zohar," 167.

74. Huss, "Text and Context of the 1684 Sulzbach Edition of the Zohar."

75. Huss, "Text and Context of the 1684 Sulzbach Edition of the Zohar," 117.

76. Abrams, "Gershom Scholem's Methodologies of Research on the Zohar," and Abrams, "Ha-Milon ha-Zohar ke-Kheli ha-Mehkar."

77. Liebes, "Sections of the Zohar Lexicon," 2. Liebes underlines that the first lexicographic attempt to incorporate the language of Kabbalah was M. Z. Kaddari's book, *The Medieval Heritage of Modern Hebrew Usage* (Tel Aviv, 1970).

78. Cited in Liebes, "Sections of the Zohar Lexicon," 1–2.

Chapter 6

1. See David Stern, *The Anthology in Jewish Literature*, and Laura, "Collected Traditions."

2. Blair, *Too Much to Know*, 175.

3. Stern, *The Anthology*, 3.

4. Stern, *The Anthology*, 3.

5. Stern, *The Anthology*, 8.

6. Elliot R. Wolfson captures this idea incisively in a recent article: "To insist on a self-awareness that is mindful of the rupture between present and past is to impose an historicist reckoning of time onto the kabbalists, which results in a skewed portrayal of their idea of personhood. I readily acknowledge that both pseudepigraphy and anonymity are forms of concealment of selfhood . . . the self-obliteration involved in distributing a text without revealing one's name demands a measure of ascesis that goes way beyond the more mundane destiny of being anonymous . . ." in "Anonymity and the Kabbalistic Ethos: A Fourteenth-Century Supercommentary on the Commentary of the Sefirot," 63.

7. Marjorie Lehman. *The En Yaaqov: Jacob ibn Habib's Search for Faith in the Talmudic Corpus*, 1.

8. See the discussion of Michel Foucault on the changing notion of textual authorship, which varied according to the genre of a particular text. Thus, while humanistic compositions were often circulated and accepted without an author, scientific works required a clearly defined authorship in order to command authority: "The author function does not affect all discourses in a universal and constant way, however. In our civilization, it has not always been the same types of texts that have required attribution to an author. There was a time when the texts we today call 'literary' (narratives, stories, epics, tragedies, comedies) were accepted, put into circulation, and valorized without any question about the identity of their

author, their anonymity caused no difficulties since their ancientness, whether real or imagined, was regarded as a sufficient guarantee of their status. On the other hand, those texts we now would call scientific—those dealing with cosmology and the heavens, medicine and illnesses, natural sciences and geography—were accepted in the Middle Ages, and accepted as 'true,' only when marked with the name of their author. 'Hippocrates said,' 'Pliny recounts,' were not really formulas of an argument based on authority; they were the markers inserted in discourses that were supposed to be received as statements of demonstrated truth." Cited in Foucault, "What Is an Author?" 125–26.

9. See Elliot R. Wolfson's recent discourse on the question of anonymous versus pseudepigraphic narrative voice, "Anonymity and the Kabbalistic Ethos: A Fourteenth-Century Supercommentary on the Commentary of the Sefirot," 56–64.

10. Laura, "Collected Traditions," 20. Laura's work on a medieval mystical compiler and Kabbalist, R. Menaḥem Ẓiyyoni of Cologne, draws attention to the cultural and theological significance of mystical anthologies that have received disproportionately scant scholarly attention in the academic study of Kabbalah. Her article mentioned above and her doctoral dissertation help to redress this important lacuna. See her doctoral dissertation, Laura, "The Ashkenazi Kabbalah of R. Menahem Ziyyoni" (2005).

11. Laura, "Collected Traditions," 19.

12. Other examples of this maximalist strategy is Abraham Azulay's Or ha-Hamah (Przemysl, 1896–1898), Simeon ibn Lavi's Ketem Paz (Livorno, 1795).

13. Azulay, Or ha-Hamah, 20.

14. [95] David Stern identifies canonization as the third theoretical variable by which anthology as a genre can be defined, "The Anthology," 6.

15. Both works were printed in the sixteenth century: Recanati's Commentary in Venice in 1523 and Ẓiyyon's Sefer Ziyyoni in Cremona in 1559, at the press of Vincenzo Conti. Shortly after its printing, however, a thousand copies of Sefer Ẓiyyoni were seized by the authorities on the order of the Dominican Sixtus of Sienna and were subsequently burned with a few surviving copies. The book was reprinted in Mantua in 1560. See Marvin J. Heller, Unicums, "Fragments and Other Hebrew Book Rarities," 16.

16. See Sefer Ẓiyyoni, fol. 7b. Additional works he mentions are, Sefer ha-Ḥayyim, Shaʾarei Zedek, Sod ha-Razim, Sefer Heikhalot, Makhberet Sekhel, Shaʾarei Orah.

17. Meir ibn Gabbai, Avodat ha-Kodesh, III chapter 23. Quoted in Scholem, "Revelation and Tradition," 299.

18. Abrams, Kabbalistic Manuscripts and Textual Theory, 575. See also the conservative stance of the medieval rabbi and exegete, Nachmanides, who unequivocally rejected the ability of the human rational faculty to formulate kabbalistic verities and therefore emphatically discouraged such a pursuit. He takes a decidedly negative stance against the use of the rational intellect in adducing kabbalistic wisdom in the introduction to his Commentary on the Torah.

And thus I attest with a faithful covenant, based on reliable advice, that anyone who looks into this book should not apply logic or reasoned thought to any of the allusions that I write concerning the secrets of Torah. For I will inform him with certainty that my words cannot be comprehended and nothing can be known at all by applying rational knowledge and understanding, except from the mouth of a wise kabbalist into the ear of a capable and understanding [receiver]. Rational thoughts regarding these [mysteries] are folly . . . causing great damage and denying all profit, one should not trust spurious falsehood, for his rational intellect will produce nothing but evil. For they will speak rebelliously against God, for which they will not be able to atone.

See Chavel, *Ramban's Commentary on the Torah*, vol. 1 (Jerusalem, 1959), 7–8.

19. On the question of authorship in kabbalistic texts see Abrams, *Kabbalistic Manuscripts and Textual Theory*, 574–85; for problematizing the question of authorship, see Foucault, "What Is an Author?"

20. For a comprehensive treatment of Recanati's sources, see Idel, *R. Menahem Recanati the Kabbalist*, 85–121.

21. Idel, *Kabbalah in Italy 1280–1510*, 118–21, and also Idel, *R. Menahem Recanati the Kabbalist*, 93–94, 146–47. For an illustration, see figure 7.1 in this section, which shows clearly the word Recanati is commenting on, the corresponding sections from the Zohar, the *Bahir*, and the Zohar on Ruth.

22. Idel, *Kabbalah in Italy 1280–1510*, 112.

23. Idel, *Kabbalah in Italy 1289–1510*, 116.

24. Idel, *Kabbalah in Italy 1280–1510*, 111.

25. In this sense Recanati prefigures Moses Cordovero who in the sixteenth century undertakes a more comprehensive assessment of kabbalistic texts and ideas in his *Pardes Rimonim*, organizing them into a topically arranged framework rather than adopting the Torah-commentary model pursued by Recanati in his *Commentary*.

26. Yissakhar Baer, *Meqor Hokhmah*, fol. 1b.

27. Yissakhar Baer, *Meqor Hokhmah*, fol. 1b.

28. See a discussion of the Zohar as midrash by Oded Israeli, *Temple Portals: Studies in Aggada and Midrash in the Zohar* (Verlag, 2016, which is the English translation of the Hebrew original, Jerusalem: Magnes, 2013).

29. Recanati, *Commentary on the Torah* (Venice, 1523), fol. 1a.

30. See Zohar 1:2b–1:3b.

31. See JT *Hagigah* 2:1, 77c; *Bereshit Rabbah* 1:10; *Midrash ha-Gadol*, Genesis 1:1, 10.

32. Oron, "The Narrative of the Letters and Its Source," 108.

33. Oron, "The Narrative of the Letters and Its Source," 109.

34. Oron, "The Narrative of the Letters and Its Source," 97.

35. Deuteronomy 5:20 in *Parashat Va-Ethanan*.

36. *Mekor Ḥokhmah*, Prague 1610, fol. 4b. Exodus 30:25.

37. *Me'ulefet Sapirim* (Constantinople, 1660), Introduction.

38. 'Shimon the Righteous was from the remnants of the Great Assembly. He would say, "On three things the world stands: on Torah, on service (of God), and on acts of lovingkindess." *Pirkei Avot* 1:2.

39. Algazi explains in the introduction that he adopts the organizational structure of *Tapuḥei Zahav* written byYeḥiel Mili as an abridgment to the ethical work, *Reshit Ḥokhmah*, and printed in Mantua in 1623. Mili's work reframes *Reshit Ḥokhmah* in a more concise format and breaks it down into thirty-day units, offering a practical curriculum for a monthly study cycle on the topic of ethical conduct.

40. *Me'ulefet Sapirim*, 1660, 44a–46a.

41. *Meqor Ḥokhmah*, 1610, 1b.

42. *Meqor Ḥokhmah*, 1610, 1b.

43. *Meqor Ḥokhmah*, 1610, 1b.

44. Benayahu, "The Book *Mafteaḥ ha-Zohar*," 37.

45. See Galante, *Mafteaḥ ha-Zohar*, 21a–29a. (1) Prayer and commandments related to weekdays, Shabbat and festivals, blessings on enjoying material pleasure; (2) Torah study, its reward and elevated status; (3) afterlife, death, reward and punishment, the soul; (4) charity and good deeds; (5) repentance; (6) the ascent of the righteous in two worlds; (7) deeds that bring a person to heaven or hell; (8) destruction of the Temple, four types of exile, in-gathering of the exiles, coming of the Messiah, resurrection of the dead; (9) the holiness of Shabbat and festivals, what they do above on festivals, and what is appropriate to do below in this world; (10) matters concerning the bridegroom and the bride, and the commandments of procreation and circumcision; (11) the exulted status of the land of Israel and the one who merits to die in it; (12) the sayings of the Sages scattered in the Zohar and other matters.

46. See Cooperman, "Political Discourse," 47–68. See also his oral comments to Boaz Huss, http://condor.wesleyan.edu/openmedia/emw/video/2004/huss_2004.mov.

On the inclusion of *zoharic* and other kabbalistic ideas in sermons, see Bonfil, "Preaching as Mediation between Elite and Popular Cultures: The Case of Judah del Bene," Horowitz, "Speaking of the Dead," Idel, "Judah Moscato," and Saperstein, "Italian Jewish Preaching: An Overview." It should be noted as well that a survey of homiletical works printed between 1540 and 1640 indicates that out of 193 sermons, 25 or close to 13 percent displayed some kabbalistic content. See Gueta, "The Hebrew Imprints of 'Shin' Years," 141.

47. Benayahu, "The Book *Mafteaḥ ha-Zohar*," 38.

48. Benayahu, "The Book *Mafteaḥ ha-Zohar*," 38.

49. See Chapter 3, p. 86.

50. MS British Library 381, which was written between the years 1562 and 1564, after he had returned to Italy from Safed. See Benayahu, "The Book *Mafteah ha-Zohar*," 37.

51. Benayahu, "The Book *Mafteah ha-Zohar*," 38.

52. See Benayahu, "The Book *Mafteah ha-Zohar*," 37–47, where he lists twenty-four different manuscript versions of indexes to the Zohar.

53. *Maftehot ha-Zohar*, fol. 44a. The topics covered by the author include: the Biblical Fathers (*Avot*); Adam to Noah; Adam in God's Image; the Land of Israel; Synagogue; Children (procreation); Noah's Sons; Animals; Blessings; Hell (*gehinom*); Metempsychosis (*gilgul*); Exile and Redemption; Reward and Punishment; Garden of Eden; Speaking and Honest Speech; Blessings/Curses/Vows/Oaths and Lies; Four Elements; Confession; Marital life; Times; Dream; Destruction; Purity and Sanctity; Fear and Love; Reverence for God's Name; Priests and Levites; Throne of Glory; Atonement; Sorcery; Writings (Psalms, Proverbs, etc.); Food; Circumcision; Death; Angels and Palaces; Positive and Negative commandments; Tabernacle, the Temple and their Vessels; the Giving of Torah and the Tablets; Prophets; Women; the Soul; the Other Side; Sukkot and Shemini Azeret; Samael and the Serpent; Books; the World; Aza and Azael; Humility; Times (months, days, nights, and hours); Pesakh; the Righteous (*tsadiq*); The Righteous and Others; Rightousness and Judgment; Aspects of Kindness; Judges and Tribulations; Charity and Acts of kindness; Plants; Phylacteries, Fringes and Mezuzah; Incense Offering; Sacrifices; Sexual Offences (*keri ve-arayot*); Shema and Other Prayers; New Year; Holy Spirit and Prophecy; Spirits and Demons; Shavuot; Tribes and Israel; Shabbat; Satan, the Evil Inclination and the Angel of Death; Peace in the Household, the Land, and with Others; Names (of the righteous, the wicked, Naomi, Ruth, etc); the Heavens; Rebuke; Torah and its Study; Resurrection of the Dead; Letters; Fasts and the Ninth of Av; Repentance.

54. *Maftehot ha-Zohar*, last unmarked page in the "Introduction."

55. Yehiel Mili, *Tapuhei Zahav*, fol. 3b–4a.

56. Pinchas Neurlingen, *Mazdik ha-Rabbim*, fol. 2a. For reference, see Pachter, "The Book *Reshit Hokhmah*," 707.

57. R. David ben Avraham Shemaryah, *Torat Emet*, fol. 2a.

58. Similarly, R. Moses Cordovero also distinguishes between a revealed-exoteric and a hidden-esoteric layer embedded within the *zoharic* corpus. In addition, R. Moses Basola defends the publication of the Mantua edition of the Zohar by deploying a twofold stratification of the *zoharic* text where the revealed aspect can benefit the many while the more *sefirotic* and esoteric portions of the text will be acquired by only a select few: "Where the *Zohar* talks about the essence of the divine, and the emanations, it speaks in an obscure language, and only one who is wise and understanding and knowledgeable in the ways of the kabbalah can understand it. And therefore, I say that the *Zohar* is beneficial to

all, because the uneducated will learn from it the plain meaning of the verses according to the way of truth." In Huss, "The Anthological Interpretation," 10.

59. Huss, *Like Radiance*, 246. It should be emphasized that mystical ideas and teachings were traditionally regarded as inherently esoteric that resisted uncontrolled disclosure. This assumption holds especially true in the field of Kabbalah, where textual sources confirm that certain topics, such as the heavenly Chariot vision of Ezekiel, were not to be expounded openly. These teachings should be imparted only in chapter headings to a student who had been found worthy of reception and one who is able to comprehend them from within one's own intellect (BT *Hagigah* 14b). Other mystical texts underline the need for strict oral transmission of mystical knowledge and only through a whisper.

60. On the question of the reception and conceptualization of the Zohar as an authoritative text, see Huss, "*Sefer Hazohar* as a Canonical, Sacred and Holy Text."

61. Idel, "Midrash vs. Other Jewish Hermeneutics," 49.

62. Idel, "Midrash vs. Other Jewish Hermeneutics," 48–49.

63. Idel, "Midrash vs. Other Jewish Hermeneutics," 56.

Chapter 7

1. *Yesh Sakhar*, Prague 1609, 1b. In his introduction to *Yesh Sakhar*, he informs the reader that it was too expensive for him to print *Yod'ei Binah* and he had to put it off until such time that he would become financially more established.

2. The National Library of Israel catalogs three manuscripts of Yissakhar Baer's works each produced in Italy. All three manuscripts were copied in Italy and are on the work, *Imrei Binah*, and two of them are abridgments. See F 47966; F 10769; and F 43027 at the National Library in Jerusalem.

3. One such Ilan was recently discovered among the books of R. Yehudah Yudel Rosenberg, a Polish rabbi who immigrated and settled in Montreal (Canada) in the first half of the twentieth century. Prof. Ira Robinson who is currently writing a biography of this rabbi found a cylinder among R. Rosenberg's books, which contained just such a Lurianic *Ilan*, which was bequeathed to and is currently stored in the collection of the Jewish Public Library in Montreal. Subsequently, the scroll was examined and cataloged by J. H. Chajes.

4. Michel de Certeau, *The Practice of Everyday Life*, 174.

5. Guglielmo Cavallo and Roger Chartier (eds.), *History of Reading in the West*, 1–2.

6. Boaz Huss, "Admiration and Disgust: The Ambivalent Re-Canonization of the *Zohar* in the Modern Period," in *Study and Knowledge in Jewish Thought*, ed. Howard Kreisel (Beer Sheva: BGU Press: 2006), 236, and especially note 85, which provides a list of works that appeared in the 1990s in Israel. Huss notes

the resurgence of Zohar commentaries and translations into Hebrew, within this decade, following the dissemination of R. Yehudah Ashlag's Hebrew translation of the Zohar, the *Sulam*. The reprinting of *Yesh Sakhar* in 1993 fits into this larger cultural process that aimed to refocus religious attention on the Zohar and its commentaries among various religious groups in Israel.

7. Ira Robinson, *Rabbis and Their Communitiy: Studies in the Eastern European Orthodox Rabbinate in Montreal, 1896–1939*, 64.

8. Yehuda Yudel Rosenberg, *Sefer Zohar Torah*, vol. 1 (Jerusalem, 1967), 9. I thank Prof. Ira Robinson for bringing this passage to my attention.

9. Based on the book list in Stephen Burnett, *From Christian Hebraism to Jewish Studies: Johannes Buxtorf (1564–1629) and Hebrew Learning in the Seventeenth Century*, in which Yissachar Baer's works are listed under #95–98.

10. Theodor Dunkelgrün, "The Humanist Discovery of Hebrew Epistolography." I would like to thank Dr. Dunkelgrün for sharing his article with me.

11. Isaiah Tishby, *The Wisdom of the Zohar*, vol. 1, 104.

12. Cavallo and Chartier, *History of Reading in the West*, 1.

13. See Samuel Cohn's review of Ginzburg's *Cheese and the Worms*, in *Journal of Interdisciplinary History* 12, no. 3 (1982): 523–25. Robert Mandrou, *De la Culture Populaire aux 17e et 18e Siecles: La Bibliotheque Bleuede Troyes* (Paris: Stock: 1964); Genevieve Bolleme, *Les Almanachs Populaires aux 17e et 18e Siecles, Essai D'histoire Sociale* (Paris, La Haye, the Netherlands: Mouton, 1969).

14. Tishby, *The Wisdom of the Zohar*, xxix.

15. Tishby, *The Wisdom of the Zohar*, xxix.

16. See the insightful foreword by Margot Pritzker that explains the reasons for her interest in supporting the project, *The Zohar: Pritzker Edition*, xiii.

17. Matt, *Zohar: Pritzker Edition*, xvii.

18. Abrams, "The *Zohar* as Palimpsest," and *Kabbalistic Manuscript and Textual Theory*, 375, 384–85, 415–16, 423–24, 465, 467, 504, 550.

19. Matt, *Zohar: Pritzker Edition*, xxiii.

20. I used the translation of Daniel Abrams with slight modification, "The *Zohar* as Palimpsest," 7.

Bibliography

Primary Sources

WORKS IN MANUSCRIPT

————. *Imrei Binah*, Ms. Moscow, Russian State Library 676, fols. 19a–80b.
————. *Imrei Binah*, Ms. Mantua, Jewish Community of Mantua Ebr. 14.
————. *Kitzur Imrei Binah*, Ms. Moscow, Russian State Library 302, fols. 60a–72b.
————. *Kitzur Imrei Binah*, Ms. London, Montefiore Library 479, fols. 12a–52a.
————. *Kitzur Imrei Binah*, Ms. Budapest, Kaufmann 560.

PRINTED WORKS

Algazi, Shlomo, *Me'ulefet Sapirim*. Amsterdam: Casper Steen, 1703 [Hebrew].
Ashkenazi, Yeḥiel. *Heikhal ha-Shem*. Venice: Daniel Zanetti, 1594 [Hebrew].
Azulay, Abraham. *Or ha-Ḥamah*. Przemysl, 1896–1897; rpt. Bnei Brak, Israel: Yahadut, 1973 [Hebrew].
Baer, Yissakhar ben Nafthali Katz from Szczebrzeszyn. *Mar'eh Kohen*. Krakow: Proshtitz, 1589 [Hebrew].
Baer, Yissakhar ben Moses Petaḥyah. *Imrei Binah*. Prague: Moses ben Betsalel Katz, 1610 [Hebrew].
————. *Meqor Ḥokhmah*. Prague: Moses ben Betsalel Katz, 1610 [Hebrew].
————. *Meqor Ḥokhmah*. Berlin: Meschullam Zalman ben Wolf Fischof, 1710 [Hebrew].
————. *Pitḥei Yah*. Prague: Gershom ben Betsalel Katz, 1609 [Hebrew].
————. *Pitḥei Yah*. Berlin: Meschullam Zalman ben Wolf Fischof, 1710 [Hebrew].
————. *Yesh Sakhar*. Prague: Gershom ben Betsalel Katz, 1609 [Hebrew].
————. *Yesh Sakhar*. Warsaw: Nathan Schriftgiesser, 1881–1882 [Hebrew].
————. *Yesh Sakhar*. Jerusalem: Torat Moshe, 1993 [Hebrew].
Ben David, Barukh. *Zer Zahav*. Krakow, 1647 [Hebrew].

229

Cordovero, Moses. *Pardes Rimonim*. Krakow/Nowy-Dwor: Prostitz, 1592 [Hebrew].

———. *Or Yakar*, ed. Menahem Zev Hasida. Jerusalem: Ahuzat Israel, 1970 [Hebrew].

Delmedigo, Joseph. *Ta'alumot Hokhmah*. Basel: Samuel Ashkenazi, 1629–1631 [Hebrew].

Fano, Menaham Azaria. *Pelah ha-Rimon*. Venice: Daniel Zanetti, 1600 [Hebrew].

Galante, Moses. *Mafteah ha-Zohar*. Venice: Giorgio di Cavalli, 1566 [Hebrew].

———. *Mafteah ha-Zohar*. *Mantua: Yehudah Shmuel of Perugia and Son Yehoshua*, 1623 [Hebrew].

Gallico, Samuel. *Assis Rimonim*. Venice: Daniel Zanetti, 1601 [Hebrew].

Ibn Gabbai, Meir. *Avodat ha-Kodesh* (*Marot Elohim*). Venice, 1567 and Krakow, 1576 [Hebrew].

Isaiah ben Eliezer Hayyim, *Yesha Yah*. Venice: Giovanni Vendramin, 1637 [Hebrew].

Ma'arekhet ha-Elohut with Minhat Yehudah, commentary by Yehudah Hayyat. Ferrara: Abraham Usque, 1558 [Hebrew].

Mili, Yehiel. *Tapuhei Zahav*. Mantua, Italy: Raphael Hayyim, 1623 [Hebrew].

Recanati, Menahem. *Peirush al ha-Torah*. Venice: Daniel Bomberg, 1523.

Rittangel, Johannes Stephanus. *De Veritate Religionis Christianae*. Franequerae: Wibium Bleck, 1699 [Latin].

———. *Sefer Yezirah*. Amsterdam: Joannen & Iodocum Ianssonios, 1642 [Latin].

Streinburg, Eliezer ben Menahem. *Petah Enayim*. Krakow, Poland: Meisels, 1647 [Hebrew].

Zeilig, Aharon. *'Amudei Sheva*. Krakow, Poland: Menahem Nahum Meisels, 1635 [Hebrew].

Ziyyon, Menahem. *Sefer Ziyyoni*. Cremona, Italy: Vincenzo Conti, 1559 [Hebrew].

Zohar, Pritzker Edition, translated and annotated by Daniel Matt. Stanford, CA: Stanford University Press, 2003–2018.

Secondary Sources

Abrams, Daniel. "Critical and Post-Critical Textual Scholarship of Jewish Mystical Literature: Notes on the History and Development of Modern Editing Techniques." *Kabbalah* 1 (1996): 17–71.

———. "The Cultural Reception of the Zohar: An Unknown Lecture by Gershom Scholem from 1940 (Study, Edition and English Translation." *Kabbalah* 19 (2009): 279–316.

———. "Defining Modern Academic Scholarship: Gershom Scholem and the Establishment of a New (?) Discipline." *Journal of Jewish Thought and Philosophy* 9, no. 2 (2000): 267–302.

———. "Gershom Scholem's Methodologies of Research on the Zohar." In *Scholar and Kabbalist: The Life and Work of Gershom Scholem*, edited by Mirjam Zadoff and Noam Zadoff, 3–16. Leiden, the Netherlands and Boston: Brill, 2019.

————. "Ha-Milon ha-Zohar ke-Kheli ha-Mehkar ha-Ishi shel Gershom Scholem." *Kabbalah* 38 (2017): 59–82 [Hebrew].

————. The Invention of the "Zohar" as a Book: On the Assumptions and Expectations of the Kabbalists and Modern Scholars. *Kabbalah* 18 (2009): 7–142.

————. *Kabbalistic Manuscripts and Textural Theory: Methodologies of Textual Scholarship and Editorial Practice in the Study of Jewish Mysticism.* Jerusalem–Los Angeles: Magnes Press, Hebrew University, Cherub Press, 2010.

————. "Orality in the Kabbalistic School of Nahmanides: Preserving and Interpreting Esoteric Traditions and Texts." *Jewish Studies Quarterly* 3 (1996): 85–102.

————. *Sefer Hibbur Amudei Sheva by R. Aaron Zelig Ben Moshe Cracow 1675: A Chapter in the History of Textual Criticism to the Editio Princeps of the Book of the Zohar Cremona 1558.* Los Angeles: Cherub, 2017.

————. "When Was the Introduction to the Zohar Written, and Changes within the Differing Copies of the Mantua Printing." *Asufot* 8 (1994): 211–26 [Hebrew].

————. "The Zohar as Palimpsest: Dismantling the Literary Constructs of a Kabbalistic Classic and the Turn to the Hermeneutics of Textual Archeology." *Kabbalah* 29 (2103): 7–56.

————. "The Zohar Dictionary as a Personal Research Tool for Gershom Scholem." *Kabbalah* 38 (2017): 59–82 [Hebrew].

Altmann, Alexander. "Eternality of Punishment: A Theological Controversy within the Amsterdam Rabbinate in the Thirties of the Seventeenth Century." In *Essential Papers on Kabbalah*, edited by Lawrence Fine, 270–87. New York and London: New York University Press, 1995.

————. "Notes of the Development of Rabbi Menahem Azariah Fano's Kabbalistic Doctrine." *Jerusalem Studies in Jewish Thought* 3 (1983/84): 241–67.

Altshuler, Mor. "Prophecy and Maggidism in the Life and Writings of R. Joseph Karo." *Frankfurter Judaische Beitrage* 33 (2006): 81–110.

Anderson, Benedict. *Imagined Communities: Reflections on the Origin and Spread of Nationalism.* London: Verson, 1983.

Ariel, David S. "*Shem Tob Ibn Shem Tob Kabbalistic Critique of Jewish Philosophy in the Commentary on the Sefirot: Study and Text.*" PhD diss. Brandeis University, 1982.

Assaf, Simha. "On the Controversy over the Printing of Kabbalistic Books." *Sinai* 5 (1939): 360–68 [Hebrew].

Avivi, Yosef. "Kitvei ha-Rama mi-Fano be-Hokhmat ha-Kabbalah," *Sefunot* 19 (1989): 347–76 [Hebrew].

Bakhtin, Mikhail. *Problem of Dostoevksy's Poetics*, edited and translated by Caryl Emerson. Minneapolis: University of Minnesota Press, 1984.

Baron, Salo Wittmayer. *A Social and Religious History of the Jews.* Philadelphia, 1976.

Baruchson-Arbib, Shifra. *Books and Readers: The Reading Interests of Italian Jews at the Close of the Renaissance.* Ramat-Gan, Israel: Bar-Ilan University, 1993 [Hebrew].

———. "Jewish Libraries: Culture and Reading Interests in 16th Century Italy." *Library History* 10 (1994): 19–26.

———. "Money and Culture: Financing Sources and Methods in the Hebrew Printing Shops in Cinquecento Italy." *La Bibliofilia* 92, no. 1 (1990): 23–39.

———. "The Prices of Hebrew Printed Books in Cinquecento Italy." *La Bibliofilia* 97, no. 2 (1995): 149–61.

Baruchson-Arbib, Shifra, and Gila Prebor. "Sefer Ha-Ziquq (An Index of Forbidden Hebrew Books): The Book's Use and Its Influence on Hebrew Printing." *La Bibliofilia* (2007): 3–31.

Baumgarten, Eliezer. "Drashot 'al ha-Ilan ha-Kabbali le-Yosef ibn-Zur." *Kabbalah* 37 (2017): 101–57.

Baumgarten, Eliezer. "Notes on R. Naftali Bachrach's Treatment of Pre-Lurianic Sources." *AJS Review* 37 (2013): 1–23 [Hebrew].

Beit-Arie, Malachi. "Publication and Reproduction of Literary Texts in Medieval Jewish Civilization: Jewish Scribality and Its Impact on the Texts Transmitted." In *Transmitting Jewish Traditions: Orality, Textuality and Cultural Diffusion*, edited by Yaakov Elman and Israel Gershoni, 225–47. New Haven, CT and London: Yale University Press, 2000.

Benayahu, M. "The Book *Mafteah ha-Zohar* and Its Recensions." *Asufot* 10 (1997): 37–47 [Hebrew].

———. *Toldot ha-Ari*. Jerusalem: Makhon Ben Zvi, 1967 [Hebrew].

———. "Vikhuakh ha-Kabbalah im ha-Halakhah." *Da'at* 5 (1980): 61–115 [Hebrew].

Ben Shlomo, J. *Torat ha-Elohut shel R. Moshe Cordovero*. Jerusalem: Mosad Bialik, 1965 [Hebrew].

Benin, Stephen D. "Search for Truth: Jews, Christians and the Authority to Interpret." In *With Reverence for the Word: Medieval Scriptural Exegesis in Judaism, Christianity, and Islam*, edited by Jane Dammen McAuliffe, Barry D. Walfish, and Joseph W. Goering, 13–32. Oxford: Oxford University, 2003.

Berkovitz, Jay R. "The Persona of a *Poseq*: Law and Self-Fashioning in Seventeenth-Century Ashkenaz." *Modern Judaism* 32, no. 3 (2012): 251–69.

Berman, Nathaniel. *The 'Other Side' of Kabbalah: Divine and Demonic in the Zohar and Kabbalistic Tradition*. Leiden, the Netherlands: Brill, 2018.

Biale, David. *Gershom Scholem: Kabbalah and Counter-History*. Cambridge: Harvard University Press, 1982.

Blair, Ann. "Annotating and Indexing Natural Philosophy." In *Books and the Sciences in History*, edited by Marina Frasca-Spada and Nick Jardine, 69–89. Cambridge, UK: Cambridge University Press, 2000.

———. "Organizations of Knowledge." In *Cambridge Companion to Renaissance Philosophy*, edited by James Hankins, 287–303. Cambridge, UK: Cambridge University Press, 2007.

———. "Reading Strategies for Coping with Information Overload ca. 1550–1700." *Journal of the History of Ideas* 64, no. 1 (2003): 11–28.

————. *Too Much to Know: Managing Scholarly Information before the Modern Age*. New Haven, CT: Yale University Press, 2011.

Blau, Joseph L. *The Christian Interpretation of the Cabala in the Renaissance*. Port Washington, NY: Kennikat Press, 1965.

Bonfil, Robert. *Cultural Change among Jews of Early Modern Italy*. Farnham, UK: Ashgate/Variorum, 2010.

————. "Halakhah, Kabbalah and Society: Some Insights into Rabbi Menahem Azaria Da Fano's Inner World." In *Jewish Thought in the Seventeenth Century*, edited by Isadore Twersky and Bernard Septimus, 39–61. Cambridge: Harvard University Press, 1987.

————. *Jewish Life in Renaissance Italy*. Berkeley: University of California Press, 1994.

————. *Rabbis and Jewish Communities in Renaissance Italy*. Oxford and New York: Littman Library by Oxford University Press, 1990.

————. "Reading in the Jewish Communities of Western Europe in the Middle Ages." In *A History of Reading in the West*, edited by Guglielmo Cavallo and Roger Chartier, 149–78. Amherst and Boston: University of Massachusetts Press, 1999.

————. "Sifriyotehem shel Yehudei Italiya bein Yemei-HaBenayim laEt haHadashah." *Pe'amim* 52 (1992): 4–18 [Hebrew].

Bos, G. "Hayyim Vital's *Practical Kabbalah and Alchemy*: A 17th Century Book of Secrets." *Journal of Jewish Thought and Philosophy* 4 (1994): 55–112.

Brenner, Michael. "Between Haskalah and Kabbalah: Peter Beer's History of Jewish Sects." In *Jewish History and Jewish Memory: Essays in Honor of Yosef Hayim Yerushalmi*, edited by Elisheva Carlebach, John M. Efron and David N. Myers, 389–404. Hanover, NH: University Press of New England, 1998.

Bues, Almut. "The Formation of the Polish-Lithuanian Monarchy in the Sixteenth Century." In *The Polish-Lithuanian Monarchy in European Context, c. 1500–1795*, edited by Richard Butterwick, 58–81. New York: Palgrave, 2001.

Burnett, Stephen G. *Christian Hebraism in the Reformation Era (1500–1660): Authors, Books, and the Transmission of Jewish Learning*. Leiden, the Netherlands and New York: Brill, 2012.

—————. *From Christian Hebraism to Jewish Studies: Johannes Buxtorf (1564–1629) and Hebrew Learning in the Seventeenth Century*. Leiden, the Netherlands and New York: Brill, 1996.

Burke, Peter. *Languages and Communities in Early Modern Europe*. Cambridge, UK: Cambridge University Press, 2004.

————. "Revolution in Popular Culture." In *Popular Culture Theory and Methodology: A Basic Introduction*, edited by Harold E. Hinds, Marilyn F. Motz, and Angela M. S. Nelson, 30–46. Madison: University of Wisconsin Press, 2006.

Busi, Giulio. *Qabbalah Visiva*. Torino, Italy: Einaudi, 2005 [Italian].

————. "Who Does Not Wonder at this Chameleon? The Kabbalistic Library of Giovanni Pico della Mirandola." In *Hebrew to Latin, Latin to Hebrew*, edited by Giulio Busi, 167–96. *Berlin and Torino: Nino Aragno Editore, 2006.*

Butterwick, Richard, ed. *The Polish-Lithuanian Monarchy in European Context c. 1500–1795.* Houndmills, UK and New York: Palgrave, 2001.

Campanini, Saverio. "On Abraham's Neck: The Edition Princeps of the *Sefer Yeṣirah* (Mantua 1562) and Its Context." In *Rabbi Judah Moscato and the Jewish Intellectual World of Mantua in the 16th–17th Centuries,* edited by Giuseppe Veltri, and Gianfranco Miletto, 253–73. Leiden, the Netherlands: Brill, 2012.

Carlebach, Elisheva. *Divided Souls: Converts from Judaism in Germany 1500–1700.* New Haven, CN: Yale University Press, 2001.

————. *The Pursuit of Heresy: Rabbi Moses Hagiz and the Sabbatian Controversies.* New York: Columbia University Press, 1990.

Carpenter, Edmund and Marshall McLuhan (eds). *Explorations in Communications: An Anthology.* Boston: Beacon Press, 1960.

Cavallo, Guglielmo and Roger Chartier, eds. *A History of Reading in the West.* Amherst and Boston: University of Massachusetts Press, 1999.

Certeau, Michel de. *The Practice of Everyday Life.* Berkeley and Los Angeles: University of California Press, 2011.

Chajes, J. H. "Kabbalah and the Diagrammatic Phase of the Scientific Revolution." In *Jewish Culture in Early Modern Europe: Essays in Honor of David B. Ruderman,* edited by Richard T. Cohen et al., 109–23. Pittsburgh, PA: University of Pittsburgh Press, 2014.

————. "'Too Holy to Print': The Forbidden Books of Jewish Magic." *Jewish History* 26 (2012): 247–62.

————. *Visualization of Knowledge in the Medieval and Early Modern Periods,* edited by J. H. Chajes, Adam Cohen, Marcia Kupfer, and Andrea Worm. Turnjout, Belgium: Brepols, 2017.

Chartier, Roger. *Forms and Meanings: Texts, Performances, and Audiences from Codex to Computer.* Philadelphia: University of Pennsylvania Press, 1995.

Considine, *Dictionaries in Early Modern Europe: Lexicography and the Making of Heritage. Cambridge, UK: Cambridge University Press, 2009.*

Cooperman, Bernard Dov. "*Amitica* and Hermeticism. Paratext as Key to Judah Moscato's *Nefuṣot Yehudah.*" In *Rabbi Judah Moscato and the Jewish Intellectual World of Mantua in the 16th–17th Centuries,* edited by Giuseppe Veltri, and Gianfranco Miletto, 79–104. Leiden, the Netherlands: Brill, 2012.

————. "Organizing Knowledge for the Jewish Market: An Editor/Printer in Sixteenth Century Rome." In *Perspectives on the Hebraic Book: The Myron M. Weinstein Memorial Lectures at the Library of Congress,* edited by Peggy K. Pearlstein, 79–129.Washington: Library of Congress, 2012.

————. "Organizing Knowledge for the Jewish Market: An Editor/Printer in Sixteenth Century Rome" (unpublished manuscript).

————. "Political Discourse in a Kabbalistic Register: Isaac de Lattes' Plea for Stronger Communal Government." In *Be'erot Yitzhak: Studies in Memory of Isadore Twersky*, edited by Jay M. Harris, 47–68. Cambridge: Harvard University Press, 2005.

Copenhaver, Brian P. *Hermetica: The Greek Corpus Hermeticum and the Latin Asclepius in a New English Translation, with Notes and Introduction.* Cambridge, UK: Cambridge University Press, 1995.

Coudert, Allison P. "Five Seventeenth-Century Christian Hebraists." In *Hebraica Veritas? Christian Hebraists and the Study of Judaism in Early Modern Europe*, edited by Allison P. Coudert and Jeffrey S. Shoulson, 286–308. Philadelphia: University of Pennsylvania Press, 2004.

Coudert, Allison P., and Jeffrey S. Shoulson, eds. *Hebraica Veritas? Christian Hebraists and the Study of Judaism in Early Modern Europe.* Philadelphia: University of Pennsylvania Press, 2004.

————. *The Impact of the Kabbalah in the Seventeenth Century: The Life and Thought of Francis Mercury van Helmont (1614–1698).* Leiden, the Netherlands; Boston; and Cologne, Germany: Brill, 1999.

————. "The Kabbalah Denudata: Converting Jews or Seducing Christians." In *Jewish Christians and Christian Jews: From the Renaissance to the Enlightenment*, edited by Richard H. Popkin and Gordon M. Weiner, 73–96. Dordecht, the Netherlands: Kluwer, 1994.

Cygielman, Shmuel A. Arthur. *Jewish Autonomy in Poland and Lithuania until 1648.* Nanuet, NY: Feldheim Publishers, 1997.

Dan, Joseph, ed. *The Christian Kabbalah: Jewish Mystical Books and Their Christian Interpreters: A Symposium.* Cambridge: Harvard College Library, 1998.

————. "Gershom Scholem: Between History and Historiosophy." *Binah* (1989): 219–49.

David, Abraham. *A Hebrew Chronicle from Prague, c. 1615*, translated by Leon J. Weinberger and Dena Ordan. Tuscaloosa: University of Alabama Press, 1993.

————. *To Come to the Land: Immigration and Settlement in Sixteenth-Century Eretz-Israel*, translated by Dena Ordan. Tuscaloosa and London: University of Alabama Press, 1999.

Davis, Joseph M. "The Reception of the *Shulhan 'Arukh* and the Formation of the Ashkenazic Jewish Identity." *AJS Review* 26, no. 2 (2002): 251–76.

————. *Yom Tov Lipmann Heller: Portrait of a Seventeenth-Century Rabbi.* Oxford and Portland, OR: Littman Library of Jewish Civilization, 2004.

Dunkelgrün, Theodor. "The Humanist Discovery of Hebrew Epistolography." In *Jewish Books and Their Readers*, edited by Scott Mandelbrote and Joanna Weinberg, 211–59. Leiden, the Netherlands: Brill, 2016.

Dweck, Yaacob. *The Scandal of Kabbalah: Leon Modena, Jewish Mysticism, Early Modern Venice.* Princeton and Oxford: Princeton University Press, 2011.

————. "What Is a Jewish Book?" *AJS Review* 34, no. 2 (2010): 367–75.

Eisenstein, Elizabeth L. *The Printing Press as an Agent of Change: Communications and Cultural Transformations in Early-Modern Europe*. Cambridge, UK: Cambridge University Press, 1979.

————. *The Printing Revolution in Early Modern Europe*. Cambridge, UK: Cambridge University Press, 1983.

————. "Some Conjectures about the Impact of Printing on Western Society and Thought: A Preliminary Report." *Journal of Modern History* 40, no. 1 (1968): 1–56.

Elbaum, Jacob. "The Influence of Spanish-Jewish Culture on the Jews of Ashkenaz and Poland in the Fifteenth-Seventeenth Centuries." In *Binah: Jewish Intellectual History in the Middle Ages*, edited by Joseph Dan, 179–97. Westport, CT, London: Praeger.

————. *Openness and Insularity: Late Sixteenth Century Jewish Literature in Poland and Ashkenaz*. Jerusalem: Magnes Press, 1990 [Hebrew].

Elior, Rachel. "The Doctrine of Transmigration in Galya Raza." In *Essential Papers on Kabbalah*, edited by Lawrence Fine, 243–69. New York and London: New York University Press, 1995.

————. "Messianic Expectations and Spiritualization of Religious Life in the Sixteenth Century." *Revue des Etudes Juives* 145 (1986): 35–49.

Evans, R. J. W. *Rudolf II and His World: A Study in Intellectual History 1576–1612*. Oxford: Clarendon Press, 1973.

Faierstein, Morris M. "Charisma and Anti-Charisma in Safed: Isaac Luria and Hayyim Vital." *Journal for the Study of Sephardic and Mizrahi Jewry* (October/November 2007): 1–20.

Febvre, Lucien and Henri-Jean Martin, *The Coming of the Book: The Impact of Printing 1450–1800*. London: NLB, 1979.

Fine, Lawrence. "The Art of Metoposcopy: A Study in Isaac Luria's Charismatic Knowledge." In *Essential Papers on Kabbalah*, edited by Lawrence Fine, 315–37. New York and London: New York University Press, 1995.

————. "The Contemplative Practice of Yihudim in Lurianic Kabbalah." In *Jewish Spirituality from the Sixteenth Century Revival to the Present*, edited by Arthur Green, 64–98. New York: Crossroad, 1987.

————, ed. *Essential Papers on Kabbalah*. New York and London: New York University Press, 1995.

————. "Maggidic Revelation in the Teachings of Isaac Luria." In *Mystics, Philosophers and Politicians*, edited by Jehuda Reinharz and Daniel Swetschinski, 141–57. Durham, NC: Duke University Press, 1982.

————. *Physician of the Soul, Healer of the Cosmos: Isaac Luria and His Kabbalistic Fellowship*. Stanford, CA: Stanford University Press, 2003.

————. "Pietistic Customs from Safed." In *Judaism in Practice*, edited by Lawrence Fine, 375–85. Princeton and Oxford: Princeton University Press, 2001.

———. "Purifying the Body in the Name of the Soul: The Problem of the Body in 16th Century Kabbalah." In *People of the Body: Jews and Judaism from an Embodied Perspective*, edited by Howard Eilberg-Schwartz, 117–42. Albany: State University of New York Press, 1992.

———. "Recitation of the Mishnah as a Vehicle of for Mystical Inspiration: A Contemplative Technique Taught by Hayyim Vital." *Revue des Etudes Juives* 141 (1982): 183–99 [French].

———. *Safed Spirituality: Rules of Mystical Piety: The Beginning of Wisdom*. New York: Paulist Press, 1984.

Fishbane, Eitan. *As Light before Dawn: The Inner World of a Medieval Kabbalist*. Stanford: Stanford University Press, 2009.

———. "Authority, Tradition, and the Creation of Meaning in Medieval Kabbalah: Isaac of Acre's *Illumination of the Eyes*." *Journal of the American Academy of Religion* 72 (2004): 59–95.

———. "Chariot for the Shekhinah: Identity and the Ideal Life in Sixteenth-Century Kabbalah." *Journal of Religious Ethics* 37, no. 3 (2009): 385–418.

———. "Tears of Disclosure: The Role of Weeping in Zoharic Narrative." *Journal of Jewish Thought and Philosophy* 11, no. 1 (2002): 25–47.

Fishman, Talya. "A Kabbalistic Perspective on Gender-Specific Commandments: On the Interplay of Symbols and Society." *AJS Review* 17 (1992): 199–245.

Flatto, Sharon. *The Kabbalistic Culture of Eighteenth Century Prague: Ezekiel Landau and His Contemporaries*. Portland, Oregon: Littman Library of Jewish Civilization, 2010.

Fontaine, Resianne, and Shlomo Berger. " 'Something on Every Subject': On Pre-modern Hebrew and Yiddish Encyclopedias." *Journal of Modern Jewish Studies* 5 (2006): 269–84.

Frank, Daniel, and Matt Goldish, eds. *Rabbinic Culture and Its Critics: Jewish Authority, Dissent, and Heresy in Medieval and Early Modern Times*. Detroit, MI: Wayne State University Press, 2008.

Foucault, Michel. "What Is an Author?" In *Language, Counter-Memory, Practice: Selected Essays and Interviews*, edited by Donald F. Bouchard, 141–60. Ithaca, NY: Cornell University Press, 1977.

Freudenthal, Gad. *Science in Medieval Jewish Cultures*. Cambridge, UK: Cambridge University Press, 2011.

Galinsky, Judah. " 'And This Scholar Achieved More Than Everyone for All Studied His Works': On the Circulation of Jacob B. Asher's *Four Turim* from the Time of Its Composition until the End of the 15th Century." *Sidra* 19 (2004): 25–45 [Hebrew].

———. "On Popular Halakhic Literature and the Jewish Reading Audience in Fourteenth-Century Spain." *Jewish Quarterly Review* 98, no. 3 (2008): 305–27.

———. "Rabbi Jeruham b. Meshullam, Michael Scot, and the Development of Jewish Law in Fourteenth-Century Spain." *Harvard Theological Review* 100, no. 4 (2007): 489–504.

Garb, Jonathan. "The Cult of the Saints in Lurianic Kabbalah." *Jewish Quarterly Review* 98, no. 2 (2008): 203–29.

———. The Kabbalists of Prague." *Kabbalah: Journal for the Study of Mystical Texts* 14 (2006): 347–83 [Hebrew].

Giller, Pinchas. *The Enlightened Will Shine: Symbolization and Theurgy in the Later Strata of the Zohar*. Albany: State University of New York Press, 1993.

———. *Reading the Zohar: The Sacred Text of Kabbalah*. Oxford and New York: Oxford University Press, 2001.

———. "Recovering the Sanctity of the Galilee: The Veneration of Relics in Classical Kabbalah." *Journal of Jewish Thought and Philosophy* 4 (1994): 147–69.

Gilmont, Jean-François, "Protestant Reformation and Reading." In *A History of Reading in the West*, edited by Guglielmo Cavallo and Roger Chartier, 213–37. Amherst and Boston: University of Massachusetts Press, 2003.

Gilmont, Jean-François, ed. *The Reformation and the Book*. Brookfield, UK: Ashgate, 1998.

Ginsburg, Elliot K. "Kabbalistic Rituals of Sabbath Preparation." In *Essential Papers on Kabbalah*, edited by Lawrence Fine, 400–37. New York and London: New York University Press, 1995.

———. *The Sabbat in the Classical Kabbalah*. Albany: State University of New York Press, 1989.

Ginzburg, Carlo. *The Cheese and the Worms: The Cosmos of a Sixteenth-Century Miller*. New York: Penguin Books, 1982.

Goldberg, Jacob. *Jewish Privileges in the Polish Commonwealth: Charters of Rights Granted to Jewish Communities in Poland-Lithuania in the Sixteenth to Eighteenth Centuries: Critical Edition of Original Latin and Polish Documents with English Introductions and Notes*. Jerusalem: Israeli Academy of Sciences and Humanities, 1985.

Goldish, Matt. "Halakha, Kabbalah, and Heresy: A Controversy in Early Eighteenth Century Amsterdam." *Jewish Quarterly Review* 84, no. 2–3 (1993): 153–76.

———. *The Sabbatean Prophets*. Cambridge, MA and London, UK: Harvard University Press, 2004.

Goldshmidt, Roee Hagit. "*Arvei Nahal* of Rabbi David Shlomo Eybeschütz: Editing of the Sermons and Their Printing as a Means of Editing of Homiletical Literature from the Sixteenth Century and Its Conclusions for the Hassidic Movement from the Foundational Figure of the Besht" Ph.D. Dissertation. Beer Sheva: Ben Gurion University of the Negev Beer Sheva, 2016 [Hebrew].

Gondos, Andrea. " 'Go Your Forth': The Construction of Meaning in the Zohar." MA Thesis. Montreal: Concordia University, 2005.

———. "Kabbala, Halakha, and the Age of Printing: Yissachar Baer's *Yesh Sakhar*." In *From Antiquity to the Postmodern World: Contemporary Jewish Studies in Canada*, edited by Daniel Maoz and Andrea Gondos. Newcastle upon Tyne: Cambridge Scholars Press, 2011.

———. "Kabbala in Print: Literary Strategies if Popular Mysticism in Early Modernity." PhD diss. Montreal: Concordia University, 2013.

———. "New Kabbalistic Genres and Their Readers in Early Modern Europe." In *Connecting Histories: Jews and Their Others in Early Modern Europe*, edited by Francesca Bregole and David Ruderman, 67–85. Philadelphia: University of Pennsylvania Press, 2019.

Grafton, Anthony. "Giovanni Pico della Mirandola: Trials and Tribulations of an Omnivore." In *Commerce with the Classics: Ancient Books and Renaissance Readers*, edited by Anthony Grafton, 93–134. Ann Arbor: University of Michigan Press, 1997.

———. "The Humanist as Reader." In *A History of Reading in the West*, edited by Guglielmo Cavallo and Roger Chartier, 179–212. Amherst and Boston: University of Massachusetts Press, 2003.

Green, Arthur. "The Zohar: Jewish Mysticism in Medieval Spain." In *Essential Papers on Kabbalah*, edited by Lawrence Fine, 27–66. New York and London: New York University Press, 1995.

Greenblatt, Rachel L. "A Community's Memory: Jewish Views of Past and Present in Early Modern Prague." PhD diss. Hebrew University of Jerusalem, 2006.

———. *To Tell Their Children: Jewish Communal Memory in Early Modern Prague*. Stanford, CA: Stanford University Press, 2014.

Gries, Zeev. "Between History and Literature: The Case of Jewish Preaching." *Journal of Jewish Thought and Philosophy* 4 (1994): 113–22.

———. *The Book in the Jewish World 1700–1900*. Oxford and Portland, OR: Littman Library of Jewish Civilization, 2007.

———. *Conduct Literature (Regimen Vitae): Its History and Place in the Life of Beshtian Hasidism*. Jerusalem: Bialik Institute, 1989. [Hebrew].

———. "The Copying and Printing of Books of Kabbalah as a Source for Its Study." *Mahanayim* 6 (1994): 204–11 [Hebrew].

———. "Kabbalah and Halakhah." *Madaʿei Hayahadut* 40 (2000): 187–97. [Hebrew].

Gross, Abraham. *Iberian Jewry from Twilight to Dawn: The World of Abraham Saba*. Leiden, the Netherlands: Brill, 1995.

Gueta, Anat. "The Hebrew Imprints of 'Shin' Years as a Resource for the Research of Jewish Society's Spiritual Life." PhD diss. Ramat Gan, Israel: Bar Ilan University, 2002 [Hebrew].

Guldon, Zenon, and Jacek Wijaczka. "The Accusation of Ritual Murder in Poland, 1500–1800." *Polin* 10 (1997): 99–140.

Halbertal, Moshe. *Concealment and Revelation: Esotercism in Jewish Thought and Its Philosophical Implications*. Princeton, NJ: Princeton University Press, 2007.

———. *People of the Book: Canon, Meaning, and Authority*. Cambridge: Harvard University Press, 1997.

Haberman, A. M. "The Printer Hayyim Shaḥor, His Son Isaac and His Son-in-law Josef b. Yakar." *Kiryat Sefer* 31 (1955/56): 483–500 [Hebrew].

———. "The Sons of Hayyim Halicz, a Family of Hebrew Printers." *Kiryat Sefer* 33 (1957/58): 509–20 [Hebrew].

Hacker, Joseph R. "Authors, Readers and Printers of Sixteenth Century Hebrew Books in the Ottoman Empire." In *Perspectives on the Hebraic Book: The Myron Weinstein Memorial Lectures at the Library of Congress*, edited by Peggy K. Pearlstein, 17–63.Washington: Library of Congress, 2012.

———. "The Intellectual Activity of the Jews of the Ottoman Empire during the Sixteenth and Seventeenth Centuries." In *Jewish Thought in the Seventeenth Century*, edited by Isadore Twersky and Bernard D. Septimus, 95–136. Cambridge: Harvard University Press, 1987.

———. "A New Letter Regarding the Debate over the Printing of the *Zohar* in Italy." In *Masuot: Mehkarim be-Sifrut ha-Kabbalah uve-Mahshevet Yisrael Mukdashim le-Zikro shel Prof. Ephrayim Gottlieb*, edited by Michal Oron and Amos Goldreich, 120–30. Jerusalem: Mossad Bialik, 1994 [Hebrew].

Hacker, Joseph R., and Adam Shear, eds. *The Hebrew Book in Early Modern Italy*. Philadelphia: University of Pennsylvania Press, 2011.

Hallamish, Moshe. "The Influence of the Kabbalah on Jewish Liturgy." In *Priere, Mystique Et Judaisme: Colloque De Strasbourg* (September 1984), edited by Roland Goetschel, 121–31. Paris: Presses Universitaires de France, 1987.

———. *The Kabbalah in Liturgy, Law, and Custom*. Ramat Gan, Israel: Bar Ilan University Press, 2000 [Hebrew].

———. "Rabbi Judah the Pious' Will in Halakhic and Kabbalistic Literature." In *Mysticism, Magic and Kabbalah in Ashkenazi Judaism; International Symposium Held in Frankfurt A.M. 1991*, edited by Karl Erich Grozinger and Joseph Dan, 117–22. Berlin: Walter de Gruyter, 1995.

Hamesse, Jacqueline. "The Scholastic Model of Reading." In *A History of Reading in the West*, edited by Guglielmo Cavallo and Roger Chartier, 103–19. Amherst and Boston: University of Massachusetts Press, 2003.

Hass, Christina. *Writing, Technology: Studies on the Materiality of Literacy*. New York and London: Routledge, 1996.

Hecker, Joel. "Eating Gestures and Ritualized Body in Medieval Jewish Mysticism." *History of Religions* 40 (2000): 125–52.

———. *Mystical Bodies, Mystical Meals: Eating and Embodiment in Medieval Kabbalah*. Detroit: Wayne State University Press, 2005.

Heller, Marvin J. *The Sixteenth Century Hebrew Book: An Abridged Thesaurus*. Leiden, the Netherlands and Boston: Brill, 2003.

———. *Studies in the Making of the Early Hebrew Book*. Leiden, the Netherlands and Boston: Brill, 2008.

Hellner-Eshed, Melila. *A River Flows from Eden: The Language of Mystical Experience in the Zohar*. Stanford, CA: Stanford University Press, 2009.

Herrera, Robert A. *Mystics of the Book: Themes, Topics, and Typologies*. New York: Peter Lang, 1993.

Hock, Simon. *Die Familien Prags (The Families of Prague)*. Pressburg, 1892.

Horowitz, Elliott. "Speaking of the Dead: The Emergence of the Eulogy among Italian Jewry of the Sixteenth Century." In *Preachers of the Italian Ghetto*, edited by David B. Ruderman, 129–62. Berkeley: University of California Press, 1992.

Horowitz, Isaiah. *Shnei Luhot ha-Brit*. Translated by Eliyahu Munk. Jerusalem, New York: Lambda Publishers, 1999.

Hubka, Thomas. "The Synagogue of Gwozdziec: The Gate of Heaven. The Influence of the Zohar on Art and Architecture." In *The Myth in Judaism [Hamitos bayahadut]*, edited by H. Pedaya, 263–316. Beer Sheva, Israel: 1996.

Hundert, Gershon David. "Jewish Urban Residence in the Polish Commonwealth in the Early Modern Period." *Jewish Journal of Sociology* 26 (1984): 25–34.

———. *Jews in Poland-Lithuania in the Eighteenth Century: A Genealogy of Modernity*. Berkeley: University of California Press, 2004.

———. "Jews, Money and Society in the Seventeenth-Century Polish Commonwealth: The Case of Krakow." *Jewish Social Studies* 43 (1981): 261–74.

———. "On the Jewish Community in Poland during the Seventeenth Century: Some Comparative Perspectives," *Revue des etudes juives* (1983): 349–72.

———. *Security and Dependence: Perspectives on Seventeenth Century Polish-Jewish Society Gained through a Study of Jewish Merchants in Little Poland*. PhD diss. New York: Columbia University, 1978.

Huss, Boaz. "Admiration and Disgust: The Ambivalent Re-Canonization of the Zohar in the Modern Period." In *Study and Knowledge in Jewish Thought*, edited by Howard Kreisel, 203–37. Beer Sheva, Israel: Ben-Gurion University of the Negev Press, 2006.

———. "The Appearance of *Sefer ha-Zohar*." *Tarbitz* (2001): 507–42.

———. "The Anthological Interpretation: The Emergence of Anthologies of Zohar Commentaries in the Seventeenth Century." *Prooftexts* 19 (1999): 1–19.

———. "A Dictionary of the Foreign Words in the *Zohar*: A Critical Edition." *Kabbalah* 1 (1996): 167–204 [Hebrew].

———. "The Formation of Jewish Mysticism and Its Impact on the Reception of Rabbi Abraham Abulafia in Contemporary Kabbalah." In *Religion and Its Other*, edited by Heicke Bock, Jorg Feuchter, Michi Knechts, 142–62. Frankfurt and New York: Campus Verlag, 2008.

———. *Sockets of Fine Gold: The Kabbalah of Rabbi Shim'on Ibn Lavi*. Jerusalem: Magnes Press and Ben Zvi Institute, 2000 [Hebrew].

———. *Like the Radiance of the Sky: Chapters in the Reception History of the Zohar and the Construction of Its Symbolic Value*. Jerusalem: The Ben-Zvi Institute and the Bialik Institute of Jerusalem, 2008 [Hebrew].

———. "Mysticism versus Philosophy in Kabbalistic Literature." *Micrologus* 9 (2001): 125–35.

————. "On the Status of Kabbalah in Spain after the Decrees of 1391: The Book *Poke'h Ivrim.*" *Pe'amim* 56 (1993): 20–32. [Hebrew].

————. "Sefer Ha-Zohar as a Canonical, Sacred and Holy Text: Changing Perspectives of the Book of Splendor between the Thirteenth and Eighteenth Centuries." *Journal of Jewish Thought and Philosophy* 7 (1998): 257–307.

————. "The Text and Context of the 1684 Sulzbach Edition of the *Zohar.*" In *Tradition, Heterodoxy and Religious Culture: Judaism and Christianity in the Early Modern Period,* edited by C. Goodblat and H. Kreisel, 117–38. Beer Sheva, Israel: Ben Gurion University of the Negev Press, 2007.

————. "Translations of the Zohar: Historical Contexts and Ideological Frameworks." *Correspondences* 4 (2016): 81–128.

Hyman, Arthur. "A Note on Maimonides' Classification of Law." *Proceedings of American Academy for Jewish Research* 46–47: 323–43.

Idel, Moshe. *Absorbing Perfections: Kabbalah and Interpretation.* New Haven and London: Yale University Press, 2002.

————. *Ascensions on High in Jewish Mysticism: Pillars, Lines, Ladders.* Budapest: Central European University Press, 2005.

————. "Differing Conceptions of Kabbalah in the Early 17th Century." In *Jewish Thought in the Seventeenth Century,* edited by Isadore Twersky and Bernard D. Septimus, 137–200. Cambridge: Harvard University Press, 1987.

————. "Italy in Safed and Safed in Italy: Toward an Interactive History of Sixteenth-Century Kabbalah." In *Cultural Intermediaries: Jewish Intellectuals in Early Modern Italy,* edited by David Ruderman and Giuseppe Veltri, 239–69. Philadelphia: University of Pennsylvania Press, 2004.

————. "Jewish Thinkers versus Christian Kabbalah." In *Christliche Kabbala,* edited by von Wilhelm Schmidt-Biggemann, 49–65. Ostfildern, Germany: Jan Thorbecke Verlag, 2003.

————. "Judah Moscato: A Late Renaissance Jewish Preacher." In *Preachers of the Italian Ghetto,* edited by David B. Ruderman, 41–66. Berkeley: University of California Press, 1992.

————. "Kabbalah and Elites in Thirteenth-Century Spain." *Mediterranean Historical Review* 9, (1994): 5–19.

————. *Kabbalah: New Perspectives.* New Haven and London: Yale University Press, 1988.

————. "The Kabbalah's 'Window of Opportunities,' 1270–1290." In *Me'ah She'arim: Studies in Medieval Jewish Spiritual Life in Memory of Isadore Twersky,* edited by Ezra Fleischer et al., 171–208. Jerusalem: Hebrew University Magnes Press, 2001.

————. *Language, Torah, and Hermeneutics in Abraham Abulafia.* Albany: State University of New York Press, 1989

————. "Magical and Neoplatonic Interpretations of the Kabbalah in the Renaissance." In *Jewish Thought in the Sixteenth Century,* edited by B. D. Cooperman, 186–242. Cambridge: Harvard University Press, 1983.

———. "Major Currents in Italian Kabbalah between 1560–1650." In *Essential Papers on Jewish Culture in Renaissance and Baroque Italy*, edited by D. B. Ruderman, 345–68. New York: New York University Press, 1992.

———. *Messianic Mystics*. New Haven, CT and London: Yale University Press, 1998.

———. *The Mystical Experience in Abraham Abulafia*. Translated by Jonathan Chipman. Albany: State University of New York Press, 1988.

———. "Mystical Techniques." In *Essential Papers on Kabbalah*, edited by Lawrence Fine, 438–94. New York and London: New York University Press, 1995.

———. "Nachmanides: Kabbalah, Halakhah, and Spiritual Leadership." In *Jewish Mystical Leaders and Leadership in the 13th Century*, edited by Moshe Idel and Mortimer Ostow, 15–96. Northvale, NJ: Jason Aronson, 1998.

———. "On European Cultural Renaissances and Jewish Mysticism." *Kabbalah: Journal for the Study of Jewish Mystical Texts* 13 (2005): 43–78.

———. "On Kabbalah in R. Judah Moscato's *Qol Yehudah*." In *Rabbi Judah Moscato and the Jewish Intellectual World of Mantua in the 16th–17th Centuries*, edited by Giuseppe Veltri, and Gianfranco Miletto, 57–77. Leiden, the Netherlands: Brill, 2012.

———. " 'One from a Town, Two from a Clan'—The Diffusion of Lurianic Kabbala and Sabbateanism: A Re-Examination." *Jewish History* 7 (1993): 79–104.

———. "Rabbinism versus Kabbalism: On G. Scholem 'S Phenomenology of Judaism." *Judaism* 11 (1991): 281–96.

———. *R. Menahem Recanati: The Kabbalist*. Jerusalem: Schocken Books, 1998.

———. "Sexual Metaphors and Praxis in the Kabbalah." In *The Jewish Family: Metaphor and Memory*, edited by David Kraemer, 197–224. New York and Oxford: Oxford University Press, 1989.

———. "Spanish Kabbalah after the Expulsion." In *Moreshet Sepharad: The Sephardic Legacy*, edited by Haim Beinart, 166–78. Jerusalem: Magness Press, Hebrew University, 1992.

———. "The Study Program of R. Yohanan Alemanno," *Tarbitz* 48, no. 3–4 (1979): 301–31 [Hebrew].

———. "Transmission in Thirteenth-Century Kabbalah. In *Transmitting Traditions: Orality, Textuality, and Cultural Diffusion*, edited by Yaakov Elman and Israel Gershoni, 138–65. New Haven, CT and London: Yale University Press, 2000.

Israel, Jonathan. I. *European Jewry in the Age of Mercantilism*. Oxford: Littman Library of Jewish Civilization, 1998.

Jacobs, Louis. *Theology in the Responsa*. London and Boston: Routledge & Kegan Paul. 1975.

Jacobson, Yoram. Along the Path of Exile and Redemption: The Doctrine of Redemption of Rabbi Mordecai Dato. Jerusalem: Mosad Bialik, 1996 [Hebrew].

Johns, Adrian. *The Nature of the Book: Print and Knowledge in the Making*. Chicago: University of Chicago Press, 1998.

———. *Piracy: The Intellectual Property Wars from Gutenberg to Gates*. Chicago: University of Chicago Press, 2009.

Kaddari, M. Z. *The Medieval Heritage of Modern Hebrew Usage*. Tel Aviv, Israel: Dvir, 1970 [Hebrew].

Kahana, Maoz. "Cosmos and Nomos: Rabbi Joseph Karo and Shabtai Zvi as Portable Heavenly Temples." *El Prezente: Journal for Sephardic Studies* 10 (2016): 143–53.

Kahana, Maoz, and Ariel Mayse. "Hasidic Halakhah: Reappraising the Interface of Spirit and Law." *AJS Review* 41, no. 2 (2017): 375–408.

Kahana, Maoz. "Mekorot ha-yeda' u-temurot ha-zeman: Zava'at R. Yehudah he-Hasid ba-'et ha-Hadashah." In *Spiritual Authority: Struggles over Cultural Power in Jewish Thought*, edited by Howard Kreisel, Boaz Huss, and Uri Ehrlich, 223–62. Beer Sheva, Israel: Ben-Gurion University of the Negev Press, 2009.

Kanarfogel, Ephraim. "R. Judah He-Hasid and the Rabbinic Scholars of Regensburg: Interactions, Influences, and Implications." *Jewish Quarterly Review* 96, no. 1 (2006): 17–37.

Kaplan, Lawrence. "Rabbi Mordekhai Jaffe and the Evolution of Jewish Culture in Poland in the Sixteenth Century." In *Jewish Thought in the Sixteenth Century*, edited by Bernard Dov Cooperman, 266–82. Cambridge, MA and London: Harvard University Press, 1983.

———. "Rationalism and Rabbinic Culture in Sixteenth Century Eastern Europe: Rabbi Mordecai Jaffe's *Levush Pinat Yikrat*." PhD diss. Harvard University, 1975.

Kara-Ivanov Kaniel, Ruth. "Between Kabbalah, Gender, and Law: Sexual Ethics in the Zohar." *AJS Review* 39 (2015): 14–51 [Hebrew].

———. "Lot's Daughters and the Mothers of Davidic Dynasty in the Zohar: The Enigma of the Word, 'Tiqla.' " *English Language Notes* 50, no. 2 (2012): 113–27.

Katz, Jacob. *Divine Law in Human Hands: Case Studies in Halakhic Flexibility*. Jerusalem: Magness Press, Hebrew University, 1998.

———. "Law, Spirituality and Society." *Jewish Social Studies* 2, no. 2 (1996): 87–98, 105–8.

———. "Post-Zoharic Relations between Halakhah and Kabbalah." In *Jewish Thought in the Sixteenth Century*, edited by Bernard Dov Cooperman, 283–307. Cambridge, MA and London: Harvard University Press, 1983.

———. *The "Shabbes Goy": A Study in Halakhic Flexibility*. Philadelphia and New York: Jewish Publication Society, 1989.

Koch, Patrick B. *Human Self-Perfection: A Reassessment of Kabbalistic Musar Literature of Sixteenth-Century Safed*. Los Angeles: Cherub Press, 2016.

———. "Of Stinging Nettles and Stones: The Use of Hagiography in Early Modern Kabbalah and Pietism." *Jewish Quarterly Review* (2019): 534–566.

Kolts, David. *Socrates in the Labyrinth: Hypertext, Argument, Philosophy*. Watertown: Eastgate, 2016.

Koren, Sharon. "Kabbalistic Physiology: Isaac the Blind, Nachmanides, and Moses de Leon on Menstruation." *AJS Review* 28 (2004): 317–39.

———. "Mystical Rationales for the Laws of Niddah." In *Women and Water: Menstruation in Jewish Life and Law*, edited by R. S. Wasserfall, 101–21. Hanover, NH: Brandeis University Press, 1999.

Kristeva, Julia. *The Kristeva Reader*, edited by Toril Moi. New York: Columbia University Press, 1986.

Kupfer, Ephraim. "New Documents on the Controversy over the Printing of the *Zohar.*" *Michael* 1 (1972): 302–18 [Hebrew].

Lachter, Hartley. Kabbalistic Revolution: Re-Imagining Judaism in Medieval Spain. New Brunswick: Rutgers, 2015.

Landow, George P. (ed). *Hyper/Text/Theory*. Baltimore: The Johns Hopkins University Press, 1994.

Laura, Heidi. *The Ashkenazi Kabbalah of R. Menahem Ziyyoni*. PhD diss. University of Copenhagen, 2005.

———. "Collected Traditions and Scattered Secrets: Eclecticism and Esotericism in the Works of the 14th Century Ashkenazi Kabbalist Menahem Ziyyoni of Cologne." *Nordisk Judaistik: Scandinavian Jewish Studies* 20, no. 1–2 (1999): 19–44.

Lehman, Marjorie. *The En Yaaqov: Jacob ibn Habib's Search for Faith in the Talmudic Corpus*. Detroit, MI: Wayne State University Press, 2012.

Lelli, Fabrizio. "Intellectual Relationships of Fifteenth-Century Jewish and Christian Scholars in Light of Contemporary Art." *Cadernos de Estudos Sefarditas* 6 (2006): 149–70.

———. "Jews, Humanists, and the Reappraisal of Pagan Wisdom." In *Hebraica Veritas? Christian Hebraists and the Study of Judaism in Early Modern Europe*, edited by Allison P. Coudert and Jeffrey S. Shoulson, 49–70. Philadelphia: University of Pennsylvania Press, 2004.

Lieben, Koppelman. *Gal-ed: Grabsteininschriften des Prager isr. alten Friedhofs*. Prague: Landau, 1856.

Liebes, Yehuda. "Hebrew and Aramaic as Languages of the Zohar." *Aramaic Studies* 4 (2006): 36–52.

———. "Myth vs. Symbol in the Zohar and in Lurianic Kabbalah." In *Essential Papers on Kabbalah*, edited by Lawrence Fine, 212–42. New York and London: New York University Press, 1995.

———. "Sections of the Zohar Lexicon." PhD diss. Jerusalem: Hebrew University, 1976 [Hebrew].

———. *Studies in Jewish Myth and Jewish Messianism*. Translated by Batya Stein. Albany: State University of New York Press, 1993.

———. *Studies in the Zohar*. Translated by Arnold Schwartz, Stephanie Nakache, and Penina Peli. Albany: State University of New York Press, 1993.

———. "Zohar and Eros," *Alpayyim* 9 (1994): 67–119.

Liebes, Yehuda, Jonathan Benarroch, and Melila Hellner-Eshed, eds., *The Zoharic Story*. Jerusalem: Ben Zvi Institute, 2017 [Hebrew].

Malkiel, David. "Rapture and Rupture: Kabbalah and Reformation of Early Modern Judaism." *Jewish Quarterly Review* 103, no. 1 (2013): 107–21.

Mann, Vivian B. *Jewish Texts on the Visual Arts*. Cambridge and New York: Cambridge University Press, 2000.

Mann, Vivian B., and Daniel D. Chazin. "Printing, Patronage and Prayer: Art Historical Issues in Three Responsa." *Images: A Journal of Jewish Art and Visual Culture* 1 (2007): 91–97.

Matt, Daniel C. "Ayin: The Concept of Nothingness in Jewish Mysticism." In *Essential Papers on Kabbalah*, edited by Lawrence Fine, 67–108. New York and London: New York University Press, 1995.

———. *The Book of Mirrors: Sefer Mar'ot ha-Zove'ot by David ben Yehudah He-Hasid*. Chico, CA: Scholars Press, 1982.

———. "The Language of Love in Christian and Jewish Mysticism." In *Mysticism and Language*, edited by Steven T. Katz, 202–35. New York and Oxford: Oxford University Press, 1992.

———. "The Mystic and the Mizwot." In *Jewish Spirituality: From the Bible through the Middle Ages*, edited by Arthur Green. New York: Crossroad, 1986.

McGinn, Bernard. "Cabalists and Christians: Reflections on Medieval and Renaissance Thought." In *Jewish Christians and Christian Jews: From the Renaissance to the Enlightenment*, edited by Richard H. Popkin and Gordon M. Weiner, 11–34. Dordecht, the Netherlands: Kluwer, 1994.

McLuhan, Marshall. *The Gutenberg Galaxy: The. Making of the Typographic Man*. Toronto: University of Toronto Press, 1962.

Meier, Menachem. *A Critical Edition of the Sefer Ta'amei ha-Mizwoth (Reasons of the Commandments) Attributed to Isaac Ibn Farhi*. PhD diss. Boston: Brandeis University, 1974.

Meir, Jonatan. "The Revealed and the revealed within the Concealed: On the Opposition to the 'Followers' of Rabbi Yehudah Ashlag and the Dissemination of Esoteric Literature." *Kabbalah: Journal for the Study of Jewish Mystical Texts* 16 16 (2007): 151–258 [Hebrew].

———. "Toward the Popularization of Kabbalah: R. Yosef Hayyim of Baghdad and the Kabbalists of Jerusalem." *Modern Judaism* 33, no. 2 (2013), 147–72.

Meroz, Ronit. " 'And I was Not There?' The Complaints of Shimon bar Yohai according to an Unknown Story of the Zohar." *Tarbiz* 71 (2002): 163–93.

———. "Contrasting Opinions among the Founders of Saruq's School." In *Expérience et Écriture Mystiques dans les Religions de Livre*, edited by Paul B. Fenton and Roland Goetschel, 191–202. Leiden, the Netherlands and Boston: Brill, 2000.

———. "Faithful Transmission versus Innovation: Luria and His Disciples." In *Gershom Scholem's Major Trends in Jewish Mysticism 50 Years After*, edited by Peter Schaefer and Joseph Dan, 257–76. Tubingen, Germany: Mohr Siebeck, 1993.

———. "The Path of Silence: An Unknown Story from a Zohar Manuscript." *European Journal of Jewish Studies* (2008): 319–42.

———. *The Pearl, the Matza, and the Fish: The Spiritual Biography of Rashbi.* Jerusalem: Mossad Bialik, 2018.

———. "'Rashbi's Biography' as a Zoharic Unit and the Epic Layer of the Zohar." In *The Zoharic Story*, edited by Yehudah Liebes, Jonatan Benarroch, and Melila Hellner-Eshed, 63–96. Jerusalem: Ben Zvi Institute, 2017 [Hebrew].

———. "The Saruq School of Thought: A New History." *Shalem* 7 (2000): 151–93 [Hebrew].

———. "Zoharic Narratives and Their Adaptation." *Hispania Judaica* 31 (2001): 3–63.

Mopsik, Charles. "The Body of Engenderment in the Hebrew Bible, the Rabbinic Tradition and the Kabbalah." In *Fragments for a History of the Human Body*, edited by Michel Feher with Ramona Naddaff and Nadia Tazi, 49–73. New York: Zone Books, 1989.

———. "Late Judeo-Aramaic: The Language of Theosophic Kabbalah." *Aramaic Studies* 4 (2007): 21–33.

———. *Les Grandes Textes de la Cabale: Les Rites qui font Dieu*. Paris: Verdier, 1993.

———. "Union and Unity in the Kabbala." In *Between Jerusalem and Benares: Comparative Studies in Judaism and Hinduism*, edited by Hananya Goodman, 223–42. Albany: State University of New York Press, 1994.

Morgan, Michael L. and Steven P. Weitzman (eds). *Rethinking the Messianic Idea in Judaism*. Bloomington: Indiana University Press, 2015.

Moss, Ann. *Printed Common-Place Books and the Structuring of Renaissance Thought*. Oxford: Clarendon Press, 1996.

Myers, David N. "Philosophy and Kabbalah in Wissenschaft des Judentums: Rethinking the Narrative of Neglect." *Studia Judaica* 16 (2008): 56–71.

———. "The Scholem-Kurzweil Debate and Modern Jewish Historiography." *Modern Judaism*, October 1986, 261–85.

Nabarro, Assaf. *"Tikkun": From Lurianic Kabbalah to Popular Culture*. PhD diss. Be'er Sheva, Israel: Ben Gurion University of the Negev, 2006.

Neher, Andre. *Jewish Thought and the Scientific Revolution of the Sixteenth Century*. Oxford and New York: Oxford University Press, 1986.

Neumark, David. *Toledot ha-Filosofiyah Be-Yisrael*. New York: A. Y. Shtibl, 1921.

Newman, Eugene. *Life and Teachings of Isaiah Horowitz*. London: E. Newman, 1972.

O'Callaghan, Daniel, ed. *The Preservation of Jewish Religious Books in Sixteenth-Century Germany: Johannes Reuchlin's Augenspiegel*. Studies in Medieval and Reformation Traditions 163; Texts and Sources 2. Leiden, the Netherlands: Brill, 2013.

Ogren, Brian. *The Beginning of the World in Renaissance Jewish Thought: Ma'aseh Bereshit in Italian Jewish Philosophy and Kabbalah, 1492–1535.* Leiden: Brill, 2016.

———. *Renaissance and Rebirth: Reincarnation in Early Modern Kabbalah.* Leiden: Brill, 2009.

Ong, Walter J. *Orality and Literacy: The Technologizing of the Word.* London, New York: Methuen, 1982.

Oron, Michal. "The Narrative of the Letters and Its Source: A Study of a Zoharic Midrash on the Letters of the Alphabet." *Jerusalem Studies in Jewish Thought* III (1983/84): 97–109 [Hebrew].

Pachter, Mordechai. "The Book, *Beginning of Wisdom* of Elijah de Vidas and Its Abridgments." *Kiryat Sefer* 49 (1972): 686–710 [Hebrew].

Pachter, Mordechai. "Kabbalistic Ethical Literature in Sixteenth-Century Safed." In *Binah: Jewish Intellectual History in the Middle Ages*, edited by Joseph Dan, 159–77. Westport, CT, London: Praeger, 1994.

Paluch, Agata. "The Ashkenazi Profile of Kabbalah: Aspects of the *Megalleh 'Amuqot ReNaV Ofanim 'al Va'Ethanan* by Nathan Neta Shapira of Krakow." *Kabbalah: Journal for the Study of Jewish Mystical Texts* 25 (2011): 109–30.

———. "Intentionality and Kabbalistic Practices in Early Modern East-Central Europe." *Aries* 19 (2019): 83–111.

———. *Megalleh 'Amuqot: The Enoch-Metatron Tradition in the Kabbalah of Nathan Neta Shapira of Kraków.* Los Angeles, CA: Cherub Press, 2014.

Penkower, Jordan S. *Masorah and Text Criticism in the Early Modern Mediterranean: Moshe Ibn Zabara and Menahem de Lonzano.* Jerusalem: Magnes Press, 2014.

Pilarczyk, Krzysztof. "Printing the Talmud in Poland in the Sixteenth and Seventeenth Centuries." *Studies in POLIN* 15 (2002): 59–64.

Polonsky, Antony, ed. *From Shtetl to Socialism: Studies from POLIN.* Washington, DC, 1993.

Polonsky, Antony, Jakub Basista, and Andrzej Link-Lenczowski, eds. *The Jews in Old Poland, 1000–1795.* London: I. B. Tauris and Company, 1993.

Price, David H. *Johannes Reuchlin and the Campaign to Destroy Jewish Books.* Oxford: Oxford University Press, 2011.

Putik, Alexander. *History of the Jews in Bohemia and Moravia: Exhibition Guide.* Prague: Jewish Museum of Prague, 2006.

———. *Jewish Customs and Traditions: Festivals, the Synagogue, and the Course of Life: Exhibition Guide.* Prague: Jewish Museum of Prague, 1998.

———. "Review of Avraham David, ed., Anonymous Hebrew Chronicle from Early Modern Prague." *Judaica Bohemiae* 49 (2012).

Raphael Posner, and Israel Ta-Shema, *The Hebrew Book: An Historical Survey.* Jerusalem: Keter Publishing House, 1975.

Raviv, Zohar. *Decoding the Dogma within the Enigma: The Life, Works, Mystical Piety and Systematic Thought of Rabbi Moses Cordoeiro (aka Cordovero; Safed, Israel, 1522–1570).* Saarbrucken, Germany: VDM Verlag, 2008.

Raz-Krakotzkin, Amnon. "The Censor as a Mediator: Printing, Censorship and the Shaping of Hebrew Literature." In *The Roman Inquisition, the Index and the Jews*, edited by Stephan Wendehorst, 35–57. Leiden, the Netherlands: Brill, 2004.

———. "Censorship, Editing, and the Reshaping of Jewish Identity: The Catholic Church and Hebrew Literature in the Sixteenth Century." In *Hebraica Veritas? Christian Hebraists and the Study of Judaism in Early Modern Europe*, edited by Allison P. Coudert and Jeffrey S. Shoulson, 125–55. Philadelphia: University of Pennsylvania Press, 2004.

———. *The Censor, the Editor, and the Text: The Catholic Church and the Shaping of the Jewish Canon in the Sixteenth Century*. Philadelphia: University of Pennsylvania Press, 2007.

———. "From Safed to Venice: The *Shulhan 'Arukh* and the Censor." In *Tradition, Heterodoxy and Religious Culture*, edited by Howard Kreisel and Chanina Goodblatt, 91–115. Beer Sheva, Israel: Ben Gurion University of the Negev Press, 2006.

Reddaway, W. F. *The Cambridge History of Poland*. Cambridge, UK: Cambridge University Press, 1941.

Reiner, Elchanan. "The Ashkenazi Elite at the Beginning of the Modern Era: Manuscript versus Printed Book." *Polin* 10 (1997): 85–98.

———. "The Attitude of Ashkenazi Society to the New Science in the Sixteenth Century." *Science in Context* 10 (1997): 589–603.

———. "Beyond the Realm of Haskalah: Changing Learning Patters in Jewish Traditional Society." *Simon Dubnow Institute Yearbook* 6 (2007): 123–33.

———. "A Biography of an Agent of Culture: Eleazar Altschul of Prague and His Literary Activity." In *Schöpferische Momente des europäischen Judentums in der frühen Neuzeit*, edited by Michael Graetz, 229–47. Heidelberg, Germany: Universitätsverlag C. Winter, 2000.

———. "The Rise of an Urban Community: Some Insights on the Transition from the Medieval Ashkenazi to the 16th Century Jewish Community in Poland," *Kwartalnik Historii Zydow* 3, no. 207 (2003): 363–72.

———. "Transformations in the Polish and Ashkenazic Yeshivot during the Sixteenth and Seventeenth Centuries and the Dispute over Pilpul." In *Ke-Minhag Ashkenaz ve-Polin" Sefer Yovel le-Chone Shmeruk*, edited by Israel Bartal, Chava Turniansky, and Ezra Mendelsohn, 9–80. Jerusalem, 1989 [Hebrew].

Richardson, Brian. *Printing, Writers and Readers in Renaissance Italy*. Cambridge. MA: Cambridge University Press, 1999.

Robinson, Ira. "Halakha, Kabbala, and Philosophy in the Thought of Joseph Jabez." *Sciences Religieuses/Studies in Religion* 11, no. 4 (1982): 389–402.

———. *Moses Cordovero's Introduction to Kabbalah: An Annotated Translation of His or Ne'erav*. Hoboken, NJ: KTAV Publishing House, 1994.

———. *Rabbis and Their Communitiy: Studies in the Eastern European Orthodox Rabbinate in Montreal, 1896–1939*. Calgary, AB: University of Calgary Press, 2007.

Rosman, Moshe. "Innovative Traditions: Jewish Culture in the Polish-Lithuanian Commonwealth." In *Cultures of the Jews: A New History*, edited by David Biale, 519–72. New York: Schocken, 2002.

———. "A Minority Views the Majority: Jewish Attitudes Towards the Polish-Lithuanian Commonwealth and Interaction with the Poles." In *From Shtetl to Socialism: Studies from POLIN*, edited by Antony Polonsky, 39–49. Oxford: Littman Library of Jewish Civilization, 1993.

Rosman, Moshe J. *The Lords' Jews: Magnate-Jewish Relations in the Polish-Lithuanian Commonwealth during the Eighteenth Century*. Cambridge, UK: Cambridge University Press, 1990.

Ruderman, David B. *Early Modern Jewry: A New Cultural History*. Princeton, NJ: Princeton University Press, 2010.

———, ed. *Essential Papers on Jewish Culture in Renaissance and Baroque Italy*. New York: New York University Press, 1992.

———. *Jewish Thought and Scientific Discovery in Early Modern Europe*. New Haven, CT: Yale University Press, 1995.

———. "Kabbalah and the Subversion of Traditional Jewish Society in Early Modern Europe." *Yale Journal of Law and Humanities* 5, no. 2 (1993): 169–78.

———. *Kabbalah, Magic, and Science: The Cultural Universe of a Sixteenth-Century Jewish Physician*. Cambridge: Harvard University Press, 1988.

———, ed. *Preachers of the Italian Ghetto*. Berkeley: University of California Press, 1992.

Ruderman, David, and Giuseppe Veltri, eds. *Cultural Intermediaries: Jewish Intellectuals in Early Modern Italy*. Philadelphia: University of Pennsylvania Press, 2004.

Sack, Bracha. "The Influence of Cordovero on Seventeenth-Century Jewish Thought." In *Jewish Thought in the Seventeenth Century*, edited by Isadore Twersky and Bernard D. Septimus, 365–80. Cambridge: Harvard University Press, 1987.

———. *The Kabbalah of Rabbi Moshe Cordovero*. Jerusalem: Bialik Institute, 1995 [Hebrew].

———. "The Mystical Theology of Solomon Alkabez." PhD diss. Jerusalem: Hebrew University, 1977.

———. *Shomer ha-Pardes: ha-Mequbal Rabbi Shabbetai Sheftel Horovits mi-Prag*. Be'er Sheva, Israel: Ben Gurion University Press, 2002 [Hebrew].

———. "Some Remarks on Rabbi Moses Cordovero's *Shemu'ah be-'Inyan ha-Gilgul*." In *Perspectives on Jewish Thought and Mysticism*, edited by Alfred L. Ivry, Elliot R. Wolfson, and Allan Arkush, 277–88. Amsterdam: Harwood Academic Publishers, 1998.

———. "Yahaso shel Rabbi Moshe Cordovero le-Sefer ha-Zohar u-le-Rabbi Shim'on Bar Yohai ve-Havurato." *Sefer Zikaron le-Ephraim Talmag* 1 (1993): 63–83.

Saperstein, Marc. *Decoding the Rabbis: A Thirteenth-Century Commentary on the Aggadah*. Cambridge: Harvard University Press, 1980.

Schechter, Abraham Israel. "Cabbalistic Interpolations in the Prayer Book." In *Lectures on Jewish Liturgy*. Philadelphia, PA: Jewish Publication Society of America, 1933.

Schechter, Solomon. *Studies in Judaism: Essays on Persons, Concepts, and Movements of Thought in Jewish Tradition*. New York: Atheneum, 1970.

Schochet, Elijah Judah. *Rabbi Joel Sirkes*. Jerusalem and New York: Feldheim Publishers, 1971.

Scholem, Gershom. "Israel Sarug: Disciple of Luria?" *Zion* V (1939–1940): 214–43 [Hebrew].

———. *Kabbalah*. New York: Meridian, Penguin Books, 1978.

———. "Le-Ba'ayot Sefer *Ma'arekhet ha-Elohut* uMfarshav." *Kiryat Sefer* 21 (1944–45): 284–95.

———. "The Meaning of the Torah in Jewish Mysticism." In *Essential Papers on Kabbalah*, edited by Lawrence Fine, 179–211. New York and London: New York University Press, 1995.

———. *The Messianic Idea in Judaism and Other Essays on Jewish Spirituality*. New York: Schocken Books, 1995.

———. *Origins of the Kabbalah*. Translated by Allan Arkush. Edited by R. J. Zwi Werblowsky. Princeton, NJ: Princeton University Press, 1987.

———. *Sabbatai Sevi: The Mystical Messiah*. Princeton, NJ: Princeton University Press, 1973.

———. "Yediot Hadashot al R' Yosef Ashkenazi." *Tarbiz* 28 (1958–59): 59–89.

Scott, Ury. "The *Shtadlan* of the Polish-Lithuanian Commonwealth: Noble Advocate or Unbridled Opportunist?" In *Focusing on Jewish Religious Life, 1500–1900: Studies in POLIN* 15 (2002): 267–300.

Segol, Marla. *Word and Image in Medieval Kabbalah*. New York: Palgrave Macmillan, 2012.

Sendor, Meir. "The Rule for the Admissibility of Kabbalah in Halakhah." In *Be'erot Yitzhak: Studies in Memory of Isadore Twersky*, edited by Jay M. Harris, 269–84. Cambridge: Harvard University Press, 2005.

Shear, Adam. Introduction to *AJS Review* Symposium: The Jewish Book: Views and Questions." *AJS Review* 34, no. 2 (2010): 353–57.

———. "Judah Moscato's Sources and Hebrew Printing in the Sixteenth Century: A Preliminary Survey." In *Rabbi Judah Moscato and the Jewish Intellectual World of Mantua in the 16th–17th Centuries*, edited by Giuseppe Veltri and Gianfranco Miletto, 121–41. Leiden, the Netherlands: Brill, 2012.

Sixtova, Olga. Hebrew Printing in Bohemia and Moravia. Translated by Pawel Sladek. Prague: Jewish Museum in Prague, 2012.

Soloveitchik, Haym. "History of Halakhah-Methodological Issues: A Review Essay of I. Twersky's "Rabad of Posquieres." *Jewish History* 5, no. 1 (1991): 75–124.

———. "Religious Law and Change: The Medieval Ashkenazic Example." *AJS Review* 12 (1987): 205–22.

————. "Rupture and Reconstruction: The Transformation of Contemporary Orthodoxy." *Tradition* 28, no. 4 (1994): 64–130.

Steinschneider, Moritz. *Catalogus Librorum Hebraeorum in Bibliotheca Bodleiana.* Berlin: Friedlaender, 1852–1860.

Stern, David, (ed). *The Anthology in Jewish Literature.* Oxford, Oxford University Press, 2004.

Stolow, Jeremy. *Orthodox by Design: Judaism, Print Politics, and the Artscroll Revolution.* Berkeley: University of California Press, 2010.

Stow, Kenneth, "The Burning of the Talmud in 1553, In the Light of Sixteenth Century Catholic Attitudes toward the Talmud," *Bibliotheque d'Humanisme et Renaissance* 34 (1972): 435–59.

Sulvass, Moses A. *Jewish Culture in Eastern Europe: The Classical Period.* New York: Ktav Publishing House, 1975.

Ta-Shma, Israel M. *Creativity and Tradition: Studies in Medieval Rabbinic Scholarship, Literature and Thought.* Cambridge and London: Harvard University Press, 2006.

————. *Ha-Nigle She-baNistar: The Halachic Residue in the Zohar.* Tel Aviv: Kibuts ha-Me'uhad, 2001 [Hebrew].

————. "The Law Is in Accord with the Later Authority-Hilkhata Kebatrai: Historical Observations on a Legal Rule." In *Authority, Process and Method: Studies in Jewish Law,* edited by Neil S. Hecht and Hanina Ben-Menahem. Boston and Jerusalem: Harwood Academic Publishers, 1999.

————. "The Open Book in Medieval Hebrew Literature: The Problem of Authorized Editions." *Bulletin of the John Rylands University Library of Manchester* 75, no. 3 (1993): 17–24.

————. "Rabbi Joseph Caro and His Beit Yosef: Between Spain and Germany." In *Moreshet Sepharad: The Sephardic Legacy,* edited by Haim Beinart, 192–206. Jerusalem: Magnes Press, Hebrew University, 1992.

Teller, Adam. "The Laicization of Jewish Society: The Polish Communal Rabbinate in the Sixteenth Century." In *Schoepferische Momente des Europaeischen Judentums in der Fruhen Neuzeit,* edited by M. Graetz. Heidelberg: C. Winter, 2000, 333–49.

————. "Rabbis without a Function? The Polish Rabbinate and the Council of Four Lands in the Sixteenth to Eighteenth Centuries." In *Jewish Religious Leadership: Image and Reality,* edited by J. Wertheimer. New York: Jewish Theological Seminary, 2004, I, 371–400.

————. "Telling the Difference: Some Comparative Perspectives on the Jews' Legal Status in Poland and in the Holy Roman Empire" *Polin* 22 (2010): 109–41.

Teller, Adam, and Magda Teter. "Introduction: Social and Cultural Borders in the Historiography of Pre-Modern Polish Jewry." *Polin* 22 (2010): 3–46.

Teter, Magda. *Jews and Heretics on Catholic Poland: A Beleaguered Church in the Post-Reformation Era.* Cambridge, UK, New York: Cambridge University Press, 2006.

Teter, Magda, and Edward Fram, "Apostasy, Fraud, and the Beginnings of Hebrew Printing in Cracow," *Association of Jewish Studies Review* 30, no. 1 (2006), 31–66.

Tirosh-Rothschild, Hava. "Continuity and Revision in the Study of Kabbalah." *AJS Review* 16 (1991): 161–92.

Tirosh-Samuelson, "Philosophy and Kabbalah, 1200–1600." In *The Cambridge Companion to Medieval Jewish Philosophy*, edited by Daniel H. Frank and Oliver Leaman, 218–58. New York: Cambridge University Press, 2003.

Tishby, Isaiah. "The Doctrine of Man in the Zohar." In *Essential Papers on Kabbalah*, edited by Lawrence Fine, 109–53. New York and London: New York University Press, 1995.

———. "Prayer and Devotion in the Zohar." In *Essential Papers on Kabbalah*, edited by Lawrence Fine, 341–99. New York and London: New York University Press, 1995.

———. *Studies in Kabbalah and Its Branches* (Hebrew). Jerusalem: Magnes Press, 1982.

———. Hebrew trans. and ed. *Wisdom of the Zohar: An Anthology of Texts*. Translated by David Goldstein. London: Littman Library of Jewish Civilization, 1989.

Twersky, Isadore. *Introduction to the Code of Maimonides (Mishneh Torah)*. New Haven, CT and London: Yale University Press, 1980.

———. "The *Shulhan 'Aruk*: Enduring Code of Jewish Law." *Judaism* 16 (1967): 141–58.

———. "Some Non-Halakic Aspects of the Mishneh Torah." In *Jewish Medieval and Renaissance Studies*, edited by Alexander Altmann, 95–118. Cambridge: Harvard University Press, 1967.

———. *Studies in Jewish Law and Philosophy*. New York: KTAV Publishing House, 1982.

———. "Talmudists, Philosophers, Kabbalists: The Quest for Spirituality in the Sixteenth Century." In *Jewish Thought in the Sixteenth Century*, edited by Bernard Dov Cooperman, 431–59. Cambridge and London: Harvard University Press, 1983.

Veltri, Giuseppe, and Gianfranco Miletto, eds. *Rabbi Judah Moscato and the Jewish Intellectual World of Mantua in the 16th–17th Centuries*. Leiden, the Netherlands: Brill, 2012.

Vinograd, Yeshayahu. *Otsar ha-Sefer ha-Ivri*. Jerusalem: Ha-Makhon le-Bibliyografyah Memuhshevet, 2006 [Hebrew].

Weinberg, Belle Hass. "Earliest Hebrew Citation Indexes." *Journal of the American Society for Information Science* 48, no. 4 (1997): 318–30.

Weinberg, Joanna. "Preaching in the Venetian Ghetto." In *Preachers of the Italian Ghetto*, edited by David B. Ruderman, 105–28. Berkeley: University of California Press, 1992.

Weinryb, Bernard Dov. *The Jews of Poland: A Social and Economic History of the Jewish Community in Poland from 1100 to 1800*. Philadelphia, PA: Jewish Publication Society, 1973.

Weinstein, Roni. *Juvenile Sexuality, Kabbalah, and Catholic Reformation in Italy*. Leiden, the Netherlands: Brill, 2009.

———. "Jewish Thought in the early Modern Period: Major currents and Trends." In *The History of Ideas: The Early Modern Period*, edited by Yosi Mali, 336–58. Jerusalem: Mossad Bialik, 2018 [Hebrew].

———. *Kabbalah and Jewish Modernity*. Oxford: Littman Library of Jewish Civilization, 2016.

Weiss, Roslyn. "Maimonides on *Shilloah ha-Qen*." *Jewish Quarterly Review* 79 (1988): 345–66.

Weissler, Chava. "Woman as High Priest: A Kabbalistic Prayer in Yiddish for Lighting Sabbath Candles." In *Essential Papers on Kabbalah*, edited by Lawrence Fine, 525–46. New York and London: New York University Press, 1995.

Werblowsky, R. J. Zwi. *Joseph Karo: Lawyer and Mystic*. London: Oxford University Press, 1962.

———. "R. Joseph Caro, Solomon Molcho, Don Joseph Nasi." In *Moreshet Sepharad: The Sephardic Legacy*, edited by Haim Beinart, 179–91. Jerusalem: Magness Press, 1992.

———. "The Safed Revival and Its Aftermath." In *Jewish Spirituality*, vol. II, edited by Arthur Green, 7–33. New York: Crossroad, 1987.

Wirszubski, Chaim. *Pico della Mirandola's Encounter with Jewish Mysticism*. Cambridge: Harvard University Press, 1989.

Wolfson, Elliot R. *Along the Path*. Albany: State University of New York Press, 1995.

———. "Anonymity and the Kabbalistic Ethos: A Fourteenth-Century Supercommentary on the Commentary on the Sefirot." *Kabbalah* 35 (2016): 55–112.

———. *The Book of the Pomegranate: Moses De Leon's Sefer Ha-Rimmon*. Atlanta: Scholar's Press, 1988.

———. "Mystical Rationalism of the Commandments in the Prophetic Kabbalah of Abraham Abulafia." In *Perspectives in Jewish Thought and Mysticism*, edited by Alfred L. Ivry, Elliot R. Wolfson, and Allan Arkush, 331–80. Amsterdam: Harwood Academic Publishers, 1998.

———. "Beautiful Maiden without Eyes: Peshat and Sod in Zoharic Hermeneutics." In *Midrashic Imagination*, edited by Michael Fishbane, 155–203. Albany: State University of New York Press 1993.

———. "Beyond the Spoken Word: Oral Tradition and Written Transmission in Medieval Jewish Mysticism." In *Transmitting Jewish Traditions: Orality, Textuality and Cultural Diffusion*, edited by Yaakov Elman and Israel Gershoni, 166–224. New Haven and London: Yale University Press, 2000.

———. "Circumcision, Vision of God, and Textual Interpretation: From Midrashic Trope to Mystical Symbol." In *Essential Papers on Kabbalah*, edited by Lawrence Fine, 495–524. New York and London: New York University Press, 1995.

———. "From Sealed Book to Open Text: Time, Memory, and Narrativity in Kabbalistic Hermeneutics." In *Interpreting Judaism in a Postmodern Age*, edited by Steven Kepnes, 145–78. New York: New York University Press, 1996.

———. *Language, Eros, Being: Kabbalistic Hermeneutics and Poetic Imagination*. New York: Fordham University Press, 2005.

———. "Language, Secrecy, and the Mysteries of Law: Theurgy and the Christian Kabbalah of Johannes Reuchlin." *Kabbalah: Journal for the Study of Jewish Mystical Texts* 13 (2005): 7–41.

———. *Luminal Darkness: Imaginal Gleanings from Zoharic Literature*. Oxford: Oneworld, 2006.

———. "Mystical Rationalization of the Commandments in Sefer Ha-Rimmon." *Hebrew Union College Annual* 59 (1988): 217–51.

———. "Suffering Eros and Textual Incarnation: A Kristevan Reading of Kabbalistic Poetics." In *Toward a Theology of Eros: Transfiguring Passion and the Limits of Discipline*, edited ny Virginia Burrus and Catherine Keller, 341–65. New York: Fordham, 2007.

———. *Through a Speculum That Shines: Vision and Imagination in Medieval Jewish Mysticism*. Princeton, NJ: Princeton University Press, 1994.

———. *Venturing Beyond: Law and Morality in Kabbalistic Mysticism*. Oxford: Oxford University Press, 2005.

Yates, Francis A. *Giordano Bruno and the Hermetic Tradition*. Chicago: University of Chicago Press, 1979.

Yisraeli, Oded. *Temple Portals, Studies in Aggada and Midrash in the Zohar*. Berlin/Boston: de Gruyter and Jerusalem: Magnes, 2016.

Zwelling, Jeremy. *Joseph of Hamdan's Sefer Tashak: Critical Text Edition with Introduction*. PhD diss. Ann Arbor, 1975.

Index